GIVE ME
A SHIP
TO SAIL

BOOKS BY ALAN VILLIERS

Give Me A Ship to Sail
Posted Missing
Sailing Eagle
The Way of A Ship
The Quest of the Schooner Argus
The Set of the Sails
Sons of Sinbad
Cruise of the Conrad
Whalers of the Midnight Sun
Grain Race
By Way of Cape Horn
Falmouth for Orders
The Coral Sea

BOOKS FOR YOUNGER READERS

The New Mayflower
And Not to Yield
Joey Goes to Sea
Stormalong

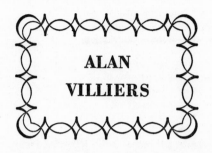

ALAN
VILLIERS

Give Me A Ship
to Sail

CHARLES SCRIBNER'S SONS

NEW YORK

A-2.59[H]

Grateful acknowledgment is made to the following for permission to reproduce the following pictures from their collections:

Figure 6: Plãtao Mendes
Figure 7: United States Coast Guard (official photograph)
Figure 8: Nicholas Horne
Figures 10 and 13: John Paul Jones Productions, Inc. (released by Warner
             Brothers)
Figure 12: Adrian Small
Figure 21: Richard Thomas & Baldwins Limited
Figure 22: P. A. Reuter Photos, Ltd.
Figures 30 and 32: Royal Navy
Figure 33: The Dicksons, Plymouth, Massachusetts
Figure 34: Socony Mobil Oil Company, Inc.
Figure 35: Louis deRochemont (from the Cinemiracle Production *Wind-
             jammer*)
Figure 36: Wilhelm Prölss

All other photographs are the author's.

Printed in the United States of America
Library of Congress Catalog Card Number 59-6176

CONTENTS

LIST OF ILLUSTRATIONS

TO NANCE

SOME WANDERING ADVENTURES

CHAPTER

1

MOBY DICK

THE wet Atlantic wind howled in the wetter rigging, and a succession of savage rain squalls drove over the ship at the coast of Wales, stinging with sleet. The rising wind tore pieces of sea from the wild waters of Strumble Race, and flung these at the little ship. Under too great a press of sail, she lurched and staggered, trying violently to roll but held down by the pressure of her sails. To seaward a wild line of blackening and broken cloud gave sure warning of yet another southwest gale, racing in from the open North Atlantic there. To leeward the rock-strewn coast of Wales offered nothing but a quick and bone-breaking, spray-choked death, if we stranded there, for the seas drove halfway up the gloomy cliffs. There were horrible rocks everywhere, without as much as a strip of sand wide enough to take the ship (if she had to beach) anywhere. The wind increased with

3

every squall. The foreyard was bending like a bow, and all the sisal standing rigging strained at its inadequate and rubberlike lanyards, iron-taut to windward and full of soft bights alee. The too-strong sails pulled too hard upon the too-light yards, and the insecure jib boom was throwing wild and anguished circles high above the sea. The cameras were in the tug, thank heavens, the tug which Lloyd's of London had insisted must stand by whenever the ship put out to sea, or she would not be insured. Far worse off than us, three of the whaleboats struggled in the sea, with the best part of my crew.

The ship was hove to, with the foresail and fore-tops'l set, the main tops'l, spanker, and two jibs—far too much sail for her. The sails forward were full on the port tack and the main tops'l was aback. The mainsail was loose, as also were the fore and main topgallants, hauled up in their gear ready to set, and blowing about and flapping in the wind. It was a fool way to sail a full-rigged ship on the lee shore of wild West Wales—a fool place to have such a ship, anyway! But the script called for all these things except the rising wind (which was a gratuitous and daily gift from the sea), and the company was working out of Fishguard.

The film unit, whose ship this was, worked desperately to photograph a scene showing the three whaleboats, just launched from the whale ship, pulling in quick succession past her cutwater towards Moby Dick. Dick himself was there, wallowing awash on a towline from the tug, blowing realistically by means of a compressed-air system ingeniously contrived inside his iron ribs. He was a brute to tow and impossible to harpoon. The new skin stretched round him to replace some that had worn off was so thick and

strong that no harpoon would go through it. No matter, for
the moment: the first problem was to get this whaleboat
scene. One thing at a time.

At a shrill whistle from one of the numerous assistant
directors, the whaleboats came smartly round the cutwater.
But they came in the wrong order. They pulled again, in
the right order this time, but a breaking sea threw Stubb's
and Starbuck's boats too close together and their oars were
mixed up. They pulled back to try again. "Only once more!"
I shout.

Do they want to drown my sailors? I have too much canvas up. The ship drives alee. The miss-rigged and ill-bal-
anced little brute, product of a non-maritime art department
and a trawler yard at Hull, will not stay properly hove to.
The tide has her at its mercy, anyway. She drives towards
the Strumble Race.

"Too dangerous," I say.

"Excellent," says the director. "Look at that glorious life
in the sea!"

"Life!" I say. "That's death! Haul down the inner jib!
Brail in the spanker!"

"Don't move those things," screams the continuity girl, a
persistent female now looking wildly aloft. "They're established in this scene!"

She means that the scene which the cameras are recording must fit with other scenes previously photographed, and
the set of the sails must remain constant throughout the
sequence. All other considerations are as nothing, which is
reasonable enough, from her point of view. But the wind
also rises and the sea continues to get up. The sea knows no
continuity. I ask a vociferous assistant director, does she

want the rigging about her ears? She blanches a little at that, for she knows the ship has been dismasted twice already.

"Just one more run!" I say. And the whaleboats form up again under my lee, to dash round into the weather when the assistant director signals. The little boats, lithe and long and sweet in the sea, are replicas of the real thing. They are all right, and there are seamen enough aboard to take care of them. But the boats are of necessity deep-laden with whale gear, insisted upon by the whaling expert (who has seen the Azoreans and the whalemen of Madeira at their work), and some of those sailors cannot swim. I know that. I have tucked life jackets beneath the thwarts, where the cameras cannot see them.

Once more it is. Surely the cameras aboard the tug must be getting magnificent stuff, the real thing! (Though what possible part of the great Pacific this Strumble Race can represent I cannot imagine, unless it be some miserable and tide-swirled cove down near Cape Horn, or south of Stewart Island). The tug comes over, the ancient tugmaster—a stalwart named Alec—looking anxiously at the ship, and the senior cameraman shouts across that those sails up front are wrong. They are spoiling his continuity, he says. Can't I fix them? They weren't like that last time he was photographing on this sequence!

Indeed they were not, for there was no gale coming up just then, and the sails were not so frantically tugging at tack and sheet. They were flat with near-calm, instead of full-bellied and pregnant with the virile wind.

It is futile to explain all this, or to point out the very obvious fact that there is nothing I can do about it. The North

Atlantic obeys no scripts. The sleet drives horizontally. The
sails blow stiff and taut like the *Conrad's* off Cape Horn.
The cameraman decides to overcome his difficulties and get
better shots by transferring to a launch. I admire his cour-
age, and ease the ship a little while the transfer is made.
The launch clouds itself in spray so much that he cannot
photograph so low down upon the sea. He calls for a plastic
camera cover, kept aboard for such occasions. The cover is
fitted, and he carries on. I bring the ship back to the required position, under the required sail, praying. The whaleboats form up, in perfect order. The wild scene is stirring, if
nothing carries away and no one is drowned. At the moment
of rounding the plunging cutwater, the seamen in the boats
straining and rain-soaked and cold but looking fiercely
grand, the sun peeps out briefly through a rent in the cloud.
In my ignorance, I think this is good—just the perfect touch.

"Damnation!" shouts the director.

"Damnation again!" shout all the assistant directors within
earshot.

The cameras stop grinding. The continuity girl looks up
ferociously at the heaven-sent sun.

"This is a gray-skies scene," she snaps.

The sun winks at them, and slips behind the cloud again.
By that time, the whaleboats are past the cutwater. They
could not stay there, lest they be run down. Alec the tugmaster has a wary eye on them, as well as upon the iron,
wood, and rubber beast of an ersatz Moby Dick, rolling in
the sea and blowing methodically, held on his wire towline
astern of the tug.

The ship has had enough. With a rather horrible, drawn-
out sound of rending wood, the foreyard breaks in two

pieces. The foresail (strong enough to round the Horn) holds it together, for the moment. Then, as a bad squall roars down, the flapping of the loose main-topgallant sail and the inability of the sisal backstays to support the weight causes the main-topgallant mast to reel over in a sort of drunken manner and break off too. The stays and things prevent it from falling right down, and I thank God that, distrusting the mast, I have had one of the rubber dummies lashed up there that very morning, instead of a live man on lookout. Upended at the masthead, the dummy stares moodily at the decks, face downwards and straw hat tied securely on. The blinding rain shuts out the land, but I know that it is perilously close.

"Brail in the spanker! Haul down the outer jib!" And damn the continuity and the cameramen, and all the assistant directors. We have to get out of this now, and run for such shelter as the port of Fishguard may provide.

I dare not clew up the foresail, for if I did the yard might fall down and the topsail blow out. Then I would have no sail for'ard at all. I run for the breakwater under the two tops'ls and one jib. Alec comes floundering along, still towing the whale.

The whale breaks adrift. Let him go! They can pick him up later. The tug must stand by the ship, entering port, for the very adequate reason that the ship cannot be anchored. Her two big bower anchors on the forecastle head are mockups, props, for photography only, and the false bow built on her has spoiled the lead for her real cables, which can no longer be worked. I reflect on these things, briefly, leaving the whaleboats to their fate. They are safe enough and can make port better than I can.

No one comes to brail in the spanker, and that big piece of unwieldy canvas must come in. My sailors are away in the boats. So are the two mates.

I am at the wheel.

"Brail in the spanker!" I roar again, above the howling of the squall.

Two spare assistant cooks, a boomboy, and a little man whose purpose aboard I never did discover come running to the poop.

"Where's the spanker?" they ask, plaintively but willing. "What are brails?"

I show them. In time, we get the spanker in, which is just as well, for the ship has a few other faults besides her inability to anchor. She will not sail properly, either. The balance of the masts is wrong and the foremast is stepped at far too great a distance from the bows. The windage of the built-up poop (she represents the art department's idea of an early nineteenth-century whaleman out of New Bedford or Nantucket) would make her hard-mouthed, even if she steered well otherwise. But she touched the ground once, coming out of Youghal, and the resulting rudder damage was not put right. To correct it meant dry-docking, and waste of the expensive cast's time. So now she scarcely steers at all. She has power, but not enough properly to control the ship. Neither the main nor mizzen yards could be properly braced round, because of the way the rigging was designed. The masts, yards, and jibboom are all too light, and the sails are the only good equipment aboard, which is wholly wrong. In an accident, at least the sails should give before the rigging does.

There were no boats save the whaleboats, and they were

away—no rafts, no rubber dinghies—and the ship was filled with people fore and aft. She had a false bow and a false stern, which a smite of the open sea could wash away. She had an overbuilt main deck which let the rain through like a fish net, and her new built-up sides spewed poor quality oakum as they worked. The standing rigging could never be set up properly. The shrouds and backstays were cut from some trawler line with soft steel cores and covered with sisal tarred to look (to a camera) like hemp. What a ship! She had a license to "ply for short distances to sea between 1st April and 31st October inclusive, during daylight hours *in fine weather.*" What is fine weather in the Irish Sea? The license is explicit on this point, for it goes on to stipulate that the ship must only go out "provided the weather is settled and the sea is calm."

What a hope! The ship, too, is required (by the certificate) to keep within strict limits—"From Fishguard not more than 15 miles along the coast to the N.E., not S. of a line 270° from Strumble Head, keeping within 3 miles of the shore." Weather settled, sea calm, within three miles of the shore! There was neither settled weather nor calm water in the Irish Sea that wild summer of 1954. The little witch of a ship just blew off the land, anyway, all but uncontrollable, almost every time she went to sea, which was daily.

I thanked God to see the hole in the breakwater loom up in the driving rain, for the clatter of the broken gear aloft was alarming. Alec passed me a line, his best towline of good nylon. It was blowing a full gale now, and a steamer blocked the way to our customary berth. There was nothing for it but to try for a buoy in the harbor. Alec towed me across, the ship taking a sheer this way and that, all but unmanageable. Ashore, the harbormaster, a master mariner of experience who had no wish to see notoriety brought to his little port by hordes of film men's bodies strewn on the rocks, seeing what went on sent his powerful launch to help. The tug was a big fellow, the *King's Cross,* bigger than our ship was, and it was as much as he could do to hold us head to wind, somewhere near the buoy. A ham-handed non-mariner, in the absence of our sailors, flung a heaving line at the launch, instead of over it, and the line got round the launch's propellor. Helpless, the launch drifted away, driving towards the rocks inside the harbor. The lifeboat was called out, and hauled the launch away from the rocks just in time.

Further inshore, a fishing vessel broke adrift and blew across the harbor with a line round his prop, too, just for good measure. Instead of helping us to get a line on the buoy, the lifeboatmen had to rescue the fishing vessel. Alec towed me right to the buoy, until the thing was just beneath the bows. The only sailor left aboard leapt onto the buoy, taking a heaving-line with him. The heaving-line broke. A sweep of Alec's nylon, as he tried to hold the ship—it was incredibly difficult seamanship—knocked my sailor off the buoy, into the sea. He helped himself, and swam to the tug.

Old Alec continued to hold us with a magnificent and quiet display of superb seamanship until at last, in an evening lull, we were able to get a nylon and then a stout wire secured to the buoy. A couple of little coasters were groping in, seeking shelter from the muck outside. The whaleboats came back, with my mariners, and we began at once to get the foreyard down and scarf the bits together, and do the same with the main-topgallant mast. Old Ted

Howard the mate and Ike Marsh the bos'n were magnificent at this(and always, for that matter). Ted was sixty-six and Ike was ten years younger. They had "bits" in the film, as well as being mariners, and since the film making always came first to the point almost of drowning, this was unfortunate.

Meantime Alec hurried off to sea again to find the whale, his decks crowded with assistant directors, cameramen, soundmen, and such. The whale had drifted into Strumble Race. Alec got alongside the thing, but could not secure a tow. The whale was perhaps a splendid beast for camera angles (though he rolled, as no real whale ever did, and nothing could get the roll out of him) and a softer spot or two could have been worked into his rubbery blubber to accept a harpoon. But he had no fitting to secure a towline, and that was fatal. He had no tail round which a wire could be passed (as it would be if he were a real whale). He was only half a whale, afloat on a complicated system of old oil drums for buoyancy and steel ribs for support. Only such parts of him as the camera could see were really whalelike.

The cameramen, sound men, and assorted assistant directors, with some of my mariners, worked valiantly to save the whale, which meant simply that they had to get a towline properly fast to him, whereafter he could be towed in. Several of the stunt men also worked like heroes, but in vain. (These stunt men, a new type in my experience, were an interesting lot. They came in two categories, the first a fellow who really was master of some "stunt" such as parachuting or frogman stuff or trick riding with motorcycles, or with horses, trapeze work, or falls, or something of the sort. This type was always a good fellow and generally developed into a good sailor too. The other type was usually a film-crowd man, an ex-extra who, after being in a film fight or two and learning how to appear satisfactorily punched and punching, to fall a little, and so forth, then becomes a minor stunt man in the sense that he will—allegedly—have a "go" at anything. Most of our stunt men belonged to the first category and were an excellent lot of fellows.)

Darkness came while they still worked at securing the whale. It was no good, and the thing drifted further and further into the hopeless waters of Strumble Race. One of the assistant directors spent an hour or two half-submerged on the whale, but he achieved nothing whatever.

At length, more than half drowned but still at least valiant, he was hauled bodily aboard the tug, despite his protests, and the ersatz half-whale was left to its fate. It had cost £5,000 and a great deal of trouble and, so far, had scarcely been filmed at all. Now it had suddenly become a menace to shipping, for its iron-ribbed solidity could cause serious grief to any little coaster that might run into it and it could not be seen in a breaking sea. Warnings had to be broadcast to all shipping to keep sharp lookout for an artificial white whale, adrift in the Irish Sea. The B.B.C., reluctant to publicize anything, not being in the publicity business, did not mention what whale it was. But the world knew, and the film men were jubilant. This was publicity worth £15,000! They smiled. The whale could be replaced.

It was never seen again.

Whatever on earth was I doing in all this flamboyant money-wasting, apparently nonsensical and utterly non-maritime melee, in the year of grace 1954, chasing a rubbery whale with a completely bogus and unseaworthy ship, in the Irish Sea? I often asked myself.

I was there for Director John Huston, because I believed in his endeavor to make a real sea film of *Moby Dick,* such as never had been tried before. I was there for John Huston, and because, with all her imperfections, this *Pequod* was trying to be a ship, a full-rigged ship, the only such offering under the Red Ensign (or any other flag) that I could hope to sail at the time. She was a ship to sail, and that was something.

John Huston was the director of the filmed version of *Moby Dick,* and I suspected that he had also produced the script, or most of it. I knew he was a clever script-writer. I knew he was a great director, and I'd heard of him (though I am no filmgoer) for years. I had no special knowledge of the cinematic world or brief for sea films, whereof in my opinion there had been but two of any validity in all history. The others were obvious tank creations, made either with models or with "ships" nailed together for the cameras and not for sea. There never had been a real endeavor to produce a thoroughly scrupulous sea film, to use a sailing ship as set and not sets as ships, actually to go to sea, the real and wild and unpredictable sea, and photograph it with imagination, as it was. Some rerigged hulks had sailed briefly off Catalina Island on the coast of California, at a convenient distance from Hollywood, where the studio crews and everyone else could come home for the night. Most—not all—such "sailing" was second unit stuff, accepted as an expensive but necessary bore to get "sea" pictures to be blended into the film in the cutting room, left entirely to assistant directors, lesser cameramen, and doubles for the players.

Then along came John Huston, one of the best directors of the lot, with an enthralling idea to make a real sea film from a great story. I met him at Claridge's in London to discuss the idea. I found him to be a long, restless man, with the garb of a horseman and the battered face of a professional boxer. He had, I knew, been amateur lightweight boxing champion of California before he was eighteen years old. He had literally sung for his supper in the London streets, too, yodeling cowboy ballads to get a bite to eat. He had also made some of the best films of the decade. Here he was in Claridge's, talking quietly about making a masterpiece from Herman Melville's extraordinary mixture of mysticism, whaling lore, sea adventure, apocalyptic meanderings, and joy in his ability to get music into the sound of English words. John Huston knew the only way really to bring such a masterpiece to life on the screen as well as I did (or a great deal better) and that was in a real ship, at sea. Where could he get such a ship? And where, he asked, were the men to sail and man her, as she should be sailed and manned?

As for this last, I was afraid I had no knowledge of the latitude and longitude of Davy Jones's locker, nor of Fiddler's Green. But I had an idea where a few good square-rig sailors might still be found, for I kept in touch with them all over the world. As for the ship, since I gathered that there no longer was even the hull of a three-masted schooner worth rigging again on all the coast of California, there were a few places where such a vessel might still be found. I meant a wooden three-master, either schooner or barkentine, that could be built up and rigged to pass with credit as Melville's whale ship *Pequod*, and be seaworthy when the job was done. Suitable schooners could be found in the Baltic, where a few remained, along the lesser ports of Sicily, and in Portugal and Spain. Where did he propose to make his film? I asked, assuming that it would probably be in the Mediterranean.

"In the Irish Sea," said Mr. Huston.

The Irish Sea! Having some experience, as master of the Outward Bound Sea School's training ship *Warspite*, sailing in that sea for a year or so, I was astonished and said as much. I was even more astonished when I learned that the base port was to be Fishguard, at the southern tip of Cardigan Bay. Why on earth choose Fishguard, of all the ports in Britain! Why commit so expensive and difficult an enterprise to do battle with the storm-tossed gray waters of the Irish Sea? What was wrong with the Mediterranean?

Not enough bad weather there, said Mr. Huston. Too much sunshine and blue sea—too much sweet stuff and not enough realism. He wanted the real thing—conflict, drama, not endless sunny seas.

Well, I wondered a little, but I approved of that in principle. As for Fishguard, he pointed out that the place had three very considerable advantages, none of which had occurred to me when I was battling the *Warspite* round that area. Fishguard Bay had a northerly aspect to seaward unimpeded by land or steamer traffic, since the place was purely an Irish ferry port (for Cork, Waterford, and Rosslare) and the ferries always sailed at night. Not even a trawler went to sea from Fishguard itself, nor a line fisherman. No round-the-harbor launches plied its waters, as they were altogether too turbulent. This meant that once she was outside the breakwater, a ship could be photographed on the open sea which could represent the Atlantic, Indian, or Pacific oceans, as required. Moreover—and these were very important considerations—Fishguard port contained excellent workshops and small slipways where repairs of all sorts could be quickly carried out (to keep an expensive concern such as a film unit on location working), and there was a large hotel then in disuse, which could be recommissioned very easily and so provide accommodation for a large film unit, right on top of the job.

I still counseled going to a port like Setubal in Portugal, rigging up an old codfishing three-masted schooner that I knew was in Lisbon, and forgetting all about the Irish Sea. Whatever the advantages of Fishguard, the disadvantage of too much bad weather could be fatal. Setubal could offer workshops and accommodation. What was more important, it could offer good light and a lively sea, not far offshore, and the chance of a real sperm whale as well, for Setubal is a whaling port.

But Setubal was not to be considered. The die was cast. As for real sperm whales, they would have no part in the picture. They were not amenable to discipline, I gathered, and could be relied upon only to add to the difficulties. Moby Dick had to be ersatz, and there was no getting round that. It would not do at all to have an ersatz whale, however satisfactory, shown up by the inclusion of the real thing. As for the whale, I gathered that Mr. Huston intended to be thorough in that field too, and had already taken expensive and far-reaching steps to see that his artificial whale looked right. His Moby Dick had to look real, to act real, and to carry off the illusion through a long film. I was not the only one who remembered a large rubbery balloon of an alleged whale which had ruined an earlier and otherwise passable attempt to film *Moby Dick*.

Mr. Huston had already sent a unit to film the activities of the open-boat whalemen of Madeira, the lovely Portuguese Atlantic island where in the early 1950's men still harpooned sperm whales from open boats. The unit spent two months at Madeira without seeing a whale, though a "pod" of sperm had been daily expected. Then Mr. Huston flew to Funchal, on the spur of the moment, and stepped off the flying boat to hear shouts of "Thar she blo-o-o-ows!" not meaning himself, but that pod of sperm. In a few hectic days, every aspect of open-boat whaling was filmed most thoroughly—the silent stalk and the thrilling chase, the turbulent tow behind the stricken whale, the whales themselves cavorting at play in the sea and then harpooned and fighting. All this was done not to cut the real scenes into the film, but to record the reality in order to perfect the sham. The artificial Moby Dick was to be designed and built to perform just as the real whales did, and to be as convincing. This thoroughness I liked, and I hoped that it would be extended to the ship.

Mr. Huston also had engaged Mr. Robert Clark, an excellent whaling expert, and was reproducing a small fleet of whaleboats. If the Portuguese coast and all the Mediterranean were not to be considered, and he remained determined on the Irish Sea, then it was imperative that the selected ship be *good*—tough, seaworthy, an able craft fit not only to sail the stormy Irish Sea but to stretch away to the Azores or down to Madeira herself, if the time came when the attempt to film in the Irish Sea had to be aban-

doned. One summer in three may offer tolerable weather in
the British Isles, at the best of times, and every westerly,
sou'westerly, or northwesterly gale that the stormy Atlantic
breeds—it is prolific—blows home on the wild coast of
Wales.

I therefore strongly advised finding a good ship in the
Baltic, with a start at Copenhagen and if unsuccessful there,
going next to Svendborg or Marstal. I knew an agent in
Copenhagen who could still be relied upon to produce a
suitable ship—an old oak Marstal barkentine or a Svendborg schooner that would be really fit for sea and worth
spending money on for the necessary conversion. There
were several useful ships lying both in Svendborg and Marstal. Charles Hvilsom's catalogue, from Copenhagen, showed
that another, and perhaps even more suitable ship, was to
be found in that port. This was a stout Arctic whaler from
the Greenland trade, a 250-ton oak barkentine with an old
auxiliary steam engine, her heavy hull strengthened to
break ice and to take the pressure of pack ice too, if need
be.

This was a ship which could be expected to stand up in
the Irish Sea! She was built in 1898 and was in good condition. I knew that, as I had had a good look at her. As for
the steam engines, they could be replaced by a handy
diesel with little trouble, and Ring-Andersen's yard at
Svendborg could be relied upon to convert the vessel into
a satisfactory and seaworthy Nantucket whale ship. True,
there was a considerable difference between an Arctic
whaler and a ship like the *Pequod*, but the old Greenlander's hull and rigging were wholly sound, her masts
were properly stepped and she could sail, and her strong
hull lent itself excellently to whatever disguise the art de-

partment might consider necessary. Much more important from my point of view, she could keep the sea when she was converted, and be a ship afterwards fit for something else.

There was not a ship in the market worth considering in all Britain, not even an Irish schooner or an Appledore ketch. The Appledore vessels were too small. The only good schooner was steel-built, and I was told that the *Pequod* must be wood since it was not possible to disguise steel vessels satisfactorily.

What about a schooner called *Hispaniola?* asked Mr. Huston. She had been used for a film already and, he thought, she might be available. She was being employed as a sort of side show in a place called Scarborough, at the moment, but her takings had dropped and perhaps she could be bought.

I was strongly against this one. I knew that this so-called *Hispaniola* was an ancient schooner called *Ryelands* which once had been an honest vessel and as seaworthy as ships come. But her days were over and had been over, then, a good ten years. She was more than seventy years old— small, strained, decrepit, and useless.

Mr. Disney had used her, said somebody.

Mr. Disney had asked very little of her, I answered, for she was used as a sailing set and not as a ship. As the alleged *Hispaniola* in his film called *Treasure Island* not much was asked of her, and she had not much to give. Under a curious rig thought, apparently, to be appropriate to the story, she had been seen briefly sailing a little round Falmouth Bay, hurrying back to moorings whenever the sun ceased to shine, which was often in those parts. No no, no *Ryelands* alias *Hispaniola*, please, if this were to be a real sea film! For she could not keep the sea. She would cost a small fortune to convert, and would be useless when the money was spent.

Mr. Huston said he would send a man to Copenhagen that evening. Could I go with him? Unfortunately, just then I could not. He also asked if I could sail his ship, look after her conversion, and so forth, and get enough sailors to form the nucleus of crew. He wanted real sailors. His policy would be to get sailors and let them be sailors, not to train actors to pretend. But I was committed already to a couple of voyages that year. One cannot drop everything merely because some more attractive or interesting proposition comes up, at the last moment. I had promised a friend to help bring his schooner up from Portugal that spring (though I do not care much for little schooners and I knew she would probably make me seasick), and the United States Coast Guard had invited me to make a cruise from New London towards Europe in the bark *Eagle* during the summer. These things, having promised, I must do.

I went off, then, to sail in the fine schooner *Bellatrix*, with an excellent crew, and was duly seasick there, along with most other persons on board, though only for a day. Then I crossed to New London and joined the steel bark *Eagle*, and sailed with the Coast Guard cadets to Santander, and Amsterdam, and Copenhagen. In Copenhagen I left, and went down to Ring-Andersen's yard at Svendborg, to see what might be there.

I saw no new *Pequod* there, nor anything like her.

The Greenlander had been sold to the Faroese for a song, said old Ring-Andersen—for about £1,000, he had heard. As for *Moby Dick*, he heard that the film people had bought an old schooner in England, and he understood that the filming had already begun, not at Fishguard but at some place called Youghal, in the south of Ireland. The schooner's name was *Ryelands*. He showed me a photograph. To a sailor, the disguised *Ryelands* looked like the devil.

She was far too small to appear authentic, for one thing. I could see at a glance that the rigging was cockeyed, the stepping of the masts was ridiculous, and the chances of that thing surviving even a summer in the Irish Sea were, to my mind, slim indeed.

It was a pity. Here at last there had been a chance to make a real sea film, as poor Ronald Walker and I had tried to do in the ship *Grace Harwar* off the Horn a quarter of a century earlier at the cost of Walker's life—with no studio, no nonsense, no mingling of the real and the false with a mixed-up sea, half tank, half real; no two winds blowing at once to catch aback the lumbering studio galleon that floundered briefly with squared yards (because none knew how to brace them properly) against a blue-sky background in some too-greatly-agitated tank. The Irish Sea would be too greatly agitated, indeed, but that would be real. The decrepit schooner *Ryelands* would be greatly agitated too, and she might, I thought, come to pieces in the process.

I put *Moby Dick* out of my mind, and hurried back to England where my wife was waiting to take the children for their summer holiday to a place called Cwmyreglwys, on the Irish Sea coast of Wales.

This is a lovely cove by Dinah's Head. We had been there before and the children liking the place, we had to go again. To get to Cwmyreglwys, we had first to go to Fishguard, some four or five miles away.

CHAPTER

2

"SOMEHOW MOST MELANCHOLY!"

THE oddest collection of human beings I had ever seen
ambled about the curious mixture of wharf and railway platforms that is Fishguard Harbor station, in Pembrokeshire in
Wales. As the train from London came in, alongside the
quay, I saw first an old steamship called *Great Western*
which Isambard Kingdom Brunel might have designed. Out
of the shelter deck of this old-timer came a mob of Irish
cattle. There was a ramp for these which led them clear
of the passenger platforms, which was just as well, for some
of those beasts had a wild look to them. A smart big motor
ship, with a black-and-white funnel, was secured a little
further along, discharging automobiles instead of cattle.
Along the quay and down the railway platforms passed
long-haired men dressed in the clothes of long ago, slouch-
ing in sea boots and old-fashioned fur caps and all sorts of

23

ragtag sailors' garments of a type I had previously seen only
in old prints. One of these men staggered by carrying a life-
size dummy of himself made, apparently, of rubber. Eleven
men in modern garb, but dressed more curiously even than
the apparently ancient seamen, pushed a railway trolley,
laden with what looked like heavy cameras, tripods, and
such stuff. An extraordinarily tall figure of a man, lean, of
ferocious aspect, heavily tatooed, his head shaven except for
a tuft like a girl's pony tail, his skin brown like a Polynesian's but his profile that of a Roman aristocrat, strode by,
looking neither to the right nor the left, with an outsize
harpoon over one shoulder. Behind him came three men,
carrying some sort of radio-telephone apparatus and, behind them again, six men carrying pieces of what might
have been blubber. It did not smell like blubber to me. I
knew the smell of blubber from a voyage I had made years
earlier with a Norwegian pelagic whaler, into the Ross Sea.
Other men were carrying or pushing little trucks of provisions, including about 300 lamb chops and several large
saucepans of peeled potatoes, as well as barrels, gas containers, and what looked like smoke bombs. All these figures
were heading towards a small ship at the breakwater end
of the quay, where the seagulls were assembled, watching
the proceedings, and a line of very large motor lorries was
drawn up in military order.

We looked at all this with the utmost astonishment, my
family and I, but it was the ship which really caught my
horrified attention. I had, I thought, a fair knowledge of
seagoing sailing ships throughout much of the modern
world, but I had never seen anything like this. She was a
small sailing ship, rigged as a full-rigged ship but with

sundry variations which looked no use to me. She had a great long jib boom set at an exceptionally high angle but far too fragile to carry sails of the size which could be set there and which were already bent, ready to set. Her masts were high, spindly, and poorly placed, with the mizzen too far forward and much too near the main, and the fore much too far aft. An enormous figurehead of an American Indian glared ferociously from the head of the raked cutwater. This figurehead was, I thought, far too large for the ship, and looked as if it was weighing the bows down.

Aft I could make out a built-up poop that resembled nothing more than a nightmarish cross between some old galleon and a Persian Gulf dhow. A steep gangway, looking rather perilous, led to the decks of this extraordinary vessel, which because of her fragility and the old-fashioned channels which supported the rigging, was held off the quay by two large catamarans. Along her pinrails I could see what looked like whale's teeth (or ersatz whale teeth) placed there instead of belaying pins. Worst of all, both topgallant masts lay over at a crazy angle, obviously adrift, and a gang of morose men appeared to be at work trying to get the broken spars down. A grizzled old man with a gray stub of beard, dressed in the sort of seafaring clothes which sailors used to make for themselves a hundred years ago, was surveying the men aloft with some contempt. Another bearded man, much younger, and in the clothing of a modern mariner, was having an altercation with a curious youth, at the foot of the gangway.

"Tell the director to take the ship out himself, if he wants!" he was saying, in a far from gentle voice. "The trouble with you people is that you never know what you want to do. When you do, it's impossible!"

The curious youth shrugged his shoulders, saying nothing.

I turned away.

"What ship is that?" I asked a railwayman who looked as if he had been to sea. I had a full grown fear that I knew what answer he would give me.

"That's the *Moby Dick* ship," he answered sadly.

Some bearded men on deck walked with difficulty, for one had crutches, another must have been in a plaster cast, and the third had an arm in a sling.

"They've been having bad luck," the railwayman continued. "Too much bad weather—and that ship! There's one of the stars got a broken back, they say, and a leading player is in hospital. The ship's been dismasted twice already, and she's only been here a couple of weeks. Look at her now!"

I looked.

"It would seem that you're still in time to be some use," said my wife, who was also looking, fascinated. "They're in a mess."

"Nobody can make anything of that ship now," I said. "Let's get on with the holiday. I've a book to begin too, you know."

"You could call John Huston," said my wife, who does not often take the side of the movie makers. "That's the least you could do. After all, it was you that said this was a sea film that was worth putting yourself out for. It looks like you've got your chance."

"You call him," I said. "I'll be working on my book. That ship's no good and I can't do anything about that."

"You could sail it."

She looked at me.

"You're always looking for a square-rigged ship to sail," my wife continued. "Well, here's one. She's British, too. Remember your idea of getting the film people to pay for a good ship, and then you make a school ship of her afterwards when they've finished their film. She might do for the Outward Bound."

"Not that thing!" I said. "I respect the Outward Bound. She's a wreck."

But I called Mr. Huston, and that was fatal. The *Hispaniola*, he said, had been acquired for reasons of expediency which now he bitterly regretted. But he was stuck with her, and she was breaking up his stars and herself. Once having assembled his cast, he had to go on and he had no time to get a better ship. A day's idleness cost £5,000 and, since she was his only set, he could not film other scenes while waiting for her masts to be set up again after one of her too frequent dismastings. He had not been able to find a sailing-ship captain or crew. She had sprained his Starbuck's back, broken some of Ishmael's bones, and put another leading player in hospital. It was then the latter part of August and he'd had the ship since June, but he doubted whether he had been able to make a fourth of the sequences that he needed.

"Look at these," said Mr. Huston, pushing across a huge sheaf of sketches. "This is what I'm after."

I looked at the sketches, and saw that they were a pictorial treatment of the story of Moby Dick, all splendidly and stirringly done. They were the work of a young fellow named Grimes, and they gave an excellent idea of the superb film that Mr. Huston was trying to make.

I joined the *Pequod* next morning, taking over from the bearded man who had been airing strong views to the assistant director. He left the ship with alacrity and obvious relief, saying that he would go off to the China Coast again where there was only a blockade to run, and know peace.

For a moment I reflected on the faulty judgement which, turning down the good ships, had so expensively acquired this wreck. "The fools spent £60,000 on her! They could have *built* a better ship for that," my predecessor said. But, as Mr. Huston pointed out, there she was, and the job now was to make the best possible use of her.

I was a little depressed when I had a close look at those too light masts and yards, and the overbuilt bows and main deck that had fouled up the lead from the windlass, and all the other exhibitions of appalling lack of seamanship. But I noted that there were three excellent Cape Horn seamen among her crew who had somehow been overlooked by the previous master, one of them with a square-rigged certificate as second mate (though he was working as an able seaman) and two of the others old sailors who were also expert riggers, though not employed at all in that field aboard.

I packed off the morose, hired riggers aloft back to the shipyard which had sent them, made these sailing-ship men my mates and bos'n forthwith and sent them aloft, took out some further life insurance, and hoped for the best. The rest of the crew were all right. Three good and well-skilled men who could lead them were a sufficient nucleus, and the ship was well manned.

By the following daybreak, we had the *Pequod* rigged again, after a fashion, and the sails stowed a little better than they had been, and the decks shipshape. Then the horde of the film people descended on her again, and all was bedlam—or nearly all. Not quite all, for the director, his stars, and the senior assistant director knew what they were trying to do and were men of the right spirit, determined to accomplish it despite the appalling difficulties. There was a considerable strain of the warrior in these gentlemen and, in a sense, working for a big film on location was a kind of warfare—neurotic at times perhaps, but a battle into which everything had to be thrown by everyone.

The *Pequod* was the oddest command I'd ever had in my born days. The job was to get her out to sea on every possible day for every possible daylight hour and sail her like a Nantucket whale ship of the 1820's, looking out for "whales," lowering boats to chase whales, towing back whales, cutting-in whales, trying-out stacks of cut-up and very artificial blubber in her deck tryworks, also artificial, while the cameras ground. She had a passenger certificate for seventy-one persons but accommodation for nobody, not even her master. She had to come back to port every night, late, in order that her people could find room to stretch out and sleep. This they did in the Fishguard Bay Hotel, but there were too many of them to fit in that large and rather gloomy place. They spread out into hotels and rooms in Fishguard itself, and a considerable bus and taxi service was organized to carry the cast and others between their widely separated apartments and the ship. Fast launches sped about the harbor, dashing out with visitors, writers, and so forth (never with late-comers of the cast, for the film discipline was strict and enforced on all save shop stewards belonging to the all-powerful unions). In addition to these speedboats there were assorted other launches— quite a fleet of them, most of them decrepit but all very profitably chartered. Most of the hands lived like fighting cocks in the Fishguard Bay Hotel, but had to sleep several to a room.

Inside the film discipline, full democracy prevailed, and the lowest stand-in (characters hired for their physical dimensions, to take the place of the chief players when lights were being set up and all that sort of interminable boring stuff was going on, which was appallingly often) or shop steward from the Electrical Trades Union could order the same sumptuous dinner as the stars were having, as often as he wished. As far as I could understand, the stars had the worst time of it, for they had to be up at five in the mornings—every morning—or earlier, to have time to get their elaborate make-up on and be ready to report aboard the ship at seven. It took two hours, for instance, every day, to put the Polynesian harpooner Queequeg's tattoos on and color his skin the proper shade, and another twenty minutes to fit him with brown eyes, for his own were blue. The brown contact lenses hurt abominably, and he usually took them out again when he was not in a scene.

Day after day, prominent—and well paid—actors rose early, were made up, and descended on the ship to spend a twelve to sixteen-hour day aboard her, and were not photographed at all because something or other went awry. This *Moby Dick* was quite something to organize, what with big hotels and full-rigged ships and tugs and launches and a pod of artificial whales, and one thing and another. Extraneous and extraordinary persons kept dropping in, bankers from New York biting their nails (for they were financing the film), an Irish peer of sorts whose photograph in long underwear had been featured in a popular illustrated weekly, magazine writers, actresses from Paris hoping to influence Mr. Huston to use them in a future film or somebody to use them anyway, persons seeking Mr. Peck's autograph, and a considerable number of undefined humans of both sexes whom somebody or other just liked to have around.

I knew I'd taken on an assignment. But when the very first morning I watched the horde of seamen stream aboard followed by actors, stunt men, cameramen and camera crews, electricians' mates, shop stewards, cooks, script and continuity girls, property men, wardrobe men, carpenters, sound men, effects men and producers of smoke, scarers-off of seagulls (equipped with revolvers), Director John Huston, radio experts, whaling experts, arc lamps, cameras, dummies (life-size, to be spewn up by whales etc.), pieces of whale, harpoons, lines, provisions, large barrels, gas containers, etc. etc., I wondered whether I was going to have room to move. Nobody appeared to trust the ship much, for they took everything ashore out of her each evening only to have to carry it all back the following morning. My mariners fought for room to work and get the gangway in. At least eighty persons crammed the decks, some of them sight-seers, as far as I ever discovered. There was one little man there for a month before I found that he was supposed to be a camera mechanic.

An assistant director proceeded to order the crew about

and send away the boats, without any reference to me. He had three parts of the *Pequod's* crew detailed for work in the boats, regardless of the ship's needs, before she left the quay. I said something to the point, whereat I was told by this youth to look after my work and he would look after his. What was my work? I asked mildly (for the moment), beginning to understand the alacrity with which my predecessor had departed. Why, steer the ship! said the assistant director.

That matter was put right, yet it was curious, seeing how close she could come to killing them, how little comprehension most of these single-minded movie persons ever acquired of the ways of the sea.

Mr. Peck the star and Mr. Huston the director were of a different caliber, but they were jammed in the milling throng, just as much as anyone else. They came aboard as early as anybody and were exposed to the elements, all day long, for the ship had no shelter. The hold was cluttered with cables, tanks, gear, property, stores. The few small dressing rooms were ill ventilated and wet. Comfort was not considered at all, which was right enough, I suppose, aboard a nineteenth-century Yankee whaler. The function of the ship was to sail the Irish Sea, look like a whaler, and get the seascape right so that no part of the coasts of Ireland or of Wales came in the background, and the sun was right so the cameramen could photograph a properly lighted foreground where, in due course, action took place.

What a business! The ship under sail proved herself awkward to the point of being nearly uncontrollable. The sea background could not be just sea, as it was. It had to be "dressed." The script called for sundry whaleboats and har-

pooned whales to be seen, too, and these had to be provided. The background for the first scene when I took
over was to represent the meeting between Captain Ahab's
Pequod and the British whale ship *Samuel Enderby*, somewhere in the Pacific Ocean, on a day when sperm whales
were unusually plentiful and the slaughter was terrific. Both
Pequod and *Enderby* crews are getting all the whales they
can until the *Enderby's* master, in a "gam," gives Captain
Ahab news of Moby Dick. At once Ahab calls off the hunt,
hoists his boats, cuts his whales adrift, and sets off on his
fatal hunt for the great white whale. It is dramatic stuff.
But it would not be very dramatic unless the real action was
all there, looking real. That was the difficulty.

The reality would be simple, but the sham was complicated because of sets and tides and wind, and the different effects of all these on ship, boats and sundry varieties of
ersatz whale. The whales were the least bother, because
they were inanimate and had only to show parts of their
dark carcasses awash in the water. But the ship, the whales,
and the whaleboats each drifted at varying rates, according
to how much of them was immersed, and the ship being
deepest drifted fastest. Since she was the studio as well as
set, she had to record sound. She had been equipped with
a soundproofed engine room where generators produced
power to record the sound, but the soundproofing was not
good enough and this could not be used. A large ocean-
going tug had to be there as well, with a cable stretched
across from her afterdeck to transmit the current she provided to the recorders who had to use it in the ship, and
the tug and the tug's smoke and the cable and the land and
all other things extraneous and unwhalelike had to be out

of the picture. The tug drifted, too, and she could not tow the *Pequod* under sail for fear of parting her electric cable. The *Pequod* could keep station, but the main trouble was to have all the whaleboats and whales staying in their proper places, too, and to keep them there all properly set up and ready for action during the appallingly long delays which appear to go with all cinematic enterprise. It took hours for the camera crews, or the lighting men, or the sound men, or the carpenters, to do anything. There was a big whale alongside the *Pequod*—the one which Ahab cuts adrift. This was a well-made beast, very realistic, but it complicated the situation hopelessly. A sperm whale lashed alongside the ship, almost the same length that she was, made it quite impossible to hold the vessel on any bearing, and she began to drift dangerously close to Dinah's Head. This bothered nobody but me, for the cameras were shooting to seaward.

Again and again the scene would be all set up, and then the whaleboats drifted one way, or the whales another. Or perhaps the "whale" alongside fouled the cutting-in stage and then swung under the bows, pinning its ersatz carcass on an underwater bracket which had been bolted to the cutwater in order that any towline that might be used during shooting would not be in the film. Then, when all was set once more, the tug's power cable parted because the tug took a sheer one way and the *Pequod*, lying more or less unmanageable, went the other. The cable was not strong enough to hold the two ships together.

So things went on, all day long. The Irish Sea is wide open to the North Atlantic where wild winds blow, and wild winds blew that summer. Indeed, we knew no summer that year. The whiplash winds from the Roaring Forties came screaming one after another over that gray waste of sea, and the foul ground and the rocks and the racing tides as the angry waters poured north and south to get round Britain made the place a seafaring hell.

"Good, good!" John Huston would say (at first) when a big sea got up, not looking at the lowering skies and the racing rack overhead, happy because this was the "real stuff." Real stuff? That it was with no shadow of doubt whatever—real enough to sink the sievelike *Pequod* any day.

She had pumps, and they worked, which was just as well.

It took three days to get that whaling scene on film, although the episode would occupy less than a minute of screening time. Meanwhile I had noted that the new topgallant masts worked alarmingly, and I knew they would never stand up to much. I hoped the summer *would* come. (It never did.) It is a mistaken idea that August is a summer month on the west coast of Great Britain. August is the month that hurricanes begin in the Caribbean, and most of them dissipate themselves over the North Atlantic. Too many blow right home towards the Irish Sea, or set up disturbances which reach boisterously there.

Beating round the Horn in a well-found ship was nothing like beating the awful *Pequod* about the Irish Sea, and the brief nightly interludes alongside the dock spoiled the rhythm of the battle. A good many of the technicians were seasick, as many a hardened mariner might well be in so small a tossing ship round those waters (I came mighty near it myself more than once). They would have got over it if we had kept the sea. The breaks ashore only made things worse. It was a good thing most of the cast (apart from the leading players) were seafaring men, or men with some maritime background.

The *Pequod* had five whaleboats, tough, lithe little things like whaleboats were, and John Huston had those boats overside and off after whales, ersatz and imaginary, whenever the sea got up and the conditions were realistic for wonderful photography. Day after stormy day the whalemen strained at the oars while the whaleboats jumped and rolled and all but capsized, or played leapfrog with each other in the horrible waste of hole-filled waters that is the Irish Sea.

To seaward near Fishguard was a notorious piece of foul ground, where the waters, ebbing out of the Bristol Channel (which is like a lesser Bay of Fundy) met the angry rollers flung before the Atlantic's sou'westerly gales. Foul ground is a place where the bottom, instead of being reasonably smooth, is like a rock-strewn canyon. This place, being shallow and standing at a meeting of the currents, was always an appalling maelstrom of seas rushing in all directions. The locals called it a "race," and even the fishermen took good care to keep out of it.

The film men tried to keep *in* it. "Good, good!" they'd say. "Let's head for Strumble Race, Alan," almost every morning, even sometimes when the coasters were coming in for shelter and the gale warnings were flying, and the weather forecast spoke of "Wind 25-35 knots S.W. veering later to W.S.W. gusting to gale force: cloud 8/8; 6/8 in afternoon: sea rough to very rough: visibility five to ten miles."

"Sounds like good visibility," was Mr. Huston's only comment to that kind of forecast. After all, if the weather did

get too bad—and it frequently did—we *could* run for shelter
into Fishguard itself. The masts might come out of the
Pequod, but she ought to float. She was built of wood. I
began to think, though, that my crew of good sailors had
a worse time chasing sham whales than any Nantucket
whaleman ever had chasing the reality! Real whalers kept
out of tidal races and shunned such places as the Irish Sea.
Real whales, too, were often in short supply. When hunted
they tired out, in time. Also they died. Our dreadful ersatz
variety neither tired nor died, but were with us always.
There were at least fourteen different varieties of ersatz
Moby Dicks, mainly experimental. One was electronic and
two were manipulated by a system using compressed air.
Another ran on a sort of switchback monorail which had
been especially contrived for him beneath the water. Some
were miniatures, and there were little model boats and
men—perfect doubles for Ahab, Starbuck, and the rest—
to go with them. There were several horrible whales of
more than life size, and these were our special curse there
in the Irish Sea.

No problem defeated those film men. One day we had to
get a couple of thousand seagulls to wheel round left-to-
right over the five whaleboats—Ahab's and his mates'—
while they looked for Moby Dick, and to keep on wheeling.
Seagulls are about as easy to handle as a pod of whales but
they are in somewhat better supply, and the couple of thousand were rounded up all right. How on earth even Mr.
Huston with his assistants, four launches, and two "special
effects" men could get them to do what was wanted of them,
I did not know. Ordinarily, as the *Pequod* was supposed
to be hunting the deep sea where no coastal seagulls fly, a

couple of grim fellows aboard were kept busy firing blanks to scare them away. After a while the gulls had caught on to the idea, and stayed away except at mealtimes. Now they were required for action, and they must produce.

Mr. Huston was never worried by the possibility that he couldn't get the seagulls to do what he wanted. It simply never occurred to him. He did it, too, in two days with the whole of one day's catch of fish from Milford Haven where twenty ocean-going trawlers were based, and all the meat the eighty of us were going to have for lunch and dinner on those two days, into the bargain. The gulls apparently appreciated meat more than fish, and Mr. Huston got the idea very quickly. Then, by setting up his scene and liberally sprinkling the area with the Milford Haven fish, he attracted the seagulls for fifty miles around, even from as far away as St. Patrick's Causeway. There had not been free lunch like that laid on for seagulls in the Irish Sea since the big four-masted bark *Hougomont* had stranded there fifty years earlier and ground up her cargo of Alaska salmon on the Nevin rocks.

Then, by alternately scaring the gulls up with the boats and the guns, and placing the food in a wide circle for them to fly over, slowly, slowly the director got those gulls to do just what he needed and, after a while, it seemed almost that the gulls themselves got the idea and performed perfectly for each retake. The only trouble was that they learned so well that after a while they were so full of food that many could no longer take off from the water, and about a thousand of them stayed in the bay for days afterwards. Whenever they saw the whaleboats launched they came screaming over, hoping for more chops and steak. We lost some time because of that, for the *Pequod* was then supposed to be out in the deep water again. Poor gulls. They looked dubiously at the director and his cameramen in the evenings when we came back to Fishguard harbor, as if they could not understand what was expected of them.

It was getting late in the year then, near the end of September. We began to meet too much wind and sea, even for Mr. Huston. Many a day I went out very dubiously, sure that we would not get far before the wind would pipe up so much that we could not carry sail and then we'd have to fight our way back again. The *Pequod* leapt as if she'd been stung with a dozen rusty harpoons, and she kept on leaping. Her motion was terrible, and seasickness, under such conditions, claimed all but the stoutest-hearted. I marveled at the immense endurance both of Mr. Huston and Mr. Peck —day after day, standing about in the windy open, in rain and misery and cold, ready at a moment's notice to get on with the film, yet often thwarted in every endeavor for days on end. The infinite patience called for to get the good sea pictures so necessary for the film would have tried Job. Dawn to dusk, every day—seven days a week, thirty days a month—so it went. The unfortunate Mr. Peck had often to stump the deck with an ivory bone for a leg, which made it not only painful and awkward to keep his balance but often dangerous, for a lurch of the ship could send him flat on his face. He was good at keeping his balance. He gained his sea legs, there in the Irish Sea.

One day we had just got nicely out to wind'ard and were beginning to get some rugged stuff, with the sea-booted mariners cavorting in the boats and the ship leaping about like a frolicsome young whale which had been drinking,

when suddenly a series of hard westerly squalls came
marching out of the sullen sky and shrieked and howled in
the sisal rigging. I got some sail off her mighty quick, despite
the customary protests of the continuity girl to keep the
canvas as it was, because it was needed for continuity. That
continuity girl never changed. She had eyes only for one
thing and that was her job, and in three months of sailing
in the old *Pequod* she never once even admitted the idea
that there were times when the ship had to come first and
the devil take the continuity. Even though the masts fell
about her ears she still shouted to get them up again the
way they had been established!

I got the sails in and saved the masts, and ran in for the
harbor to get behind the big breakwater. We got off the
breakwater and the sea quieted a bit there, because there
was a lee. An assistant director suggested that we could get
a shot in there—all I had to do was keep the ship in the
same place, he said. How do you induce a full-rigged ship
to stand still in a tideway with a gale of wind? I'd like to
know! She could not anchor—even if she could, her one
anchor would never have held her there.

I backed and filled and kept a weather eye lifting for the
tug, hoping that I could keep the *Pequod* off the rocks until
it came. It took all the rest of the day to extricate the ship
from the position and get her safely into shelter.

In all this rain-soaking, gale-howling, frequently miserable and (even more often) somewhat dangerous time—it
went on for weeks and months—Director Huston stayed to
the last, helping with the awkward jobs always, never spar-
ing himself, always energetic and optimistic, always in the
best of humor. He seemed to be grateful for the chance of

working like a galley slave in a gale of wind and to exult in defeating the sea's challenge. It never occurred to him that we might not defeat it, one of those over-boisterous days.

It was all no use. In October, the wind howled all night almost every night among the wet Welsh hills, and the rain streamed against the windows in the Fishguard Bay hotel, but in the mornings we would be off again. October is a miserable month in the Irish Sea. This was a color film, and with the sun so far south as the year advanced, there was not strength enough in the light to photograph action in color, even if the sun came out, which it very seldom did.

There were all sorts of heartbreaking difficulties. One day, with the weather bad but just usable, everything was set to film an important scene when Mr. Peck's false nose came slightly adrift. A skilled make-up man attended Mr. Peck at all times but, try as he could, the poor man was too seasick to get the nose properly in place again. He tried to do the job, most courageously, despite the seasickness. But his hands had temporarily been bereft of their skill and it was useless. We had to come back to shelter for him to recover, and by then the light had changed too greatly and it was no use to go out again.

Another scene called for a man to fall from aloft. This took a week. Dummy after dummy was tossed out violently, but they all fell like dummies, or landed on deck. The "rushes" showed that they were not good enough. None of the stunt men aboard was a satisfactory high-faller, though many tried. A special falling man had at last to be brought from London, at an agreed price of £150 the first fall and £100 for each retake. The rigging was so shaky that it was

difficult for the bos'n to rig up a firm line for the stunt man
to hold to, on a yardarm sufficiently outboard to be certain
that he would not fall on deck, while he poised himself for
his work. A dummy dropped from the selected position did
fall on deck, most lugubriously. The dummy bounced, but
stunt men do not. However, after many days our stunt man,
who was Irish, climbed nonchalantly aloft and made a most
realistic and horrible fall, with appropriate sound effects,
landing on his back in the sea. It was an excellent performance and he was congratulated on all sides, but Ishmael
was heard to remark that he had already lost the £150 in
the poker school and, having fallen so well the first time,
there would be no retakes.

Using the ship as studio, recording the sound and photographing the action and everything, proved an infinitely
difficult business. No one expected it to be easy. The
weather was the effective enemy—the weather and the ship.
Now the whaleboats were getting smashed up and several
of the leading players had not had a chance to recover from
the serious injuries which they suffered when it was supposed to be summer. Starbuck was still in a painful plaster
cast, and Ishmael's broken foot was far from mended. Poor
Ishmael had to shuffle about on crutches the best way he
could, which meant that he could be photographed only
from the knees up until he was properly recovered.

I admired the way these actors and the film crews generally stuck to the job. It seemed to me that the stress of
their jobs must be nearly unsupportable. All day, every
day, week after week, month after month, a man like
Gregory Peck was called upon to wait about on the windy
poop or the tossing main deck of that inadequate ship, wait-

ing, waiting, waiting—while the gales blew or the sun was shining when continuity called for it not to shine, or in when it should be out, or the well-fed gulls persisted in getting into the film when the ship was supposed to be a thousand miles from land, or a jet aircraft screamed overhead—waiting for the light to be right, for the ship to be right, for the whole dressed-up and drifting scene to be set and lit to the director's perfect satisfaction. Unless it was perfect, the director would not begin to film.

Hour after hour would pass in the most trying and frustrating circumstances, yet upon the instant, when things were ready, there was Mr. Peck suddenly and perfectly (except for a disconcerting resemblance to a good-looking Abraham Lincoln) transformed into Captain Ahab. A somber, powerful figure in his dark clothes, one leg hitched up painfully behind him and hidden beneath the skirts of the long coat, his handsome face livid with a great scar and his nose altered in shape—it occurred to me that the real Ahab had led a better life than this actor did. Ahab lived only one life, after all, and had to die once only. It was simpler to be Ahab than to act the part for a film. In time, I realized something else. It was really Mr. Huston who was Ahab—Mr. Huston, projecting the story through Mr. Peck. It was Mr. Huston who was everything, even the spirit of Moby Dick himself.

But Mr. Huston could not be the ship, and she defeated him—had defeated him before he began to make the film. She was partly useless for his real purposes and, in the end, he was forced to admit the fact. An extension to work longer in the Irish Sea was sought and not granted, for the authorities could not accept the risk. Fishguard itself was an unsafe port in the winter months, and there was no other haven.

Very well, said Mr. Huston. We will sail down to Madeira, or to the Canary Islands.

Not with this ship, I had to say, for she is not seaworthy. She will come to pieces in the Bay even if the Ministry of Transport allow her to sail, which they would not dream of doing, naturally, at that time of year.

So Mr. Huston had to go off to a studio near London, with great reluctance, to film there what he had been unable to get at sea. He had always planned to use a studio for some of the scenes, and stages had been hired, very expensively, for some time. But he had had no intention of photographing "sea" scenes under cover. Now he had to construct mock-ups of his *Pequod* and get on with them.

Later he took the company to Las Palmas, flying them down there in a chartered airplane which also took the boats. Skilled carpenters could build another Moby Dick or two down there, and the whaleboats were at last in their element. They had to manage without a ship. By that time the shrinking hulk of the built-up *Pequod* was chained in a Cardiff dock, where after some months she was sold to a television company to make "sea" films of the utmost banality, and profit. She had cost the *Moby Dick* company £65,-000, I was told, what with her soundproofed engine room and generators, over-built bows and main deck and full-rigger's spars and all the rest. The television filmers paid £4,500 for her; but they got no bargain.

I suppose that Mr. Huston's idea really was impossible, from a film maker's point of view. It was a grand idea and

I thought it should have worked, but with all that enormous staff and gang of hangers-on which is considered necessary, apparently, for the making of any film (or enforced upon the makers by union rules), he would have required either a very big sailing ship, which would be quite wrong, or a passenger liner chartered to keep in company to accommodate them all, if he really meant to make the film at sea. It was inevitable that he should allow his art department to decide the design of the whaler, but it was a pity that the technical qualities of the ship, her ability to sail and so forth, had not been checked by a competent naval architect who really knew square-rigged ships. The *Moby Dick* film was excellently served by its art department, which did a splendid job, for the art direction was superb. But art directors can scarcely be expected to know much about the practical points of sea-going sailing ships. That is not their job. Neither had they anything to say in the ship's selection, and the choice of ship for Mr. Huston's *Moby Dick* was fatal. So, as things turned out, was the choice of Sea.

I saw the film, eventually. It was a wonderful film, I thought, but somehow, it was not the compelling masterpiece it should have been. I remembered Melville's words describing the *Pequod*—"long seasoned and weather-stained in the typhoons and calms of all four oceans. . . . Her masts —cut somewhere on the coasts of Japan, where her original ones were lost overboard in a gale—her masts stood stiffly up like the spines of the three old kings of Cologne. Her ancient decks were worn and wrinkled, like the pilgrim-worshipped flagstone in Canterbury Cathedral where Beckett bled. . . . A noble craft, but somehow most melancholy!"

Aye, a noble craft, but somehow most melancholy. That seemed to me to sum up the film.

At least the poor *Pequod* had been a ship to sail, and to keep together for a little longer the skilled nucleus of a deep-sea sailing-ship crew. I reflected on these things as I hurried off to the quiet beaches and the sunny harbors of lovely Portugal, to see what might offer there and to restore my tranquillity.

CHAPTER

3

"GOD HELPS HIM
WHO WORKS"

THE first soft streaks of a lovely dawn showed the dark sails like detached wings close upon the sea, standing silently, with the vessels which bore them still hidden from view. There were many such sails, some with the high peaks of the swift lateen, others more rounded. At that soft hour no wind blew. The Atlantic murmured gently on the shelving beach, as if loath to waken land and people to the new day. Many people were already awake, not only in those silent, softly moving ships. The soft padding of a hundred barefoot fishermen and their wives passed beside me in the street, as the fisherfolk headed for the beach and the day's work there. Some were leading cattle, a pair of bullocks yoked together, but with no other harness. Many men carried round fishing baskets, as the dorymen do in their little boats on the Banks. The women were bundled up in black

against the cool of the dawning, and some of them were
speaking in quiet voices to their men. The men wore stocking caps, heavy shirts of bright plaids, and colorful trousers,
though a few were dressed in black.

The graceful sailing ferry which had brought me across
the channel from near Aveiro came gently alongside the
quay without a sound, and I stepped very quietly ashore.
Nearby were several of those lovely sailing boats which hail
from Ilhavo and Gafanha, and ply the river-fed, landlocked
arms of the Atlantic there. In the soft light these boats were
beautiful, with their grace of line and decorative coloring.
Nothing was to be seen that did not fit in, not mariner nor
fisherman nor boat, and the reek of diesel and of petrol was
not allowed at all.

I made my way behind the fishermen towards the beach
of Costa Nova, one of those grand and shelving beaches,
wide open to the Atlantic swells, where I knew the companies of cooperative fishermen still launched their great
barcos do mar on such mornings as this and fished in the sea
as Christ's disciples had done almost 2,000 years before. I
wanted to see this fishing, and this was a good place.

Facing the Atlantic, on the shelving beach, were several
extraordinary craft—big fellows, sixty to seventy feet long,
flat-bottomed, beamy, built solidly of enormous hand-hewn
planks of heavy wood, their bows drawn upwards in long
slender lines which rose gracefully twenty feet or more
above the sand. Their double-ender sterns swept up a little
too, to offer a little shelter to a steersman there. These boats
were gaily painted, and a garland of fresh flowers hung
from each lofty prow. Two of the boats stood by the water's
edge, on rollers of fresh-cut pine.

Along the beach came thirty or forty men in a long line, carrying an enormous fishing net, in line ahead, all walking on the good firm sand with a sort of rhythm as if this was a movement in a ballet, and the net was looped in graceful patterns, shoulder to shoulder. Other men came behind these, in pairs, carrying what looked like long coils of rope, on sweeps. In the distance and the half-light, the great net looked at first like an enormous serpent, undulating along towards the sea under its own power, and the heads of the fishermen were excrescences on its round back. Here and there, groups of well-fed bullocks stood, heads down a little and staring out to sea, as if all this were a familiar sight to them.

At the water's edge further along, some fishermen were using teams of bulls to swing one of these Phoenician landing boats (for such they seemed to me), head to seaward, through the surf, having loaded it first with some miles of net and line. The boat had four great sweeps like solid pine trees shaped to thrust back the water at one end and rounded a little for the men to work them, at the other. Here there were no sails, for these were surf boats. Of course there were no engines. I could scarcely understand how such enormous surf boats could be launched out through the surf at all or brought safely in again, for such surf riding as I had seen had always before been in slim and lithe long boats with a great sheer, beautifully designed for their work, like Yankee whaleboats. These Portuguese boats had to carry an enormous load of net and line, for their work was to go out some miles from the beach, dropping a long rope astern of them as they went and then, when far enough out, to drop the huge nets parallel with the beach. The last stage was to run another tremendous rope from the net's extremity back to the beach, and coming through the surf to land, this end was passed to a team of waiting bulls, which began at once to haul away on it and so bring in the net. Other bull teams also took the first rope and, between them, bullocks and men hauled in the great net across the floor of the bay, scooping up all the fish in its way.

All this took time, a great deal of time. It took time to launch the boat through the surf—time and the village, as far as I could understand. The boat was manhandled and shoved and pushed until finally it stood on its massive rollers at the edge of the surf, the tide making and the seas slowly growing beneath the flat bottom until every surge of the ocean swell set it to jumping lightly. Two oxen, yoked together, waited patiently at either quarter, ready to haul away when the order came. The oxen were hitched to the boat's quarters by ringbolts in its sides. They paid no attention to the white water swirling round them, so long as they could keep their faces clear of the spray. Some forty men were also there—the same men who had been carrying the gear—all in their gay fishing shirts and all with their trousers hitched well above the knee.

As soon as a sea running in gave a lift to the bow, one among them who was master gave a great shout. The bullocks strained, the forty men strained, the boat lurched, the spray drove white all round it—nearly afloat! Next sea should do it. A wild-looking figure in the bow of the boat tossed a stout line to a party of women by the water's edge.

In came another Atlantic swell, greater than the last. Up rose the high prow. Again the oxen and the forty men strained at the task, while the women took the weight of the line, upwind of the boat, to keep it headed exactly into the run of the surf lest it broach to. The forty men shoved mightily, while agile small boys dashed among their legs moving the rollers towards the stern, the better to keep some way on the boat. In came another breaker, now lifting the fat stern as well as the bows. The master roared his orders, the men shouted, the oxen were unhitched before the sea swept over them, the women all shrieked together, straining at their line, while the garlanded prow bucked and leapt in the surf.

Now! yelled the master.

Immediately the men, most of them wet through with the spray and sea, leapt into the boat and, each taking his appointed station like a perfectly drilled gun's crew, fiercely grasped the enormous sweeps, ten men to each, and began to flail mightily at the foamy sea with these.

Let go! shouted the master to the gang of women, and immediately they did so.

I jumped over the stern, from which a heavy rope was trailing, the inshore end far up the beach and miles of it coiled down aboard. The forty men stood perched on heavy thwarts, laughing as they shoved at the sweeps.

In comes another swell, a little higher and longer than its predecessors. The prow rises high, the stern sinks, the men flail at the water, the master exhorting them. If the boat swings broadside-to now she may roll over, and some of them will certainly be crushed. The great fat rump of the laboring boat strikes on the sand once, hard, shaking me to the teeth but with no effect on the fishermen. The sea boils all around. But the boat is gaining, and keeping straight.

The master, an imperious figure dressed in black rags and a black stocking cap, has no long sweep to help to keep the vessel straight. His control is by spoken order only. No sweep that a single man could wield would have any useful effect on the boat, while she is so near the beach and in the surf. The men at the sweeps know their business. Eighty strong brown arms, forty straight strong backs work together as a splendid team with the rhythm of an Oxford eight, and the power they impart pushes the boat steadily to seaward. In a few moments, she is beyond the surf and, on this bright morning, there is no broken water.

The sun is up now—well up, and the morning mists rolling away show a four-masted schooner, a Grand Banker, anchored off the bar of Aveiro. Steadily the boat ploughs along to seaward, two men under the master's eye paying out line. The line slips into the sea with a swoosh, and the sides of the boat inboard are scored with its countless passages. Ashore, on the beach, I see that oxen and women are sitting now, the women making a meal for some children who have joined them, all laughing merrily and happy in the morning sun. The master keeps a sharp eye to seaward, looking for the slightest sign of a break in the weather. This is open sea here, and the boat can know no haven. She must come safely back to the beach, for there is nowhere else for her to go.

I read the name of this vessel, painted on the end of the covering at the bows. DEUS AJUDA QUEM TRABALHA, it reads. God Helps Him Who Works. This is the spirit of the companions.

For an hour or more, the boat thrusts seawards and the line runs out. Then it is time to launch the net, a great tarry, bulky thing, and the boat turns on a course parallel with the shore the better to lay the net for a good drag. The net all out, shoreward it turns again, precisely at a right angle, and runs steadily in, headed once more towards the surf. I watch all this carefully. The surf has risen considerably, for no cause that I can see. The boat is light now, and must come through that surf and beach with care. I see the oxen are standing by, waiting, and the women and boys are ready to put down the wooden rollers. As she runs in, sometimes riding up on the crest of a breaker like a surfboard at Manly Beach or Waikiki, the rope to the net still trailing astern helps to keep her straight, together with the skillful handling of the men at the sweeps.

In she runs, quickly, bows high on a great swell that turns over feet from the beach in a roaring smother of foam and spray. Back the water runs, in strong undertow. The boat strikes the beach. Out leap the forty men. Working so quickly that I do not follow everything, in a trice the oxen are hitched, great ropes are secured on either side of the bow, up runs the boat beyond high-water mark, safe on the sand!

At once she is swung by the oxen and the youngsters' skillful use of the rollers, for her bows must face seawards as quickly as possible. She is hauled a little up from the surf and left there, for the moment, while the oxen continue with the endless task of hauling in the net lines. There is a rhythm to all this work, and it is carried out by the villagers —men, women, and children—with the air and the competence of people to whom all this has been handed down through centuries. While the oxen, three pair a side, haul in the net lines, sinking knee-deep in the sand, the forty men who landed begin at once to load the boat again with a fresh net, which had been spread on the beach to dry.

Further down the beach, another boat exactly similar was being launched, in precisely the same manner, and more oxen were standing by to haul in its lines. Hour after hour, the strong beasts steadily hauled in the line on a sort of endless chain of rope and oxen. Boys hitched them by a special kind of hitch to the rope at the water's edge whence the oxen trudged and tugged stoutly up the beach as far as they could go. Here the boy unhitched again, very smartly, and the oxen hurried to the water's edge once more. Always there were two pair hauling in and one pair running to the water's edge. A girl in black coiled down the recovered rope. A man drove each pair of oxen, while the fishermen's wives waited quietly for the catch (if any) to be landed. Then they would load their fish baskets on their heads and trudge off for miles, selling the fish at nearby towns. The net was marked by a pair of brightly painted barrels, and these bobbed slowly on the sea as the oxen hauled the net shorewards.

As the markers reached the nearer waters the tempo quickened. Now the oxen ran! Men stripped to their checked underwear and dashed into the sea as the net approached. Women and children thronged towards the place where the cod-end of the net would land. A *guarda fiscal*, his duty to assess and collect the tax, appeared from nowhere and now watched everything. The owner of the gear, a lean dark citizen who also conducts the best pension in town, came out to watch. Oxen, men, women, children, owner all become excited. Children dash into the surf to rescue sardines flapping out before the net. Now the net is landed, and the cod-end lashings are quickly slit. Inside is a mess of fish, flapping and gasping—big skate, squid, mackerel, some hake, gummy sharks, a score or two of large flatfish, and many stone of sardines. The catch is auctioned off forthwith, in many lots, the tax is paid, and the fish-wives are soon on their way inland to sell their wares.

In the meantime the boat is ready to launch again. It is midmorning now, and hot—pleasantly hot. I sit in the shade of an old *barco do mar* and learn what I can of this ancient industry from the pleasant young owner of the gear, whose sister, a pretty schoolteacher at Aveiro close by, comes to join us. There are eighty companions in each boat's team at Costa Nova, I am told—eighty companions, forty-two for the boat and thirty-eight ashore and, with them, four sets of nets, two sets of the ropes (very expensive, all this), a wagon for the nets, and eleven pair of oxen. All these are financed from the catch of fish, the profits of which are divided between the owner and the companions on a fixed and time-honored basis, one-third to the owner, two-thirds to the companions, with the state taking 12 per cent as tax —tax which in most cases includes rates, land tax, income tax, and everything else, for it is all that the companions pay. The companions form close-knit communities in all the fishing villages up and down the coast, dedicated to prosperous and hard-working fisheries, and to mutual aid. In good times, all prosper. In bad, all pull together for the common good.

Often there may be bad times, for the Atlantic can roar upon the coast for weeks on end in the fishing months, and make fishing impossible. The companions are fishermen and highly specialized, not farmer-fishermen. They rarely have

any land to till, but live by the success of the fisheries. This
kind of fishing is called, in Portuguese, *Artes de Grande
Xavega,* and it can be most successful. Eight companies
were still engaged in it, a year or two ago, at beaches in the
jurisdiction of the captain of the port of Aveiro alone—at
Costa Nova and Furadouro, at Torreira, Mira, Leirosa,
Vieira de Leiria. At most of these beaches two boats were
working. As recently as 1957, the companies in the Aveiro
district landed fish worth the best part of four million escu-
dos. But here and there I saw the darkening ruins of abandoned boats, where a stretch of beach had given up the
Xavega, and the picturesque big vessels were rotting in the
sun.

"Too much trawling, and too successful with the new
gear," the companions said. "Everyone can't catch the same
fish. If the trawlers take them before they can reach our
beach, why, we will have to turn ourselves into trawlermen
too."

I saw little sign that any had taken such a step. The companions of the fisheries were too old and too well-knit communities to disband lightly. At some ancient ports such as
Povoa de Varzim, north of Oporto, they practically gov-
erned themselves by ancient usage, and had a dialect of
their own.

Elsewhere other fishing methods prevailed, as at Nazare
(full of artists from France, painting industriously, and large
motor coaches of tourists from all over Europe, for whom
the little barefoot girls and boys of the *Ta-Mar* danced
busily by the beach), and Costa da Caparica just south of
Lisbon (where there were also some smaller *barcos do
mar*), and Sesimbra and Setubal and Sines, and all round

1. The *Pequod* was terrible.

2. The net looked like a sea serpent on the Costa Nova beach.

3.
Fishing
from a
beach in
Portugal

4.   On a Portuguese beach.

the coast of the beautiful Algarve from the Point of Sagres
to the Spanish border. Nazare is God's gift to marine artists,
a crowded, glorious beach of gold, teeming with picturesque
life. Flat-bottomed, high-prowed boats stand everywhere, or
dot the waters of the open bay, beamy to accept their
heavy loads of fish and men and gear, graceful and strong to
survive in the sea, flat-bottomed to slide over sands. In
Nazare the companions take the names of the fish they seek,
and it is Senhor Pedro de Bacalhau who is master of the
nets, maybe, and Sehnor Affonso Bonito who is second assistant.

At Albufeira, in the south, I found the beach full of
lateen-rigged sailing craft, eighty or a hundred of them
packed together occupying every available piece of sand,
all gaily bright with colorful patterns which included always an eye on either bow, for the boat to "see." There were
over 200 boats on the beach there altogether, and when they
launched together of a sunny evening or came running in
like a wonderful and organized fleet for market in the
dawns, the sight was beautiful. There was something very
Arab about these vessels. They were all open boats and
their rig was pure Arab. None had power: eight or ten men
seemed the average crew. The whole of the fishing commu-
nity turned out to haul in the boats in the mornings and to
help launch them in the late afternoons. Albufeira was a
lovely place, perched prettily on its Atlantic cliffs and gaz-
ing out to sea.

Quarteira, further to the east, was also most interesting—
a flat, easy beach with a uniform good surface, and no cliffs.
Here I watched a hundred dhow-rigged little fellows come
sailing in from sea, their high peaked sails incredibly pic-

turesque and the silver fish gleaming beneath the thwarts, the hulls painted in many soft and lovely colors, the sails browns and tans and sometimes purest white. Once a black squall whipped suddenly up: how the villagers rushed to the beach! Upon the instant, a hundred peaks of wind-stiff sails broke out upon the sea as sail was made from vessels which had been lying anchored, sails down and fishing. With a pother of flying foam and the wind rising and crying with the wet sigh of threatened gale, the little chaps came rushing for the beach where the villagers ran out to attach beaching lines, to haul them ashore.

For half an hour or so the beach was packed with excited life. The oldest women I had ever seen, all dressed in black with the big black felt hats of the Algarve surmounting ancient heads that seemed to be carved from mahogany, stood in the long hauling lines with the children and all the men, as boat after boat was hauled to safety up the beach, and not a man nor woman nor child desisted nor bothered with the fish until all the boats were in.

CHAPTER

4

THE TUNNY RUN

AT QUARTEIRA I heard about the Tunny Run, the tuna-fish bullfight which was due any day, men said, in the corrals off Faro—that same Faro where the Elizabethan Earl of Essex had raided and stolen the learned books which founded, later, John Bodley's great library at Oxford. From time immemorial the tuna corral had been put down there in the sea off Faro and Tavira. Once Prince Henry the Navigator had owned these fishing rights and farmed them out for revenues to finance his sea expeditions. Drake and Essex must have known how to avoid the wide area of the heavy nets, for they are large enough to trap unwary ships. Nowadays their position is carefully charted.

Apparently, nobody knows much about the habits of tuna fish. One thing is certain, and that is that each year countless thousands of them pass along the southern coast of

Portugal, bound inwards towards the Mediterranean, to spawn. They come from the southwest, and they are in a hurry. It appears, from what I was told, that they swim with the land on their port side, and they head into soundings until they get in the shallow water off Cape St. Mary, which is about halfway between Cape St. Vincent and the Spanish border—not far from the Straits of Gibraltar. They like to make a landfall in that area, and then they head seawards again for a while before continuing towards the east. Later, many are seen off the south coast of Spain and off Sicily, and, I believe, round the Bay of Naples. They come out from the Mediterranean along the Moroccan coast, after spawning, bound back for the mysterious haunts somewhere in the North Atlantic from which they came. It is all a silent, pulsing, fishy mystery: but the fishermen know that they are there. They are expected each year about May 15, and usually they come fairly punctually.

When they come they are fat, healthy, and single-minded, with one aim only—to reproduce their kind in peace and then get back to the depths again as quickly as possible. When they are inward bound, the tuna are timorous, afraid of shadows, easy to catch. A barrier of nets is put up in the deep water off Cape St. Mary in their path, and the whole barrier is contrived to induce any tuna fish which strike it to make for the gates of the corral at its center. Once they pass through these, they are doomed.

The tuna trap consists, in the main, of a great L-shaped line of nets, each arm of the L about three miles long. The arms are not straight, for then the tuna could find the way past them and be gone. Each few hundred yards there is a pocket where the net suddenly turns back upon itself, like the eye of a crochet needle. At each end of the nets, there is another of these pockets. The tuna wants only to pass the obstruction and continue towards the east. At any point along the whole of the trap (except in the corral) it could turn back, or swim right through the nets, for the mesh is big and the nets are not strong. The nets form a barrier only, to cast shadows in the sunlit sea, and the shadows are enough to stop the tuna. It swims along, looking only for a way out to the east, and finds itself again and again in the pockets, always nearer to the corral. At last it approaches the gates of the corral, which are never closed. They are hung skillfully in such a way that they throw no shadow when the tuna is entering them but there is always a shadow across the aperture when seen from inside. The tuna goes in but it will not swim out. He swims and swims and swims, looking for a shadowless passage. There is none. He is trapped—doomed.

It is a silent business. From the sea there is nothing to be seen but a line of yellow corks bobbing in the water with, here and there, a heavy cork buoy to mark a mooring an-chor.The hundred miles of heavy wire, the six hundred big iron anchors, the thousands upon thousands of acres of wide-mesh net, are all hidden from view. A line of black launches, dhow-rigged, silent, apparently unmanned, marks the corral. They wait there, watching for a sign of the tuna. The black dhows lie low upon the sea, hitched to the sides of the corral. Aboard them, keen-eyed men keep constant watch on the clear depths. Seated in a small dinghy in the southeastern corner of the corral is another keen-eyed man, called an "idler," whose business it is to signal any tuna movement he might see. He knows the fish will make for the southeast corner, seeking the way out that is not there.

Also at the corral is the Master of the Nets, a most experienced tuna fisherman whose word is law. The Master also watches the water. Nothing disturbs the surface but the movement set up by the wind. The inexperienced could watch all day and see nothing—not the slightest sign of a tuna fish. The tuna has a blue back and is difficult to see from above. The "idlers" and the Master can see him—how, I don't know—and they know that, if they see one, a school is there. How big a school they do not know, but a school, anyway, for the migrant tuna does not swim alone.

Sometimes, days pass without sight of a tuna. The worst thing that can happen, from the watching tuna men's point of view, is to sight a killer whale. The killer is the great enemy of the tuna, and he likes them best when they are fat for spawning. If the trappers know the tuna's movements, so also does the killer whale and, far too often, he is patrolling off Cape St. Mary, too. If the tuna sight a killer even when they are in the corral, they will become completely mad and break a way out of the nets, causing a great deal of damage. It takes six weeks to get the trap laid properly, and damage to it is a serious thing. Big anchors, long steel wires, acres of mesh have to be recovered, repaired or replaced, and the whole lot put down again, exactly as it was. There is one place for the trap and one only, and a surveying vessel attends each year to assist in getting the trap down in that place.

I went out to the nets off Faro, in the Algarve, half a dozen times, hoping to see the manner of taking the tuna, for I had been told that the actual catching in the corral was a dramatic business. They called it the "tuna bullfight."

Not many people ever saw it, for the corral is a long way at
sea, and visitors are not encouraged. One could go out ten
times and not see a tuna. The sun was hot and the sea had
a considerable swell, even though the weather was almost
calm. None but the hardened tuna men could stand the
motion day after day. The first time out I was lucky, for the
"idlers" had seen tuna. There was an air of silent excitement. A large net was being rigged hurriedly at one end
of the corral, to drive the fish towards the furthest end.
Until this net is cast, all is strict silence. The men believe
that the tuna can hear them, even when it is still deep in
the sea.

A hundred and fifty men are gathered about the corral.
Once the net is cast they are all free to make noise. The
surface is beaten to alarm the tuna and make them go towards the corral's further end, where the bottom will be
hauled up under them. The bottom net stretches only a
third of the way along the corral, for it would be unwieldy
if it were any bigger. Now it all lies on the sea bed beneath
the fish, but the outboard end has lines to the surface,
which are buoyed. When the tuna are driven along before
the loose net, these lines are taken inboard on the launches,
and a hundred men get hold of the bottom net and begin
to lift. Slowly, slowly, they haul the net in, chanting a wild
and ancient chant, working in rhythm. Slowly more and
more of the bottom net comes to the surface, while the corral space is steadily lessened. Still I see no sign of fish.

I see nothing, though I look most closely. Ah, there is
something! A fish—a *big* fish! But a second look, and even
I can see that it is a languid shark, a gummy about three and
a half feet long. Where *are* these tuna? Steadily the men

chant; steadily the net comes in. The corks bob upon the blue surface of the sea: a line of piratical fellows, stripped to the waist, now appears on the dhows round the business end of the corral, flexing muscles, grasping wrist hooks which look big enough to stun a bullock. All peer into the water—tense, determined, alert.

Now comes something! Not a languid shark this time but a school of fish—big fellows. Not tuna yet, though. *Are* there any tuna here? I begin to wonder. I catch a glimpse of the Master's set countenance. He looks satisfied, though these are flying fish which are breaking surface and—to me at any rate—there is still no sign whatever that there is a tuna within miles. Flying fish? What are they doing in the corral? When we tried to catch tuna, bonita, or albacore with a hook and line from the bowsprit end of a big sailing ship, our "bait" was always a piece of white cloth which we made to skim the seas like a flying fish. That was what the tuna ate. Yet here now was a school of flying fish—big fellows, wild-eyed, beautiful—swimming round and round and round. Why didn't they fly out? They could do that easily enough. Indeed they need never have been stopped by the trap at all—by any trap. They could swim through the mesh without noticing it. They could fly over any net. Yet here they were, with their archenemies, the tuna, close behind them. It was a mystery. Afterwards I asked the tuna men. It was equally a mystery to them.

"As far as we can make out, these flying fish guide the migrating tuna," the master told me. "But we don't know. We always see the flying fish first. If there are flying fish, there are tuna with them. The more flying fish, the bigger the school of tuna. No, they never fly out. Do the tuna eat them? Not the flying fish that come with them. They don't touch them. There's never anything in the stomachs of the tuna when we get them. They don't seem to eat at all when on the move."

Within a moment of the flying fish coming up, suddenly the surface gives a wild flurry as if an eruption was under the corral. At once there is a breaking of the sea by a score great dorsal fins—two score, three score, hundreds of them! Wilder and wilder the surface grows until it is lashed as if by a storm. Spray and foam fly everywhere. The great tuna dart here, leap there. The line of the launches approaches ever nearer, nearer, the net rising, the tuna men chanting that same old wild chant, louder and louder. Then I do not notice the rising net any longer. The last roundup begins— the slaughter of the tuna. Near-naked men leap onto the sides of the net, lean far from the inboard gunwales of the deep launches, thrust deftly with their hooks and long gaffs among the tuna, cutting at them with swift blows, the red blood spurting thick. Here and there a great tuna of three hundred pounds and more breaks away and swims in furious circles with a hook hanging from its gills and the blood turning the water ever a warmer red.

These tuna are huge fish, weighing up to 400 pounds and more. The smallest of them is over a hundred pounds. I see the hooks torn from men's wrists time and time again. I see tuna swimming round with great gaffs hanging to them and other gaffs afloat in the pool of the corral, floating by their wooden handles.

I noticed, as the wet and bloodstained men secured tuna after tuna, that they weren't actually hauling them into the boats at all. What they did was to hook a tuna in the gills, hold on for their lives, lift the tuna's head in the water, and then guide the huge, struggling body while the fish, with its thrashing tail, propelled itself up over the low gunwale and into the launch. The tuna flicked themselves up into those launches. His own wildly beating tail sends him up over the side of the boat. He goes up with his own way. His own strength dooms him. Great shapely blue bodies are everywhere, with wild staring eyes, and the water is soon tinged and then stained all red with the tuna's blood. Everywhere where there is room, a man crouches over the corral; and still the space narrows. The tuna are strong. Some men are pulled in, even though the loop round the hook is designed to be disengaged easily. Men can be badly injured among a school of maddened tuna. The tuna bullfight, they call it, not without reason. Sometimes bones are broken in the corral and men may be drowned.

Swiftly, the number of the swimming tuna declines as they are hauled into the launches, where they thrash violently until the whole launch shakes and trembles with the magnificent pulsating life flung so violently into it—trembles a little while, as the blood in the scuppers and the bottom of the boat thickens and deepens. No sound comes from the tuna except this terrific thrashing. They thrash and tremble for perhaps fifteen minutes, after the corral is cleared: then all is quiet. The wide-eyed, handsome tuna are all dead. There is escape for none.

A fisherman hoists the lateen yard of the largest dhow at an angle which indicates the size of the catch, to be signaled to the canneries ashore. The dhows, deep laden with the dead tuna, detach themselves, make sail, and slip away towards Vila Real. Other fishermen get quietly on with the task of relaying the corral and the hoisting launches drop back into position, letting the corral bottom fall into place again as they go. The bloodstains disperse slowly from the pool, while the Master and the idlers go back to their silent, deadly watching again, as if appalled at the slaughter they have just seen.

The Tunny Bullfight was a bit of a murder, and I was sorry for the poor tuna—unfortunate fish, that its solid and abundant flesh should be both nutritious and tasty, and its desire for a peaceful spawning so overpowering that it was temporarily timorous, afraid of shadows, and so easily caught. Poor fish! Yet some schools escaped—many schools, indeed, for there were many other traps along Mediterranean coastlines, many other murderous corrals. Yet there always were tunny to come back again from the deep Atlantic towards the Mediterranean, at the proper season of the year.

I left the Algarve, bright with its sunshine and its flowers, and went to Lisbon to join the new Grand Banks assistance vessel *Gil Eannes* for her maiden voyage towards the Banks and Greenland. While other countries were consuming their resources in preparations for war, Portugal had built a new hospital ship to accompany the dory fishermen in their fleet of schooners to the Banks. This was the 4,000-ton motor ship *Gil Eannes*, a handsome white vessel of unusual appearance, built in a dry dock at Viana do Castelo. Replacing an ancient steamer of the same name, the new *Gil Eannes* was equipped both as hospital ship and assistance vessel. She had surgeries, operation rooms, X-ray equipment, a forty-bed hospital, a chapel, and salvage gear. She had con-

siderable refrigerated space to carry bait replenishments
for the thirty schooners and three thousand dorymen who
fished from them. She had a powerful radio installation, to
keep in touch with a Portuguese fleet of sixty-five fishing
vessels spread from the Banks off Nova Scotia to north of
the island of Disko, in Davis Strait. She had three surgeons,
a priest, a staff of male nurses. Her captain was an experienced codfishing schooner master, and she carried also
the admiral of the fleet, a senior naval officer charged with
the administration and the care of all the Portuguese deep-
sea fishermen.

I had been invited to sail in this unusual vessel by my
friend, Commander Henrique Dos Santos Tenreiro, the dy-
namic head of the Gremio of the Grand Banks and Greenland fishermen. I had been to the Banks some years earlier,
in the beautiful schooner *Argus,* and saw the six-month
season through off Newfoundland and Greenland. It was a
stirring and heart-warming experience, and I was pleased to
go again to see, in part, whether there had been any deterioration among these last of Europe's sailing adventur-
ers, these 3,000 dorymen who faced the bitter and relentless
sea week after week, month after month, and took the sailing of their stout schooners and barkentines in their capable
and fearless stride. Where all around was so much change
and—in a sense—character deterioration in the ancient
ways of the sea, what had become of these? I knew the
Newfoundlanders had given up dory fishing, and their
wooden schooners were now motor ships which carried a
little steadying sail and stayed in port if the motor was
defective.

I knew the Nova Scotia men no longer had schooners and

dorymen fishing the offshore banks, and all the Gloucester-men and the St. Malo men, all the Americans and the French, had gone. I had been told that the government of a recently federated Newfoundland, alarmed at the decline of time-honored, local skills, had made a tentative approach to Portugal for the loan of some dorymen, to restore those skills. For interested governments, with a stake in the fishing wealth of the great Banks area, had noted the decline alike in quantity and quality in the catches of their too-efficient draggers, trawling methodically over the same ground, while the dorymen brought in splendid catches of fat cod. The dorymen fished on foul ground where the draggers could not work, and the older methods were slowly proving to be really the best.

The Portuguese still operated their fleet of dory fishing schooners. All had left Portugal some time before the *Gil Eannes* sailed from Lisbon. We plugged across to the west'ard over the windy sea for a week or more, and then suddenly one day, in a swift clearing of the cold Banks mist, we saw the first schooner—a low-sided wooden three-master, graceful of line and perfectly proportioned, her three lofty trucks rising to the highest aft on the tall mizzen, and her forty dories spread about the sea all round for miles. There was a restless surge on the cold old sea and a big swell ran, for it had been blowing hard earlier and the sea takes time to go down on the Banks. The schooner lay to a long scope of coir, wire, and chain cable, to which she plunged and rolled like a restless thing held by the nose. A dory was alongside her, on the lee side, jumping and rolling twice as much as the ship, while the oilskinned, sea-booted doryman, upright in his tiny boat, pitched up his catch of fish skillfully over the schooner's rail.

As the mist cleared we could see a host of dories, little red and yellow boats of incredible minuteness in the waste of gray waters, some lying to the grapnels of their 600-hook lines while the dorymen handled their jigs, hauling in the fat and flapping cod, hand over hand. Here and there, other dories broke out the triangular pinpoints of their little sails as they skimmed home towards their schooners with a fresh load of fish, or shifted ground. Some passed us very closely, and the *Gil Eannes* slowed down for them as they stood by their thwarts and smiled and waved. What a life! It was cold with a cheerless and quite hopeless intensity, and the wind from the north brought the freezing breath of ice. The men, I saw, were at work barehanded. Nothing was in their tiny boats save their fish and their fishing gear, a bit of a compass, and the doryman's pail with his bite of cold food and small flask of cold water. They had been fishing there for many weeks before the *Gil Eannes* arrived: the campaign would go on for months—for half the year and more until the schooners were all filled, come what may.

Here and there all round the horizon, other schooners showed—there a graceful four-master of perhaps 600 tons, with what looked like a sister ship anchored close by her (I recognized these as the famous sister schooners *Argus* and *Creola,* commanded by the Ilhavo brothers Paiao), and further off, a white-painted barkentine looking very gallant and romantic though, being anchored, she carried only a triangle of riding sail. We counted seven ships, and perhaps 400 dories, each with one man.

We passed one dory very close. Its little sail was painted

with a cross and its red sides bore a painted motto. DEUS
AJUDA, I could read, with difficulty: yes, there it was—DEUS
AJUDA QUEM TRABALHA. God helps him who works.

Later, after a week or so on the Banks, we went into the
crater port of St. Johns, Newfoundland, for in the chapel of
the *Gil Eannes* was an image of Our Lady of Fatima which
the dorymen were offering to the cathedral at St. Johns.
When we came in all the schooners followed us, rust-
streaked and storm-marked from the sea, and the ice growl-
ers in the Labrador current swirled in our way. The
schooners came in and the dorymen landed, 3,000-strong,
lusty, able, gentle men from their frail open boats, and they
carried their image through the streets to the cathedral,
chanting—3,000 fishermen in their plaid, gay woolen fishing
shirts and sea boots and Nazarene caps, sea-booted still
because most had no other footwear, dark men with strong
faces that shone with sure faith, and among them, their one
priest, and their admiral, and their thirty captains. The captains had the faces of priests, and the chanting of that great
concourse of those simple and God-fearing men was so moving that, though the procession had been routed by back
streets to avoid a traffic jam, all St. Johns hurried out to
watch.

Carrying the image were four captains, well known to
me, for each I knew had commanded a schooner that had
been overwhelmed in the sea in recent years. (They must
fish through the hurricane season, and keep the sea: the
Grand Banks knows little summer and the Greenland banks
none. They are assailed by ice, gales, fog. Each year one or
two ships is lost—but rarely a man.) I knew their schooners
—*Senhora da Saude, Julio Primeiro, Infante de Sagres.* And

I knew also that they had not lost a man. The men were marching there, behind their captains, singing through the gray streets of St. Johns and, below them in the harbor, were the new schooners, built to replace the old.

I stood on a vantage point and watched the men go by, and I found this procession of the dorymen very moving. Below me the schooners lay quietly to their anchors, a graceful, brave, and *living* fleet, their high-sheered decks crowded with the stacks of flat-bottomed boats called dories, their graceful cutwaters and sweet flowing white lines a challenge to the stumpy and stub-nosed vessels of the newer commerce all round them. I knew that here at least was a fleet—a last fleet—of working ships under sail from Western Europe, getting on with a share of the world's hard work, which could be depended upon to survive at least for a while—for a long while, I hoped.

Here at least were good ships to sail, and the men to sail them.

CHAPTER

5

THE RACE OF THE SAILING
SCHOOL SHIPS

BACK in England, there was a deal of talk about a race of big sailing school ships, being organized in that country to take place from Tor Bay, in the western end of the English Channel, towards Lisbon in the summer of 1956. This news struck me with some mild astonishment, for I wondered how it came about that a country which (alone among the great maritime nations), never had had such a ship for its merchant service and had had no naval sail training ship since Admiral Fisher scrapped the brigs fifty years before, was now proposing to be host for a rally and race among the more enlightened nations that had kept such ships. The very mention of the words "sail training" to the average British shipowner or merchant seaman was like waving a red rag before a bad-tempered bull. Britain had steadfastly refused to have anything to do with any of the many efforts made to restore some measure of sail training for character building and the imagined good of its merchant service. Efforts such as the late Sir William Garthwaite's Sea Lions had come to nothing, and my own attempt to provide a ship had been pretty effectively ignored. My beautiful *Joseph Conrad* was the perfect sailing school ship for British boys when I bought her from the Danes in 1934. She was a school ship designed and tested, fitted out for eighty boys. There were twenty years of good life in her when, at the end of my circumnavigation, I had to sell her in New York because of the total absence of British interest or support.

If Britain had no use for any sort of ocean-going sailing school ship and the great majority of its shipowners abominated the very idea (no one could prove that their ships had suffered from the lack), what on earth was going on with this race? There were, in the world, some thirty large seagoing sailing ships used for training in some way or other, by the Japanese, the Germans, Russians, Italians, Spanish, Portuguese, Brazilians, Chileans, Norwegians, Danes, Swedes, Finns, Poles, Americans and Indonesians, among others. I knew all this very well, having sailed in several of their school ships; in the Danish ship *Georg Stage*, the big Portuguese naval bark *Sagres*, and the United States Coast Guard's bark *Eagle*. I had remained good friends with the Danes after buying their old *Georg Stage* and had twice sailed on passages in their new vessel of the same name. I had made a pleasant run from Lisbon to Madeira and the Cape Verde Islands in the *Sagres*, which is school ship and seamanship training center alike for the Portuguese Navy. I had made a summer cruise in the *Eagle*, from the Coast Guard Academy at New London across the Atlantic to Santander, Amsterdam, and Denmark.

In addition to the considerable fleet of the larger sailing
school ships—six four-masted barks, another six or eight
full-rigged ships ranging in size from the 3,000-ton Italian
Amerigo Vespucci to the 400-ton *Georg Stage*, a dozen or so
barks with an equal variation in size, half a dozen big steel
barkentines and tops'l schooners such as Brazil's *Almirante
Saldanha*, Chile's *Esmeralda*, Spain's *Juan Sebastian del
Cano*, Belgium's *Mercator*, and Indonesia's *Dewarutji*—
there were many smaller vessels, in Sweden, France, Denmark, and other countries, and one or two ex-yachts in
Britain too. There were plenty of real sailing school ships to
choose from, if any cared to enter. In Britain there were several small vessels, not ocean-going—craft such as the ex-
yachts *Warspite* and *Moyana* working for the Outward
Bound School at Aberdovey and the Southampton School of
Navigation, another ex-yacht working out of Falmouth, and
a fourth sailing out of Poole in Dorset, for girls.

All these were doing good work in their own way. The
Outward Bound Trust had then recently acquired a former
Danish three-masted schooner to use in Scotland, and had
the damaged hull of another laid up in the south of England
after a fire, awaiting funds for conversion (three years later,
no funds had been forthcoming and the *Hans Egede* still
waited). I had sailed the *Warspite* for the Outward Bound
in '49-'50, and enjoyed the experience, for she was doing
a splendid job for a very real and enterprising organization
which seemed to me to have the answers to many of the
problems of modern youth: but the very excellence of the
job she was doing put all hope of racing to Lisbon beyond
her. The same thing applied to the three-master *Prince
Louis* in Scotland. These Outward Bound ships sail in close
connection with shore establishments on short-term courses,

and their purpose is to bring the fullness and the shock of living into the lives of youth—not for them any gallivanting off on a fascinating race, no matter how exciting the prospect. They could not be spared.

Despite my wonder, I found the plans for the international sail training-ship race well advanced and going splendidly. The English are a curious lot. Perhaps any sporting event would appeal to them, but the enthusiasm for this event was a surprise to me and to others who had spent the best part of their lifetimes trying to induce the English to support just such ships. Indeed, had I been asked to organize the race when it was first thought of (by a London solicitor, apparently), I would have been most dubious about the prospects. Let us have a real ship of our own first, before we ask others to bring their ships here and race, I might have said.

I would have been wrong. The British Admiralty, the British Foreign Office, several British pre-sea training schools, and an influential group of naval officers got behind the idea. So did the Portuguese Ambassador in London, Dr. Pedro Theotónio Pereira, G.C.V.O. Becoming the first patron of the organization which titled itself the Sail Training-ship International Race Committee, he brought in the first big entry—his own country's naval training barque *Sagres*, which was a beauty of a big old Cape Horner but not noted much for speed. That great maritime people, the Portuguese, took up the idea with enthusiasm. Other nations followed their lead with splendid entries. Norway came in with two full-rigged ships, the *Sörlandet* and the *Christian Radich*, Belgium came in with the *Mercator*, a sleek 700-ton barkentine. Sweden entered three school ships, two of them naval (the sister-schooners *Gladan* and *Falken*, lovely 200-tonners built a few years ago) and one a merchant-service training ship, the *Flying Clipper*, school ship of the Flying Clipper Line. Denmark entered the *Georg Stage*.

Many other countries were interested. The U.S. Coast Guard wanted to enter the bark *Eagle*, which stood an excellent chance of winning. Captain Karl Zittel would have given a good account, and so would his officers and cadets. But the *Eagle*, like most other school ships, cannot do what she wants or go where she pleases. She has to fit her schedule into the academic year of the training establishment she serves. Being an official ship, a flag-shower, she has also, pretty well, to go where the authorities want her to, and it had already been arranged (she had been to Europe at least for six years before that) that she was to cruise to Central America that summer. It was a pity. The *Eagle* should have been there.

Spain's bark *Galatea* and four-master *Juan Sebastian del Cano*, Italy's full-rigged ship *Amerigo Vespucci*, Chile's new *Esmeralda*, Brazil's *Almirante Saldanha*, Japan's *Nippon Maru*—all these might have come, but they were caught in the same difficulty as the *Eagle*. They had other places to go, other things to do, and they could not alter their carefully arranged schedules. There were one or two countries, I heard, which could have entered their ships but hesitated to believe that the race would ever happen. Perhaps these were sorry, afterwards.

By this time, there was a new patron—His Royal Highness the Duke of Edinburgh, himself a keen sailor and a former crew member in one of Britain's few attempts at using a sailing school ship of any kind, the earlier *Prince Louis,* which was a former North Sea pilot schooner used by a famous Scots school to foster leadership and develop character and initiative in boys. This school, to some degree, was associated with the Outward Bound Trust, a movement dedicated to the development of better citizenship in youth, and the founder of the Trust was the headmaster of the school. This was Dr. Kurt Hahn, famous German educationist. The Outward Bound movement flourished in Britain and ran sea schools both in Wales and in Scotland, operating a ketch and a three-masted schooner, not as sailing school ships in the more usual sense, but as tenders to establishments ashore which provided, by challenge and unforgettable experiences, chances for boys to find themselves, not only at sea.

Neither the ketch nor the three-masted schooner could be spared for the race, which was a pity but understandable. There remained one other British possibility. There *was* a sort of British square-rigged sailing ship building at the time, right on the shores of Tor Bay—a wooden curiosity publicized as a "precise replica" of the original *Mayflower.* I looked at the interesting little vessel as she stood bareribbed on the Brixham ways. It struck me that she might make a good sailing school ship for England, at that, for she would be difficult to handle and could be relied upon to provide plenty of challenging and unforgettable experiences for not only the young—the purpose of a sailing school ship. But the new *Mayflower* was far from ready. I thought this a pity, but I could find no locals who shared this view. For the little *Mayflower,* finished or not, was stacking the tourists into Brixham from both sides of the

Atlantic and—just then at any rate—it was obvious that this was at least an important part of her purpose.

If there was no square-rigged ship there was at least another ketch, an ex-yacht, which served to provide training through sailing for cadets at a remarkable establishment on Southampton Water. This was the School of Navigation of the University of Southampton, directed by an enterprising master mariner named Wakeford. This unusual school had been using a ketch for outside work since 1942, when the idea was pretty generally scoffed at in the United Kingdom.

Captain Wakeford became the treasurer of the Sail Training-ship International Race Committee. Could he enter his school's ex-yacht? She was considerably smaller than the national school ships. She had no regular crew assigned to her, being handled always by the school's own instructors. (So is the U.S.C.G. training bark *Eagle*—it is an excellent idea.) In a race, she could hardly be described as in the same class as a 2,000-ton Cape Horn bark or a couple of Norwegian full-rigged ships. However, a system of handicapping could get round that. She was a full-time school ship. Why shouldn't she be entered? So she was. The committee arranged to run the race in two classes, one for vessels of over 100 tons regardless of rig, and the other for smaller sailing vessels, yachts and such.

But they didn't lay down what sort of tons. The Southampton ketch, the name of which was the *Moyana*, was just over 100 tons by a rule of computation known as Thames measurement, used for yachts. None of the other entries (at the time) was a yacht. The *Moyana* was welcome, although there were a few old sailors who maintained that, since this was an international event and might be setting some precedents, there ought to be a class for square-riggers and another for fore-and-afters. The square-riggers offered a wide variety in themselves. How was anyone going to handicap this mixture? As somebody said, it was rather like having a race of all the animals in the zoo. The Swedish tops'l schooner—not a genuine square-rigger, of course—was an ex-yacht of a different class from the *Moyana*. She had been built as the private cruising yacht for a British shipowner, in the days when the scale of taxation allowed British shipowners to run such things and they had the inclination.

At any rate, the *Moyana's* entry was accepted and, once she was in, other fore-and-afters, ex-yachts and present yachts, former sailing trawlers, and one or two specially designed racers began to come forward. What sort of school ships some of these were I don't know but, at any rate for the race, they had to be manned, at least in part, by cadets or boys under training. Or girls. One, named the *English Rose*, was "manned" entirely by young women. The only man aboard was the master, an old Cape Horner aged more than seventy, who declared that girl crews were all right. Another, entered by a sailing school, had two English girls as mates and a third as cook.

Most of these yachts were small fellows, well under 100 tons. One was the Portuguese Ambassador's, and he shipped Portuguese cadets as crew for the race. (He also shipped myself, to be his navigator and, thanks to his kindness, I made the race.) The Ambassador's yacht was the American-built *Bellatrix*, a John Alden schooner of over twenty years ago, with a nice turn of speed. She was small—only forty-five feet waterline—but she was a big vessel compared with one or two of the others. There was a little Italian yawl called the *Artica II* which claimed to be sixteen tons Thames measurement but looked about six real tons.

It was a brave show of fine vessels when all this heterogeneous fleet got together in the River Dart, during the first week of July, 1956. The old port of Dartmouth hadn't seen the like, said the locals, since the days of the Spanish Armada in Queen Elizabeth's I's time. In fact Dartmouth hadn't seen it then, either. There had never been anything quite like this before, anywhere. The scene was breathtaking—a forest of masts, a galaxy of shapely hulls with the noble swelling cutwaters of the square-rigged ship, the sigh of the Devon breezes through taut rigging and high yards. When the ships all loosed their canvas to dry after a squall of rain, they made a noble picture against the backdrop of the parklike Devon fields and hills.

The crews were as unusual as the ships. Here was a great fleet of sailing ships, yet not a single one of them was interested in training sailing-ship sailors, as such. Here were more than fifteen hundred boys and youths, serving these ships (forgetting the girls for the moment), and not a single one of them was intended to become a sailing-ship sailor. Here were twenty large and small sailing ships, and only their bare minimum nucleus of professional-officer crew were sailing-ship men at all. Here were fifteen hundred boys (and twenty girls) and the whole lot were there, in those ships, for the value of the experience and the good of their souls. In a sense, too, they used sailing ships for training as a surgeon studies anatomy: the wind-driven ship provided the anatomy of seafaring, the simple elemental things which all seamen must grasp if they are to be of real use in their

exacting profession—to have some comprehension of the
element their ships must defeat, to develop the ability to
lead, to do the right thing, to stay one jump ahead of the
ferocious and devil sea which becomes no more tractable
with the passing years, no matter what manner of fresh in-
vention those years may bring—atomic power, electronic
navigation, automation on bridge and engine room, and all
the rest of it.

That fleet of ships was a soul-stirring sight in more ways
than one, and the public responded by coming by the thousand to see it. The vision which assembled the ships was
rewarded. Mr. E. Bernard Morgan, the retired solicitor who
had done so much to organize it all, bought himself a
yachting cap and gazed at the ships with affection and
amazement, perhaps astonished at what he had done, and
passed the technical details over to those competent to deal
with them. He had done a good job! Those ships were a re-
assuring sight, not only to me.

It was one of the most stirring seafaring sights—any kind
of sight—I can remember. I had been in half a dozen of
those big Grain Races from Australia, but the greatest number of sailers that I had ever seen manage to start together
then had been two. Now there were a dozen big fellows and
another twenty small fry. The big fellows included another
British entry—a sleek three-masted stays'l schooner-yacht
named *Creole* which the Greek shipowner Mr. Stavros Niarchos had made available, having another large schooner-
yacht for his own passage, and a large airplane. The *Creole,*
which was designed and built by Camper and Nicholson's
regardless of expense some years before the war, was
manned for the race by a crew of cadets drawn from the

Royal Navy and Merchant Service, and there was keen competition to get a place aboard. The lads had had a week or two to become accustomed to the ship, and Mr. Niarchos' regular master and crew were also there.

All the crews had a wonderful time in Darmouth, where the Royal Naval College had assisted in arranging an inshore regatta and entertainment of all kinds. There was not a hotel room to be had for miles around, for the whole area was crowded with visitors. The R.N. did its usual splendidly efficient job, arranging a ferry service for the fleet at its buoys, providing sports activities, and all sorts of things. Indeed the inshore regatta, in a sense, was probably the best part of the proceedings, and it was the Navy which made this a success. The race itself could easily have been a fiasco with such a diversity of ships, craft, and temperaments entered, and it was encouraging to see the preliminaries go so well.

The usual appalling English summer weather persisted almost throughout the week of the inshore regatta and continued until the day of the race. Then it blew fresh from southwest. When it blows fresh from southwest in the English Channel it generally blows fresher, with bad visibility and sometimes half a gale to follow—often a whole gale. At such times the English Channel is hard for any ship to get out of, and next to impossible for square-riggers. The wind is right against them. There are four- and five-knot tides. There are rocky and dangerous lee shores on either side, and a lot of wicked rocks round the Channel Islands, with another lot, even worse, waiting at Ushant to take a gash at any passing ship which may come too near them.

The race was arranged to start like a yacht race, but

those square-rigged ships were not yachts. There was a five-minute gun and then a starting gun, fired by the First Lord of the Admiralty aboard a naval minesweeper moored to mark the starting line off Tor Bay. Almost the whole of Tor Bay was covered with small craft of all sorts, even to canoes, so that some of the competitors had difficulty in getting about. In such conditions, the square-rigger captains could take no chance maneuvering round the starting line. There was too grave a risk of collision. The gunned start was left to the fore-and-afters. The old black ketch *Moyana,* the three-masted *Creole,* a Bermuda-rigged double-ender from Holland named *Maybe,* and a lovely and mysterious big Turk—a yawl named *Ruyam,* with a hull obviously designed for racing, and a beautiful blonde in the crew—had the start to themselves.

This *Ruyam* was listed in the official program as entered by the Turkish Commercial Navy School, but she turned out in fact to be the former yacht *Thistle,* a big, bronze-hulled beauty, a magnificent racing yawl which had been expensively refitted in Germany. When I watched her come storming for the line under a cloud of beautiful (and costly) sails, magnificently cut and drawing perfectly, with her perfect racing hull and her noble proportions, I thought that I was having a good look at the winner. She was about the *Moyana's* size, so under the rating rule that had been worked out (with much burning of midnight oil and many headaches) to take care of so diverse a fleet, she had a time allowance of thirteen hours on Mr. Niarchos' big schooner. I thought the *Creole* should have had some time on her, regardless of her "rating."

It was half an hour after the start of the big ships that

the smaller fellows—*Bellatrix* and the rest—were due to cross the line, but the larger square-riggers stormed over just a little in front of us. They could afford no chances, nor were they paying much attention to starting guns. They were not used to that kind of thing. In the *Bellatrix* we were given wonderful views of the full-riggers crowding all sail for the starting line, heeling to the fresh head wind, their white bows treading back the gray old Channel water, the southwester crying in their high rigging, the big sails straining! Last came the bark *Sagres*, tearing along with the spray driving over her and wetting the great cross of Christ emblazoned on her forecourse, as it always was on the ships of the Portuguese discoverers.

When it was our turn, we pitched and staggered beneath a press of sail, with some racing yachts round us which we knew we would be hard pressed to beat. In addition to the little Italian racing yawl, with her ultra-modern (and to my eye) rather ugly hull, there was a beauty from the Argentine named *Juana* that was crewed by Argentine naval officers. This *Juana* had already, we knew, won three hard ocean races, and we suspected she had been designed and built for just that purpose. The *Ruyam* and the *Juana* made the ketch *Moyana* look like a stately and dignified old lady, which in fact she was. She was nearly sixty years old, but she *was* a school ship and no doubt about it.

We were all there to do our best and we got on with it, *Juana* or no *Juana*, *Ruyam*, *Creole*, *Artica*, and all the rest of them. We belted along under every sail we could carry, trying to guess what that southwester would do next. We were not left long in doubt. It brought down a miserable and all-embracing fog. The clouds of lovely sails were soon lost in clouds of unlovely fog, which persisted. The wind dropped, nothing was in sight, and there we wallowed— right there in the Channel mouth, the ocean highway of the world, packed tight with more ships to the square mile than any other piece of watery highway on earth except just off the entrance to New York harbor! Ships roared, grunted, and bellowed on full-powered sirens all round us —big ships, little ships, trawlers, line-fishermen, cross-channel ferries, liners. We hoped they all had efficient radar, well maintained. More than that, we hoped they all kept radar plots, and had enough competent officers to do it. There had been a special warning broadcast about us, asking powered ships to give us a berth; but first they had to see us, in vision (preferably) or on a radar screen. Some did not, and there were several very narrow escapes from collision that first night out. When suddenly we heard a voice call MAYDAY! MAYDAY! on the radio, early that first night, we thought that it was one of us. But it was a coaster that had got herself on the rocks off the Lizard in the fog and wanted a lifeboat, quickly.

The fog lasted two days—two rather worrying days. I thought of all those boys in all those ships, lying stopped (when the wind dropped) and so liable to collision. The girls, we heard, had gone back. They had stayed five hours at sea, and then their ketch had sailed smartly back to its home port.

After the fog we had two good sailing days and bowled across the Bay of Biscay towards Finisterre at ten knots, which was good going for the *Bellatrix*. When the fog lifted we were up with the *Creole*, which pleased us. We reckoned on getting the usual north wind called *Nortada* down the coasts of Spain and Portugal and so, when we ran bravely past Finisterre four days out from Tor Bay, we were in high spirits and a good place. But the *Nortada* was not there. Its last dying breath expired as we got there, and we were stuck in head winds and calms throughout the following three days. A few lucky ships had picked up a breath of the *Nortada* before it died, and dribbled on southwards down the Portuguese coast. As things turned out, these were the winners. The best of them was only twenty miles ahead of us off Finisterre, but she came in to Lisbon two days before we did. That's the luck of ocean racing.

We were just over eight days altogether. With the slightest help from the missing *Nortada*, we would have made it easily in six. The conditions did not suit the square-riggers at all. First that beat in the Channel, then the fog and calm and, last blow of all, the absence of a reasonable sailing breeze where we all expected to find one—these things quite spoiled their chances. We were not surprised at all to hear on the radio that, just as at the start, it was a fore-and-aft finish. Argentine's racing *Juana* was first to cross the line, beating everything in both classes though she rated only twenty-five tons. Next across the line came the swift Turk, that handsome, lofty *Ruyam*, and after her, Mr. Niarchos' schooner *Creole*. Then came more fore-and-afters— a couple of the Swedish schooners, and then the little Italian (which had twenty-four hours' allowance on *Juana*). The poor square-riggers were out of it. The Oslo ship *Christian Radich* was the first of them to show up, many hours behind the leading fore-and-afters.

There was one big surprise. Those early fore-and-aft arrivals included one ship that had not been expected to be

with the leaders at all—the old ketch *Moyana*, from the
Southampton Navigation School. For all her sixty years and
her inexperienced boy-crew, there she was, keeping up with
the leaders, bowling along with the best of them into Cas-
cais Bay by the Tagus bar! Her crew were fifteen boys
aged sixteen, whose first sea experience this was and first
voyage. The captain was the deputy director of the school,
and the officers were instructors who were taking time off
for the sail. The *Moyana* (as befitted her quality) had a
generous time allowance on swift modern yachts like
Ruyam. When all the ships had arrived, it turned out that,
on time allowance, she had won.

It was a grand result. Everyone was delighted. *Moyana*
took first prize in the big class, with the ship *Christian
Radich* second and the *Ruyam* third. In the small class,
the little Italian took first prize on corrected times, with
Juana second and a British naval yawl named *Marabu* third.

Not even the fact that the old *Moyana* sank in a gale on
her homeward passage from Lisbon towards Southampton
spoiled the wonderful effects of the race. Indeed, since all
her boys were taken off safely by a passing steamer (and
showed themselves agile and resourceful young seafarers
in the rescue), there were a good many old salts who reckoned it fitting that the *Moyana*, if she had to go, should pass
in the hour of her glory. There were some others who asked,
if she had to be abandoned in a gale, why was she there? If
she could not stand a gale of wind, then what sort of ship
was she to take young boys on their first voyage to sea?

But these were unwarranted queries. The facts of her loss
were very simple. There was a wild summer gale, the back-
lash of some blowing-out Caribbean hurricane screaming

5. The tunny "bullfighters" ready for the fray.

6. Last pure sailing-ship left in the North Atlantic, the Portuguese cod-fishing schooner *Ana Maria* on the way to the Grand Banks. The *Ana Maria* was built in Dundee in 1873 and reconstructed as a cod-fisherman in 1924. She was lost in 1958.

7. I think the *Eagle* could have won, but she could not be entered.

8. The start of the Tall Ships Race from Torbay to Lisbon.

9. Frigate at Palermo. Hull-planks were peeled away. The figurehead was weathered like an old and battered doll.

10. Director John Villiers Farrow (left) and Alan Villiers study a chart for the historic sea battle in the film, JOHN PAUL JONES.

into the chops of the Channel, and she found herself on a lee shore with poor prospect of clawing off, if a showdown came. She had some rigging damage, and she was making water. If she got on any of those savage French rocks she would grind to pieces in an instant, and no one would walk away from her. The sensible thing for her master to do— the decision was entirely his, and so would the blame be if he lost the boys—was to abandon her while this could be done in some degree of safety, and this he did early on the Sunday morning of July 29. The wind was a full gale out of the northwest then, with a steep, cross, and (for small ships) dangerous sea. There was a question whether the *Moyana* would drive ashore or founder before she drifted there. In either case she had to be abandoned. The Clan Line steamer *Clan Maclean,* summoned by radio, came up and, maneuvering perfectly, brought the old ketch to a position where the lads could jump for it and scramble up cargo nets rigged on the cargo liner's sides. This they did, the whole lot of them, with such alacrity and efficiency that all hands were saved within a matter of moments, and no one went in the sea at all.

It was a stirring rescue, and it was a grand job the old ketch had done, winning the extraordinary race of the sailing school ships. Now, I thought, surely the lesson will be learned! Out of this colorful rally of extraordinary ships great and small, almost fortuitously assembled, has come this unlooked-for but compelling example of the real value of sea sailing for boys. If the English are logical, now is the moment to replace the *Moyana* with a real sailing school ship for England—not a half-converted ancient yacht nor a transformed motor fishing vessel, but the real thing such as the Norwegians had, and the Danes, the Portuguese, and all the rest. The vast crowds on Berry Head, which was black with cars and citizens when the ships set out, augured well for England's interest. The enthusiasm with which the spectacle of the tall ships had been acclaimed surely indicated real support for the idea.

But it was not to be. The enthusiasm was just that and nothing more. The *Moyana* had gone and, though an appeal was made for funds to provide an adequate replacement, it was a failure, and the Southampton School had to content itself with buying another yacht, mainly with funds of its own.

In the meantime, the three-masted *Hans Egede* continued to languish at her forlorn berth, and for her there was not even an appeal. The committee for the race remained in being, and began to organize another, this time in '58, from France towards the Canary Islands, with talk of another in the Pacific later on. To what point now? I wondered.

Our romp in the *Bellatrix* had been grand sport and enjoyable, for she had a congenial crew and is a noble little schooner. We had sailed with her before, when she came up from Lisbon first under the Ambassador's command, and knew her good qualities well. I had toyed with the idea of acquiring some such ship and sailing her as a sort of school ship myself, as I had with the rather different *Joseph Conrad* years before. (Where were the Foreign Office and the Admiralty then? Perhaps I was too fresh from sea to know about big committees and famous names, and the manner of finding the proper measure of acceptance for strange schemes in England: by the time I had learned, it was too late.)

The *Bellatrix* and her class of ship are too small for me, too small and too expensive. I wished that I had been able to keep the *Joseph Conrad*. I had bought her for less than £2,000, and her entire running costs did not exceed £100 a week. In 1956, even an ancient Baltic schooner cost £8,000 and crew costs were quite out of the question for the private citizen.

Maybe, I thought, I had better take a look at that *Mayflower* again, building at Brixham. Here at least was some sort of venture aimed, apparently, at providing a British square-rigger, if only to sail once across the North Atlantic. But I could find nobody in the shipping world who knew anything of this strange enterprise nor who was running it, nor why. I could let that project bide a while, to see if it really looked like happening or would fizzle out.

CHAPTER

6

TWO FRIGATES, PLEASE

In the meantime a man called at my home in Oxford, from Hollywood, to ask if I could find him a couple of frigates, please, for a new sea film.

I get a number of these rather unusual requests—more as the years pass. The man from Hollywood, indeed, followed hard on the heels of a chap from Virginia, who was at one of the Oxford colleges at the time and had a bright idea to build some new kind of craft described by himself as a catamaran, which he proposed to sail down the River Po in Italy, thence south through the Adriatic, and afterwards head east. This young fellow had an elderly truck at the door, laden with balks of lumber and some old oil drums. He was, I gathered, then on his way towards Italy, with this cargo, which was to be the makings of his "catamaran." All he wanted to know from me was how to rig and sail the thing, if it would sail, and where were some good places to go? I told him, and he went, and I heard no more of him or his peculiar vessel, but if his old truck ever reached the banks of the River Po I would be surprised. However, he had the right spirit, and at least the type of vessel he proposed to build would not cost him much, except perhaps his life.

I was ruminating on the idea of setting up something of a logwood raft myself, in the absence of any better vessel, but the idea did not appeal to me at all, nor to my wife. The *Kon-Tiki* expedition was a good lark, but it was also a raft-drift to end all raft-drifts, and it was not to be copied. The telephone rang and some fellow wanted to know why did Cape Horn sailors wear gold earrings? But I knew only one who did, and that was old Charlie Muller from Hamburg, Count von Luckner's bos'n. I gave my inquirer Charlie's address at the Old Seamen's Home in Hamburg: and then there was Mr. Gordon Griffith at the door, a motion-picture production manager direct from Hollywood, asking about those frigates for a film to be made, he said, about John Paul Jones.

A motion-picture production manager, apparently, is the unfortunate fellow charged with assembling all the immensity of expensive and bothersome paraphernalia—cameras, lights, generators, sets, props, costumes, food, somewhere for the cast to live, locations, art directors, sound equipment, transport, extras, and so forth and so on—without which a picture worth the name cannot be made. It is a herculean and a profoundly discouraging task. Mr. Griffith had, I gathered, recently been production-manager for some stupendous and colossal Hollywood musical, on which his two immediate predecessors had died from heart attacks in their early forties. Now Mr. Griffith wanted ships. Surely, I thought in my ignorance, there was nothing that Hollywood could possibly want which it did not already have. The place must abound with models of everything that ever floated and a lot that never did or could, and sets of all manner of ships from Ulysses' double-ender to the deck of an ocean liner. I'd seen such things on sets, more than once; and what about the hulls of the three-masted schooners which were built up to resemble pirate vessels, whaling vessels, slave ships, clipper ships, and the *Bounty, Pandora,* and *Constitution?* Come to think of it, had not the Metro-Goldwyn-Mayer company recently produced a complete new *Mayflower*—another "precise" replica, I supposed—and ought that not be laid up somewhere in San Pedro, or some such port convenient to Hollywood?

But apparently not. The *Bounty, Pandora,* et al., had been overbuilt on the hulls of old West Coast schooners, but they had been allowed to rot away. There was not as much as the single hull of a worn-out three-masted schooner anywhere on the coast of California, nor in all America, as far as Mr. Griffith knew, and he had looked. As for the *Mayflower,* if MGM still had her, she was a hull-form and two centuries wrong for conversion into a frigate. I gathered that the profligate motion-picture industry was not accustomed to preserve its sets even at their most expensive, although the attempt was sometimes made. It just did not work. Sets deteriorated. Makeshift art work and nailed-up ships came unstuck very quickly under the hot Californian sun, and they stayed unstuck. In any event, this John Paul Jones film was not for MGM but for an independent company, and they needed two ships—three, if they could get them.

It seemed incredible to me that there was not a single schooner hull available anywhere in the whole U.S.A. which could be converted into a movie-type frigate, in the year of grace 1956. What about those old codbangers out of Seattle? Were they all gone? It seemed that they were, except for one big four-master which was more motor ship than sailer, and one bald-headed three-master lying in Seattle that was not available. As for San Francisco, there was not a seaworthy schooner of any size in the whole beautiful bay, though there was one very old and very worn-out four-master that had been on the mud for years and was a write-off. This, and some rotting pieces of a few old schooners and one Islands brigantine, used as houseboats in some lonely corner of the harbor, were all that the once great sailing-ship port could show today.

The production manager had already scoured the seaports of the whole United States and communicated with everybody who could possibly give him a lead on available schooners, square-riggers, hulks, etc. I could not mention a clue in his own country which he had not already looked into. What about the dude schooners out of Maine, or on Chesapeake Bay, that take holiday makers in the season? Would a couple of them perhaps suit? What about Mystic seaport, and the *Joseph Conrad* and *Charles W. Morgan?* These were good ships. He'd been there: he hoped to use Mystic in the story, but neither the *Morgan* nor the *Conrad* could be made to sail any more, and so they were out. What about the West Indies? Yes, there were some schooners there, but only one was big enough and she had no engine.

The movie frigates had to have power. (I agreed to that, after experience in the *Pequod*: there has to be power.) Other West Indies schooners were too small, or the wrong shape (old Grand Bankers and such), or they had no power. What about Nova Scotia, then, and Prince Edward Island, and Newfoundland? The so-called schooners round those parts nowadays are two-masted bald-headed motor ships, my friend said—and I knew that that was true, though I thought that surely one or two of the old-timers were still to be found at places like the North Sydney mines, loading coal for coastwise passages.

No, said the film man, he had had to come to Europe, and his first call there was me.

Of course, I keep as well informed as I can about the usable sailing ships in the world. But just where was this outfit going to get its ships? They had to be in reasonably good order, to sail: they had to be auxiliaries: they had to be available, in the market, for sale or charter: and they ought to be seaworthy wooden ships, for steel ships could not be converted satisfactorily into frigates, not even by a Hollywood art department. They had, too, to be somewhere where they were readily filmable, in color, in wide-screen (which adds greatly to the difficulties of keeping stray pieces of land out of the picture, when they ought not to be there), and, if at all possible, there had to be some ports, towns, beaches, and scenic spots round the area where the ships were which could serve as locations for the film.

This was a big order. There *were* a couple of actual frigates, as a matter of fact—the rerigged *Dom Fernando y Gloria* lying at moorings in the Tagus off Lisbon, and the remains of the Danish *Jylland* at Copenhagen. The *Dom*

Fernando y Gloria was a boys' school, and it was doubtful whether she could be made available, while the *Jylland,* I had heard, was to be restored in Denmark as an historic monument. In any event, one ship at Lisbon and the other at Copenhagen would not be much use, though I gathered that Mr. Griffith would not be appalled at any reasonable conversion job on a three- or four-masted schooner, or brig or brigantine or barkentine, if he could find any. So long as the ship or ships were about 300 or 400 tons, seaworthy, and built of wood, somehow he could manage. As for the Baltic, where the best schooners were to be found, he was afraid that would be an unsuitable place to make the film— too much bad weather, too much commercial traffic with consequent difficulty in getting other non-period ships out of the picture, too much indifferent light. His company planned to make the film during the European winter. That meant working in one place only—the Mediterranean. What about ships down there?

Well, there were the codfishermen of Portugal, I said, which might be available for winter charter since they fished only from spring to autumn. There was a thriving motor-schooner commerce on the Spanish coast, too, out of Palma in Mallorca and Barcelona, Tarragona, and such parts. Stout two- and three-masted schooners up to 300 tons or so could be found by the dozen in that corner of the Mediterranean, but the trouble was twofold there—first, to get the Spanish mountains out of the picture with the sun behind the ships, and secondly to acquire the ships at all. They were doing well, and it was doubtful whether their owners would sell. I was against chartering, for motion-picture conversion cuts a ship about and is difficult to make good on a chartered vessel. Motion-picture directors, too, may take what chartering owners regard as unjustifiable risks with their vessels, and the owners could object and so hold up production. Once a motion-picture unit was committed to a location, there could be no holdups. The expense would be ruinous.

Well, what about Italy? There used to be a considerable sailing commerce there, too, and beautiful brigantines and barkentines flourished under the Italian flag, all built of wood, almost any one of them well suited to conversion into a frigate, with a built-over waist and great quarter-deck, a false bow of the period, new masts and yards, and the side pierced for the necessary gun ports. This sort of conversion could be managed by any good wooden shipyard. (The production manager refused to consider the British Isles, after Mr. Huston's experience with the Irish Sea weather. There were not two suitable vessels available on the market in Britain, anyway.) But I had been in Viareggio, once the principal port of Italian sailing seafaring, and I knew that its sailing days were gone. A few old schooners, more motor ship than sailing vessel, still crept about the coast and to the nearer islands, but as a sailing-ship port Viareggio was done. It was a yatching center now, and a flourishing one, but that was no help to Mr. Griffith.

There was one lead he had obtained in Hollywood, however, which seemed promising. A few years earlier there had been a minor spate of sea pictures, beginning with one made by Warner Brothers, based on the Hornblower stories. For this, at least one frigate had been rigged, and another smaller ship. These had featured briefly afterwards in three other films as pirate ships and so forth but, by dint of much telephoning—I would hate to pay a production manager's telephone bills—my friend had discovered that these ships were in Palermo, in Sicily. Some fellow in Paris, apparently connected with Messrs. Warner Bros. or possibly representing some jobber who had acquired the ships later as a speculation, alleged that they were in perfect condition, fit for immediate use, and still in their full motion-picture appearance.

We checked this report at once, by telephone to Lloyd's agent in Palermo. Yes, he said, there certainly were two such vessels lying in the harbor at Palermo. He seemed rather pessimistic about them, I thought, and declined to say anything about the larger ship. But my production manager stayed not to listen. It was enough for him that there were two ships in Palermo and, that very afternoon, we were in a British European Airways Viscount airliner flying to Rome for onward routing to Palermo. (I'd hate to pay my friend's transport bills, too: he was always ready to go anywhere.) If all passenger flying was like it is in Viscounts, I wouldn't mind the jammed-up seats and the shut-up drainpipe feeling that sitting uncomfortably inside a noisy metal fuselage always gives me.

We were in Rome in a few hours, looking for a flight to Palermo. But there was an Italian airlines pilots' strike in progress. No flights to Palermo. My Hollywood friend, at that, said that he had not been in a train or a ship in years, but we would have to find some way to get to Palermo. If there was a train, he was going in it. There was a train from Rome, about 5 P.M., that went down the coast of Italy and crossed in a railroad ferry from Reggio to Messina and so went on to Palermo. It took time. We caught the

train. Fortunately, before we got to Naples we heard there
was a nightly steamer from Naples to Palermo too. We got
out at Naples and took the steamer. It was a comfortable
ship, and a night's good sleep (which I gathered was an
unusual event in a production manager's life) brought us
into the stately, mountain-surrounded harbor of the capital
of Sicily the following morning.

From the incoming ship we could see some bare spars,
and there on a berth hauled out near a power station was
what looked like an ancient frigate—*very* ancient. I hoped
she was not hauled out for the horribly adequate reason
that she could not float. We could not see her state from
the ship, but it did not look very good from what little
we could see.

We saw as soon as we hurried ashore. The movie frigate
was there, all right, and she was just the right size and
shape of ship for this new film. But she was a wreck. She
was hogged, twisted to such an extent that her poop fell
away downhill, and the lines of false gun ports on both
sides were curved like a switchback railway. Her three
sparless masts were out of line. Her gingerbread scrollwork
and carving, etc., round the built-over stern and all the
galleries aft had peeled like the skin of an old orange. Her
standing rigging hung in bights and her running rigging
was absent. There were great gaps in her underwater
body where the planking—long worn out, doubtless—had
been peeled off and not replaced, though a little work
appeared to be going on, slowly, putting in some new ribs
and a few planks. The line of her worm-eaten keel was like
a fiddle bow. The brackets for her twin propellors stuck
out from either quarter, forlorn and unadorned, for there

was no sign of the screws themselves. Both the false rudder, built on to the additional stern, and the real rudder of the original ship were adrift. The cutwater was sheered off halfway and the plaster-cast figurehead was a pathetic and weather-worn wreck, like a child's painted toy that had been left out in the rain for years.

Aboard, the ship was a shambles. All the gear of any value had been removed. You walked in peril of your life on her broken planks. The ship, in short, was a thorough and completely unseaworthy wreck—not irreparable, perhaps (for movie purposes off Palermo breakwater) but, in my opinion, not worth anyone's while to think of making good again. We learned that she had, indeed, been capsized and below the surface, through neglect. This had ruined her. She might have served, if she had been looked after.

At least she sufficed to show, in some measure, how to convert an old ship into a photogenic frigate. This vessel had begun life as a French codfishing tops'l schooner, sailing out of ports like St. Malo across to the Grand Banks off Newfoundland and fishing with dories for cod. The draggers put her out of that business, and she had then been given an engine (of sorts) and gone coasting. Hard times made that a poor-paying proposition—hard times and small hatches, expensive upkeep and a slow turn-round, port delays and sea delays too, with an inadequate engine. So she had been sold to Warner Brothers for a movie ship, for the Hornblower film. Her "frigate" bow and stern were completely false, built onto her: her steeved-up bowsprit and long jib boom were movie additions. Her quarter galleries were stuck on, and an extra false deck had been built up on the old main deck to provide a waist and the places for the lines of gun ports on either side. Steel supports gave some strength to the channels to which the new rigging— old wire, disguised with older rope—was set up, and the masts had been disguised with sheets of light steel, welded round to make them look like the built-up, wooden masts of a ship-of-the-line. Her fighting tops were wood on steel. Her "cannon" were of aluminum. Her capstan was a prop (there had been a petrol engine to weigh anchor), and her spars lay in the hot sun on the quay nearby, where they had looked as if they had been for years.

She *had* once been a tolerable job, for local use only in fine weather. She had once looked the part of a Revolutionary warship and maybe, with a lot of money and time— especially time—she could be fixed over again. But first she would have to be made seaworthy (if that were possible, which I doubted), and then all the conversion would have to be done again, as well. It would probably be cheaper to build a new ship from scratch.

After this disappointment we were astonished when the other vessel turned out to be afloat and all right. But she was impossibly small. She was an old Biscayan crabbing ketch of typical French Biscayan lines, which even the most thorough conversion could not quite hide. She was a fore-and-after, and nothing short of a lot of money and a bit of rebuilding would ever make into her a satisfactory square-rigger of any kind.

These disappointments my friend the production manager took in his stride, like a man used to hard knocks. We looked round the harbor. In the fishing basin there were four or five old laid-up schooners, but the biggest was far

too small to think of making into a frigate. They were
little things of eighty or ninety tons—not much larger than
the crabbing ketch. Where were the good brigantines and
barkentines that used to be such picturesque frequenters
of Sicilian ports before the war? All gone? It seemed that
they were. Nobody could tell us where a single such ship
was still to be found, anywhere in the Mediterranean. We
had looked in Naples and there was nothing there. We asked
Lloyd's man in Palermo. He said they had all gone, as no
longer economic.

Then I remembered, when we landed at Augusta (maybe
it was Syracuse but I think it was Augusta) in Sicily during the war, there had been a couple of big brigantines
lying there—wooden ships, graceful, lofty, in good order.
I could see them clearly in my mind's eye, and I remembered that their port of registration was Trapani. We were
not allowed to keep diaries then, but I remembered that
the name of one was the *Fratelli Ciotta*. It was just a wild
idea, perhaps, but this place Trapani was not so far from
Palermo—a hundred kilometers or so. Why not go there
and see if any big brigs or such still existed there, in any
form? Trapani had been a big sailing port. The commerce
across to the small islands of Egadi and Levanzo, and
Ustica, and the coal trade from Sardinia, gave them work
to do. It was the sort of place that such ships would survive
in longer than most others, even if they were cut-down,
bald-headed powered barges.

It was a forlorn hope, maybe, but we were stuck anyway. So we hired a car and drove at once to Trapani, and
I became aware of another hazard in a production manager's
life, for that was a dreadful drive! The hairpin bends, the

steep mountain roads, the picturesque but so crowded high-
ways, the profusion of prettily painted horse-drawn carts in
which the occupants frequently appeared to be asleep,
and the unbounded optimism of the horn-honking hire-car
driver, made the trip a dangerous nightmare. There were
bandits in the area, he said, and he hurried. When we got
to Trapani at last, we felt like wrecks ourselves.

But there, across the river harbor, the very first thing we
saw was a big wooden brigantine and the name on her stern
was *Fratelli Ciotta*. Along the waterfront road, their shapely
cutwaters and sawn-off bowsprits jutting across the highway, were two more ships of the right hull form and about
the right size. We had come to the right place. Here were
the answers, at last. Were the ships available? Had they adequate power? They were cut down, as we saw them—two
of them crossed a couple of yards and the third no yards
at all—and the topgallant masts were gone. But the hulls
were in good order. Two were hauled out on a slipway,
ready for inspection. They were the *Marcel B. Surdo* and the
Angiolina H., both registered at Trapani. The *Fratelli Ciotta*
was afloat, and we could not easily get a close look at her.

The others were all right. Discreet inquiries showed that
though employed (mainly hauling coal from Sardinia to
Sicily) they were not making much money. They were old
ships—one built in 1904, another in 1915, but they were
still seaworthy and in class. The day of the brigantine was
obviously gone, even in Trapani. We were, I gathered, lucky
to find the ships there at all. There was no other port in all
the Mediterranean where we would have found three ex-
brigantines in one afternoon.

There were other advantages. Working out of Palermo

would be all right, for a sea film. The cameras would have open sea to the north, east, and west—and plenty of it— just beyond the breakwater. Usually there was plenty of good weather, too, and sunshine guaranteed for the color film. There were good berths, docks, transport, hotels, electrical and maintenance resources—all those many things which the big film needs. There were excellent odd spots of scenery, such as ancient quays and fortresses which could be made to represent the West Indies or even—one of them—the quays of Whitehaven in the north of England, all within a few miles of Palermo, and Mr. Griffith said that there were studio resources available in Rome. There was a shipyard at Palermo which, though small, could do the necessary conversions.

My Hollywood friend negotiated an option on two of those brigantines—the *Marcel B. Surdo* and the *Angiolina H.*—that very afternoon (not without difficulty, for one of them proved to have at least eighteen owners, all members of the same family but by no means a harmonious or even united whole, and the third ship was involved in such complicated ownership knots that we thought better to forget her altogether). Anyway, he got his option, and that was that problem solved. It might take months to convert the old wooden brigantines, but it could be done. Perhaps when they were converted they might provide me at least with a ship to sail temporarily, to keep my hand in. I was grateful for the memory of the wartime incident of the big brigantine which I had glimpsed so briefly years before, in the smoke and noise of a Sicilian landing.

In due course, executives flew over from New York, complete with art directors, assistants thereto, assistants to

assistant directors, secretaries, and so forth, and the options
on the two brigantines were taken up. It was considered
far better to buy than to charter, and I toyed with the idea
that at least the stouter of the two could be made over so
thoroughly and well that afterwards she might be worth
acquiring for a school ship. She could be kept in the Mediterranean: perhaps future film hires might help to pay for
her running and make it possible to take lots of boys. But
an art director arrived from England with plans of the
Hornblower conversion which he had somehow acquired
and, with these as his stock in trade (for he was neither
sailor nor naval architect), set up to make the two ships
over with sheets of plywood and overbuilt sterncastles,
complete with ornate plaster-of-Paris carvings and God
knows what kind of rigging. The ships were taken away to
a yard at Fiumicino, instead of being left at Palermo, and
this unseamanlike conversion was begun. Instead of just
one *Pequod,* this time there would be two. They might do
for the Bay of Palermo, but they were not for me.

Months passed and grew into a year, and I heard no more
about them, nor of the project to make the John Paul
Jones film. This was to come to life again, later—a long
time later—and the indifferent work of the art man would
be scrapped and replaced by real. In the meantime I was
not to know that. So I thought I would go down to the
Maldive Islands, where there was a brig.

I went to the Maldives, in due course. There was a long-
ish interval. Then, later, I sailed the new *Mayflower* to
America (by God's grace) and returned from there, and
still I heard no more of the pretty brigantines and their conversion into cinematic ships. But it *did* happen, in the end.

It all came about as planned, and I was able to use some of the excellent *Mayflower* sailors in the enterprise.

The idea of using these two Sicilian brigantines as 18th century frigates at last come to fruition, early in 1958. By that time the ships were at a place called Fiumicino on a mouth of the Tiber, near Rome. This was the last place on earth where I would have expected to find them. The muddy Tiber swirled past their haystack hulls, where some fellow, obviously not a seaman, had been allowed to begin their 'conversion' into the usual maritime atrocities associated with the worst of sea films. Their counters had been cut away to carry built-up poops and their sides were carried up with the thinnest of nailed planking, far too high, until the windage the sides must cause would have made the ships unmanageable in a seaway, if they ever went to sea. They were sheerless, shapeless, rigged down, bogged down, and apparently derelict, for the work had been at a standstill for months. A good wooden windlass, sheered off at deck level from one of them—doubtless by the man who had 'planned' the conversion—lay on the muddy bank ashore, and behind the ship was a hoisting bridge under which they could not pass with their masts in. They were in a mess, and my first inclination, seeing them in such a place and in so seemingly hopeless a condition, was to leave them there and go about more sensible business.

But after all, I had caused them to be bought. Fiumicino though a dreadful hole (as a port) and a disgrace to lovely Rome, was not wholly without some merit. There was a Florentine named Corti, Luigi Corti, who had a shipyard converted from a former seaplane station on another mouth of the Tiber, near Ostia, close by. This Corti was a wizard with wood, and he had an excellent wooden shipyard. It was used mainly for turning out boats and large motor-yachts of shallow draft suitable for those parts, but well designed, well built, and well finished. Luigi Corti was an enterprising man, head of a co-operative ship and boat-building firm which could do something about those brigantines, if something was to be done. Much more important than this, the John Paul Jones film now had a director from Hollywood who knew ships. My cousin John Villiers Farrow came from Hollywood, to be sure, but he was an Australian by origin like myself, *and* a sailor who had served in big sailing-ships, and that not for just a dog-watch. Axed in an economy drive from the early Royal Australian Naval College at Jervis Bay in New South Wales when he was 15, he went off in real ships, big skys'l yard barquentines out of San Francisco and other West Coast ports, heavy big heart-breakers which looked beautiful under their clouds of sail in the Pacific trades but were under-manned and brutish to handle. He had sailed in ships I wouldn't go in. Well, they had done him no harm and there he was. He knew his business and I felt that I could work well with him.

He was even more disgusted with the state of those poor ships than I was. These frigates had to go to sea and be able to keep the sea, properly, like real ships. They had to be *real ships*. In the first place, they had to sail direct to a port in Spain 800 miles away, and it was still winter then. So John Farrow had all the rubbish ripped off those two good ships until their true grace of line showed again and, with Corti contracted for the work, we started in to make a proper job. The job was done, but it was far from easy! Calling in master shipwrights from Torre del Greco to help his own men, and a few riggers and riggers' laborers from Viareggio, Corti did his part splendidly. For my part, I got hold of all the real sailing-ship sailors I could find, under sixty, who were available. I scoured the world and got five. It was Ike Marsh, now mate of one of the frigates, who really did the rigging, assisted by Joe Lacey and Graham Nunn.

The enterprise was further assisted by a competent naval architect, Ing. Enrico Fea, who had seen naval service in the Italian sailing school-ship *Amerigo Vespucci* and knew something of sail, and worked through many weeks of long and trying hours to make a good job of the ships. An enlightened art department was a tremendous help. Led by the art director, Franz Bachelon, and including the English marine artist Peter Wood, I had never worked with so sea-minded an art department before. Everyone was for *real* ships, real ships which could sail.

There were many troubles at Fiumicino, most of them avoidable if the ships had not been flying their own flag. I have heard many arguments against the practice of putting ships under flags of so-called 'convenience', but I can think of none for keeping any vessel under a flag of such whole-hearted maritime inconvenience as the Italian was for those poor ships. The Italian flag, for one thing, meant Italian crews even to the officers, and shipping an individual called a *padrone* considered, apparently, to be fit as master. There are no sailing-ship officers in Italy today and there certainly are no *padrones* experienced, or fit, to handle a full-rigged ship even if their certificates qualified them to do so, which they do not. The ships were small. Their former classification entitled them, apparently, to be commanded by *padrones*

and, though they were now radically changed from the
simple motor-schooners they had last been and were as
awkward little full-riggers as anyone was likely to be asked
to handle, the padrones still had to be aboard, in nominal
if not real command. Foreigners had to be "passengers".
I demanded a flag of convenience forthwith and this was
promised, as many things may be promised in the film industry, but it was not forthcoming in time to be of any use.
So I had to sail both ships, one at a time, from Fiumicino
towards Denia in Spain with the handicap of a *padrone*
aboard each of them. I could get no other square-rigger
master, with actual experience of handling a full-rigged
ship, to take either ship.

The *padrones* could certainly be trusted with no such
activity, and they were well aware of that. Poor men, they
did not appoint themselves, nor keep the ships under the
Italian flag. The first took one glance at the *Angiolina*—
by that time a pretty little ship, and taut and stout and
strong—and, hearing that I would sail direct to Denia,
rushed back to his sunny home remarking, on what basis
I could not imagine, that I was a very brave man, and he
was not. The second was a pierhead jump from Fiumicino
who should have known what he was doing. He, too, had
a profound belief that all passages anywhere should be
made by coasting, and screamed excitedly upon the poop
about his tremendous responsibilities, etc etc, while the
little ship wandered along pleasantly under sail, out of
sight of land, bound on the simple summer run (it was summer by that time) south of Sardinia and the Balearics,
towards Denia.

But I had some good Italian seamen too, including a

couple of excellent young fellows from the well-run naval school-ship *Amerigo Vespucci* who regarded the *padrones* with the same astonished horror that I did. We arrived. We arrived, indeed, without trouble at all, except those imagined by the fellow from Fiumicino who had acted as *padrone*.

So I flew back from Barcelona to Rome and brought the other, the larger *Marcel* now disguised—and very well disguised—as the frigate *Ranger* of the very first United States Navy, and the wind blew hard from south-east and east and we stormed across under fores'l and sprits'l and two full tops'ls, in less than five days, which was very good going indeed. It was near the end of June then, and through the summer months I continued to sail the *Marcel/Ranger/Serapis*—same ship—out of Denia, which is perhaps not the easiest port in the Mediterranean, though a peaceable and friendly place. Captain Adrian Small handled the *Angiolina,* and the *padrones* were reduced to bo's'ns which they were happy enough to be. (Apparently, it was the fear of actual imprisonment for some infringement under Italian maritime law which mostly alarmed them. There is no *habeas corpus* act in Italy. One *had* been imprisoned for some slight transgression—not his fault—some years earlier, and had sworn never to be a *padrone* again. It was really an act of grace on his part to assist the ship to clear Fiumicino, that he consented to be entered as *padrone* at all.)

Film ships with a unit embarked are not perhaps the easiest ships to handle. A film unit is a large and unwieldy organization, intent upon its own expensive and difficult business. It was a bit of a tough job, handling those full-riggers out of Denia. We had a Spanish brig as well, for good measure. That John Paul Jones film was made by John Farrow with proper ships in the proper manner—no miniatures, no fake. We had 44 guns in the *Serapis*, all of which worked, and what with their protruding muzzles, the ship's wide channels carrying the vast array of her standing rigging that supported her great lofty masts, the elaborate stern castle with its period carvings, and the figurehead and the enormous length of the bowsprit and jibboom out ahead, she was no simple vessel to handle, or to put alongside! the *Angiolina* was very similar.

It was wonderful sailing. There was a good sailing breeze and plenty of it in the Mediterranean off Denia every day, and the ships presented many a noble and wonderful spectacle, station-keeping under sail, running in for a landing at beaches representing Nassau or raid upon Whitehaven, tacking about under every stitch as the *Bon Homme Richard* and *Serapis* sparring before the beginning of that famous fight in the grim old North Sea. It was a delight to be there, a source of pride to handle real ships upon the real sea for John Farrow, at last a real sailor making a real sea film.

There were plenty of problems. It is natural that a motion picture director wants to get the most compelling, and the most moving, compositions on the screen which he can possibly contrive, with the aid of brilliant cameramen, perfect lighting, and every other factor that can be brought to help him. But ships are apt to be recalcitrant properties, and working even on well organized land locations can be tough. When the sea comes into it—the unpredictable, refusing-to-be-directed sea, where every ruffle upon the surface can make a difference—of course it is ten times tougher. In Mr.

Bronston's production of the epic JOHN PAUL JONES, there were many scenes that were hard to get, battles *at sea* between real ships, not fakes in tanks, flames roaring mast-high when the *Bon Homme Richard* and the *Serapis* come to grips, the *Alfred* and the *Ranger* within stone's throw of a Nassau beach to make an early attempt at amphibious war-fare, the *Ranger* running into harbor under a press of per-fectly-controlled, wind-filled sails, to salute the French fleet and come brilliantly, with perfect seamanship, to a flying moor. Where did I get the perfect seamanship from, when I had twelve in the crew? And how to run in and bring off a tough maneuver like that, when Denia was entered by a dog's-leg channel to stray a fathom off which was to go aground? At the end of the channel was the full stop of the quay. There was no room to moor. The *Ranger* had had a crew of fourscore and more, all good men—seamen enough to make her spin like a top and handle those sails as if they were Venetian blinds.

Well, we did our best. Adrian Small, who was in the *Pequod* and the *Mayflower* later, had command of the smaller ship, after I had brought her from Italy. (The *padrone*, after sundry unhelpful attempts at trouble-making, had retired sick ashore.) His crew did well, and mine were better, for the *padrone* of the big ship was an excellent bos'n and the Viareggio riggers were grand fellows and good sea-men. With the *Mayflower* veterans and Carpenter Otto Stoltenberg from Kalundborg in Denmark, who had been Chips of the ship *Tusitala*, we were as well off as could be hoped and, with such good direction, everyone did their best. The sailing conditions off Denia and round those parts were generally excellent, and it was a first-class place to make a film, but it could blow pretty hard in the Gulf of

Valencia. Well, that put life in the sea: but it added some-times to the difficulty of sailing. Director Farrow knew the difficulties as well as I did (or better, for he knew his own as well). We must take some risks, but they were calculated risks, reasonable chances which we generally brought off.

All this John Farrow understood and appreciated very well. In all these problems and a host of others he was assisted by a gem of a production manager, Mr. Emmett Emerson from Hollywood, who I am sure could have pro-duced an oasis a mile square in the middle of the Sahara Desert if he were given twenty-four hours notice. Emmett Emerson was a delight to work with, and the actors made pleasant shipmates too—Robert Stack, who played the lead, Peter Cushing from London, cheerful Bruce Cabot, and all the rest of them. They were not above lending a hand aboard, and neither were the large crowds of bit-players and extras of twenty-nine assorted nationalities, who came storming aboard every day.

Sometimes the film-making was even more interesting than perhaps the film itself, and adventures came our way all too often which had no place in the script. The *Alfred,* for instance, got on the rocks in Benidorme Roads, sailing in towards the beach to land her troops, and it was a matter of luck that she came off again. Sailing the two ships to-gether well out in the Gulf of Valencia, cannon blazing and battle ensigns flying, was nerve-racking at times. We used no engines, not only to avoid their give-away exhaust smoke but to make the scenes more real. There was a good sailing breeze, so we used it, but that same wind brought up a sea in which the camera boat jumped so much the poor cameraman had the greatest difficulty keeping the ships in frame, nor could the director let the motion be recorded for too long or too vividly. The wide-screen picture can be altogether too effective and make the audience seasick. We had to make several runs to get things right, wearing the ships round at the end of each run and sailing hours to get back into position again, always getting further and further out to sea. In the end we must have been halfway to the Balearic Islands. Well, they are a mighty nice place to go. This was good sailing, and I was being paid for it. Tourists by the thousands spent vast sums just to be in such places a week or two. We were there for months.

On another occasion, coming back to Denia from Benidorme, a hard northerly sprang up which was tough to slog against, and I was being slowly forced in towards the land when at last I could just make the shelter of a minute harbor under Cape St. Anthony, called Javea. It was a *very* small harbor, under a great cliff, with a mudbank filling the half of it, a 180° turn to get in, breakwater rocks on one hand and too many small boats on the other, with no room to maneuver in between. I took a pilot, of course (pilotage being compulsory for merchant vessels, and good sense anyway) but as soon as the pilot opened his mouth I realized with horror that he had not the slightest clue how to direct a sailing-ship! It was the deuce of a job, backing and filling in there, now within an inch of the rocks or all but smack into an expensive motor fishing-vessel, and the wind tumbling so hard all down the cliffs that two anchors would scarcely hold her inside the breakwater. But the wind eased, in due course, and we sailed to Denia again.

In the battle scenes, I marvelled at the apparent reality which those Hollywood special effects men could contrive— flames mast-high, great masts and yards gone by the board (but the ship's rigging all still standing, practically undamaged), "dead" bodies everywhere and live bodies fighting in the smoke and heat and flames of battle right in the cannons' mouths, bodies (live and dead) hurtling out of the rigging, a hundred cannon belching flame and smoke and everything but projectiles, the whole risky and most complicated business kept under the strictest control by two wizards from California named Sas Bedig and Rocky Kline. The fires were real and they were really in the ships, but they were suffered to do very little damage.

It was all absorbingly interesting and even thrilling, but it was also very tiring and very tough. The cast slept at Benidorme which was a lovely place but miles away. We crewmen stayed on the job. It was a delight to be there for John Farrow, and I hope those ships will last forever. They were good ships, doing all that was asked of them and doing it bravely. They were laid up at Valencia in the end, where they are ready for more good sea films.

All in all, sailing for JOHN PAUL JONES was a well worthwhile experience in more ways than one. It showed that a proper sea film *could* be made, using ships and neither tanks nor miniatures, provided the ships were good and, above all, the director knew his sea as well as his cinema. What made this job so satisfying for me was just that fact. I was on an equal footing with the art director, and so had a real say in decisions which could not afterwards be thrust aside. Maybe it helped to have a bit of a part, too, in the sea battles, for in the last analysis the film industry has real understanding of, and respect for, those who can sustain a scene when the cameras are grinding. After all, that's what the expensive great industry is all about.

CHAPTER

7

THE BRIG
IN THE MALDIVE ISLANDS

Not long before the outbreak of the Second World War,
I set out on a five-year plan to study Eastern shipping.
Beginning with the dhows of Arabia, I meant to go on to
the Indian coastal and deep-sea trades, to the Maldives and
Malaya, to the Celebes and the Philippines, and then to the
junks of China. But I had time only to study the Arabs
before I was caught in the war and compelled to give up
the plan. During the war, when I had a squadron of landing craft on the coast of Burma based on Mandapam in the
Palk Straits, between southeastern India and Ceylon, I
kept watch for the Burma rice barks and the Indian brigs
which I knew were sailing up to 1940. There were no
barks in the Burmese ports I managed to visit, with my
LCI(L), but there were several interesting square-rigged
ships on the beach at Mandapam. One was a big wooden

bark, hove-down in a sort of natural dry dock there where she was being repaired. Sometimes small wooden brigs and brigantines came sailing through the railway pass into the northern roadstead. I saw a jackass bark there one day, and a barkentine on another, but all these vessels carried single tops'ls on spindly yards and, though interesting and well-run ships, had a look of mixed European and Eastern origin about them which made them neither one thing nor the other—Eastern hulls and an Asianized European square-rig, not really suitable for beating about the Indian Ocean nor the Bay of Bengal, frequently with very deep courses and single topsails and no topgallant sails at all. Sometimes they were fitted with an additional light mast which was stepped abaft the main, or the mizzen, on the poop, apparently at the whim of the sailing master.

None of these ships, as far as I could see, was then in ordinary trade, but there were some good ships trading to Colombo—sturdy vessels of the dhow type (lateen-rigged on a kind of galleon hull), a well-kept brigantine, and a beauty of a brig. I had not seen this brig, for our LCI(L) were not encouraged to go to the crowded and overstrained port of Colombo. I had been told of her and had seen photographs. She was a *real* brig, complete in all respects, sailed by men who respected her and knew how to handle her. She was kept up like a yacht, run like a training brig, had the lines of a clipper and the full sail plan of the opium smuggler which—according to some—she once had been. Her name was the *Attiyathur-Rahman,* her port of registry a place called Malé in the Maldive Islands, and she was flagship of a little group of *buggalows* and one brigantine which traded between the Maldive Islands and Ceylon.

By 1956, as far as I was aware, she looked like being the last brig left in the world. There were no such ships in Europe, and the Indians, I knew, were building none—not even big *buggalows*. An Indian governmental inquiry into the state of the Indian sailing-vessel industry had shown in the late 1940's that this once great shipping industry was in a precarious condition. An independent and perhaps not wholly patient new India was more interested in powered vessels and mechanized shore transport than in the heritage of her own sailing fleet, and was, apparently, prepared to see these upholders of her great maritime tradition forced out of business. Her vast sailing fleet, so valuable to trade through many small ports difficult of access by road, was purely indigenous in construction and methods of navigation and everything else (apart from those few square-riggers), and there were many who hated the idea that such an industry should be allowed to die. Fraudulent practices on the part of a proportion of these shipmasters and some owners, insufficiently controlled in time of war and war's immediate and profitable aftermath, had caused merchants to lose confidence in the ships themselves after the war—in such matters as falsified insurance claims, lack of uniform trade practices, and the widspread habit of allegedly jettisoning valuable cargo for the "safety" of a vessel beset by a "storm" which went unnoticed ashore, the ship later returning to pick up the cached goods to sell for her own private profit. The loose organization of the so-called country craft, with its opportunities for fraud in times of shortage and insufficient control of ships and men, could not be allowed to continue. But neither seamen nor ships were amenable to too strict control and India's sailing ships seemed doomed. The new insistence was everywhere (or almost everywhere) on engines, as more modern and befitting a newly independent country.

If there were any Indian brigs left at all in '56, they would soon be gone. Therefore I decided to go down to Colombo and if necessary to the Maldive Islands to find this beautiful brig *Attiyathur-Rahman* and sail in her, for she was a vessel of historic interest. I had also in the back of my mind then the idea that if the *Mayflower* "replica" were ever finished in the Devon port of Brixham, I might find myself sailing her. (Who else was there, if she were to be sailed by Britishers?) The Maldivian brig, if she still existed, was the nearest thing to the *Mayflower* left sailing anywhere, for she had rigging of cordage and masts and yards of wood. Her sail plan was modern, to be sure, but the manner of working it and of staying her masts was as near to pure Seventeenth century as I was likely to find. Except for the Arab dhow, I had been in big sailing ships with steel masts and steel-wire rigging, many of them with brace-winches as well, which were horribly Twentieth-century. A month or so aboard the *Attiyathur-Rahman* would teach me a lot. I could also make a photographic record of her, on stills and with color film, while the chance remained to do such a thing.

Of course, I tried to find out where the brig was, or indeed whether she was still in commission, before leaving England. I could find out nothing. Although the Maldive Islands had been under a form of British protection since 1887, apparently there was no representation there, and since the granting of independence to Ceylon a year or two earlier, the British High Commissioner at Colombo had an officer who kept in touch as well as he could with affairs in the Indian Ocean islands. No one in London knew where the brig was. She was reported variously as having been torpedoed by the Japanese during the war, sold to a film company making a Conrad motion picture of the *Outcast of the Islands* after the war, and—in November, 1955—missing in the Bay of Bengal.

This last report I could track down at Lloyd's, where I found that a Maldivian brigantine named *Fathur-Bahari* (spelled variously as *Fatulbari, Faht-ur-Bahar,* and so forth) *was* reported to be missing after a cyclone in the Bay of Bengal, while on passage from the Maldives towards Calcutta with a cargo of a million coconuts and a million cowrie shells, and even then, aircraft of the Indian Air Force were looking for her. By mid-November she had been written off—declared a total loss with her twenty-five-man crew, her million coconuts, and her million cowrie shells (whatever they might be), for no aircraft and no searching ships could find anything of her. How well they looked I don't know, but she turned up off the Sandheads on the following day, none the worse for having ridden out the cyclone and sailed calmly and sedately into the Hooghly, quite unaware that she had been declared missing.

A brigantine is not a brig. This was a different vessel. But if she were still in trade, I thought, so might the brig be. So one midnight I climbed into a horrible big aircraft at London Airport and, with brief stops at Rome and Cairo, was over Suez soon after daybreak, on a nonstop flight from Egypt to Pakistan. Inside the aircraft I sat in the middle of the three-seat front row on the port side, from which crowded seat and with the greatest difficulty I could see a little cloud out of the inadequate window. It was a most uncomfortable seat, apparently designed to accommodate a child and, in front there near the engines, the aircraft was abominably noisy. A noisier, more boring, or more utterly soulless form of transport could not be imagined, but I was in Karachi less than twenty hours out from London. There were no *buggalows* in the harbor and no sailing craft of any kind, except the sailing ferries. From Karachi I continued in a small four-engined aircraft called a Heron over Pakistan and then over the sea, towards Diu, Damão, and Goa. These relics of Portuguese India were shut off by blockade from Mr. Nehru's India, and the only access was by flight from Pakistan.

I had heard that there were fine deep-sea *buggalows* sailing out of the picturesque old fishing port of Diu and more at Damão, while the Goans still shifted much of their iron ore down the Mandovi River by an interesting fleet of sailing craft. I could rely upon the Portuguese to maintain the sailing tradition but, though I saw some magnificent big *buggalows* both at Damão and Diu, the blockade was making it impossible for them to go to sea. At Diu a shapely big beauty lay by the beach where the fishermen dried their fish, flying alike the flags of Portugal and India, and there were photographs of President Craveiro Lopes, Dr. Salazar, Mr. Nehru, and Mahatma Gandhi in the great cabin, and no animosity among the large and happy crew towards anyone. At Damão was another large *buggalow* which ought to have been in the Mombasa trade, and in Goa a fleet of ore-stained dhows, big and small, passed constantly up and down the river. Many of these were pretty little things sporting big main lateen topsails, but they were not going further than Mormugao, the port of Goa. Here their iron ore was transshipped to steamers. As far as Goa's own sailing commerce was concerned, the Indian blockade seemed effective. But the dhows were well employed bringing the ore down river, and there was no scarcity of Panamanian, Liberian, Honduran, and Costa Rican tramps to take it away.

I continued to Colombo in a Portuguese liner, and looked in the corner of that crowded harbor where I knew the Maldivian sailing ships usually berthed. There was no sign of either brig or *buggalow*, nor as much as a Tuticorin *buque*. The tiers of buoys in all directions were filled with large ocean liners, British, Dutch, French, German, American, and Indian, but the only things under sail were a couple of fourteen-foot dinghies being sailed about the place by bareheaded Englishmen with red faces, contentedly smoking pipes. Ashore the harbormaster had no knowledge of any brigs, though he did have a vague memory of having seen the smart Maldivian at the buoys within the past year or so, and the officials at the High Commission though helpful, had no better knowledge. Who should be interested in last brigs? I searched the ancient sailing ports of lovely Ceylon, from Galle in the south to Jaffna in the north (this Jaffna once had a splendid fleet, and Galle was a port long before Colombo). There were Jaffna barks in the Burma trade after the war, but I found nothing in the old port save a few tile-carrying local dhows, open-decked, of no particular interest to me, and some fishing craft.

At Galle there were two Maldivians—little things with wide-flared hulls, a grass house built on deck, and a rig

consisting simply of a deep and narrow square sail on the
foremast and a lateen on the main. I had no opportunity to
examine these closely, for they were putting to sea as I arrived. From what I could see, I would hate to sail overnight
in one, though they were bound on a 400-mile open-sea passage. Usually they arrived, the harbormaster told me.

Galle was a fascinating place, and the harbormaster said
that he still saw the occasional bastard-brigantine from Man-
galore or Cochin, in with tiles. While I was there a straight-
stemmed vessel with a lateen rig, called a *buque,* was discharging tiles into sewn surf boats built up on the split
halves of a couple of dugout canoes with some planking
between that was caulked with coconut leaves tightly
packed, paid with some black stuff, and sewn in with a palm-
frond fiber. The sides were built up and sewn in the same
manner.

Eventually, I found a Maldivian government office in a
place called Bambalapitiya, a suburb of Colombo, and here
the Maldivian representative, Mr. Zacki, received me most
kindly. He stamped my Australian passport with the necessary permit to visit the Maldive Islands, but how, I asked,
was I going to get there? By government *buggalow,* said
the helpful Mr. Zacki: there would be one arriving at Colombo within a day or so. It was then twenty days out from
the Maldives, beating against the monsoon. The brig? He
was afraid I might wait some time for her, if she ever came
again. His latest news of her was that she was laid up in
the lagoon at Malé in a very unseaworthy condition, while
the government debated whether she was worth fitting
with an auxiliary engine or would have to be broken up as
irreparable. She was a very old ship, said Mr. Zacki, and she

had already been extensively rebuilt at Chittagong thirty or forty years before—perhaps it was fifty.

I suggested going to Calcutta to join the brigantine as a vessel more interesting to me than a *buggalow* (for *buggalows* have no square canvas, and I had sailed for eight months in a somewhat similar Arab vessel). Mr. Zacki said that a Calcutta voyage occupied the whole monsoon, and he had no idea when the brigantine might be sailing, nor how long she might take to make her way down the Bay of Bengal, round the top of Ceylon, to the Maldives again. She would go direct, with no ports of call, and it could take months.

So I waited at Colombo for the government's *buggalow*. Weeks went by, and still I waited. Well, I had learned how to do that with the Arabs, and Ceylon is a lovely island. I studied what I could of the beach fishing craft, at Mount Lavinia beach and Negombo and in the north past Jaffna, and I read all that I could find about the Maldive Islands. This was not much, for the islands have been little written about since the great Arab traveler Ibn Battuta was there in the middle of the fourteenth century, and the French castaway Pyrard de Laval in the early sixteenth. What I read was fascinating and, brig or no brig, it seemed that the Maldives were a good place to go at least once in a wandering lifetime. I read of Malabar pirates basing themselves on the lonely atolls, of the wrecks of treasure galleons on the many reefs and the gold from these galleons still circulating among the islands, of famines, and poisonings and intrigue among the ruling dynasty, and massacres long ago. I read also that the Maldivians were the finest seamen and fishermen in the Indian Ocean, which was a considerable reputation if it

were true. I read of fevers, especially a sickness called the
Maldivian fever which—it was said—was often fatal, and
struck all Europeans who stayed more than three weeks
ashore in the islands. I made a note not to exceed that brief
period, no matter how interesting the place might be.

But for some time it looked is if I would never arrive to
begin my visit, in any case, for the long-expected *buggalow*
was very late. When she finally did arrive, her discharge
was leisurely and her loading more so, through no fault of
hers. I finally joined her on Tuesday, February 21, 1956,
and we sailed that day, towing out of Colombo harbor, as
befitted a large government *buggalow*. Her name was the
Fath-ur-Rahman, which may be translated as the *Glory of
Mercy,* and she was a vessel of 145 net tons, 194.43 gross,
with a waterline length of just over 81 feet, an over-all
length of 100′ 8″, beam to outside planking 25′ 6″, and
a depth of 12′ 3″. She was manned by a crew of twenty-one
all told, all Maldivians.

The crew included the master, M. A. Muhammed Maniku;
a juvenile called a mate who seemed to act as assistant
navigator, had been (I discovered later) nineteen months at
sea only and that in the one ship, and was then learning to
steer; a serang of competence, long experience, and with
excellent power of command; four quartermasters; one
muallim (the Islamic prayer announcer, who seemed also
to do most of the praying, and little else); two cooks, and
the rest mariners. Below the poop was a sort of great cabin
without headroom in which were eight bunks, allocated to
the eight seniors—the master, mate, serang, *muallim,* four
quartermasters. Cooks and such fended for themselves and
so did the quartermasters on this passage, as the vessel was

carrying seven passengers. These had priority for bunks, if they cared to use them. Most of them did not. These passengers included two men from Malé who had been sent to Colombo for necessary medical or surgical treatment, one of whom was now fit again and the other, his case being inoperable, was returning home to die. This man turned out to be a professional storyteller and was a most cheerful old fellow. Often he had all hands in fits of laughter while he spun a yarn to them in the lee of the longboat.

The *buggalow* was a well-built vessel, built—the master told me—somewhere near Calicut about eleven years previously, at a cost of 90,000 rupees. She was a very much stronger, better-built, and better-rigged vessel than any dhow I had previously seen. She had properly caulked teak decks, real hatches and proper waterways, an efficient ship's pump (used very little: she was tight), a good compass marked with the London maker's name in an excellent brass binnacle, an efficient capstan of wood and brass, and her fresh water was carried in good steel tanks, on deck. Her "galley" was an adequate firebox with an open hearth, on the foredeck, and her cooks were industrious, well equipped, and competent. Her mainmast was either stepped in, or at any rate well supported by, a strong steel sleeve which extended about four feet above the main deck, and her rigging was exceptionally good and well cared for. Her large assortment of equipment included an old speaking trumpet, a full set of new International Code flags (and the books), a telescope, binoculars, a roll of well-kept and corrected charts kept in an ancient copper cylinder attached to the deckhead in the great cabin, and a number of umbrellas used, I suppose for going ashore in the S.W. monsoon. All of these um-

brellas were decorated with little photographs of the Queen
and the Duke of Edinburgh, set in silver in the handles.

The master had a sextant, deck watch, and the necessary
nautical tables, almanac, etc. He had an advanced textbook
on arithmetic (in English) and two different Oxford dic-
tionaries. He spoke English well. He was a very quiet little
man and I did not discover that he could speak English at
all until we sailed, though I had known him in the agent's
office ashore for some weeks. He also spoke Hindustani,
Arabic, his own Maldivian, and some Singhalese. His am-
bition was to see his native islands acquire a motor ship
and to serve aboard her some day as master. He was a
good navigator, working up star sights night and morning
and noon sights, position lines by Marq St. Hilaire from the
sun, ex-meridians, and anything else he considered necessary. He had to be a good navigator as the passage was of
some 415 miles across open sea, with a difficult landfall at
the end which had, if necessary, to be made by night.

He did not seem to bother much about the International
Rule of the Road, nor did the ship show colored side lights,
though these were aboard and kept ready trimmed at night.
He said it was the custom to show these only when sailing
into Colombo. He always had two good hurricane lamps
lit and ready for use, and he had a large torch which, he
said, he flashed on the sails if he saw a steamer approaching too close. He said that if steamers came close, it made
no difference whether he burned side lights, for he was sure
that no watchkeeping officers kept any lookout for such
antiquated sea lights as the red and green lamps of a
sailing vessel. The torch was much better. They sheered
off when they saw the sails. As for possible risk of collision

11. Ike Marsh was Bos'n and Chief Rigger.

12. The *Marcel B.* made a splendid frigate.

13. The old brigantines made a handsome fleet, in the Roads off Benidorme.

14. I sailed by *buggalow* to the Maldive Islands.

with other such vessels as his own, he knew where they all were, and he had confidence in their masters.

The master had been only nine years at sea, and that all in the one ship. He was, he said, not less than thirty-five and not more than forty years old: he was not quite sure. He had previously been a clerk in the customs and had studied navigation under a competent instructor ashore at Malé. He did not have any experience of sailing small vessels. His title of *Maniku* was a rank which was, apparently, the right rank for the sailing-master class, and it was not considered at all odd in the Maldives, where all had the sailing tradition, that a master would not have gone to sea until he was twenty-six. He was a quiet little man most interested in his profession, and he told me that he had two special friends in Colombo, the master and chief officer of a large steamer belonging to the Union S.S. Co. of New Zealand and trading regularly to Colombo, who visited him in the *buggalow* and he visited their steamer, where they were instructing him in such things as RDF and radar. I formed a high opinion of this master and his ship.

On the passage, she rolled a lot, running deep-laden before the wind. She set a lateen topsail on the main, which was a sail I had not been with before. She had a main topmast not much stouter than a flagstaff, and the tops'l yard was hoisted on this. It was very light. So was the sail. I slept in the open in preference to the great cabin, which was hot. She steered like a witch and ran like a clipper, and very little rudder movement was necessary to give her a good course. We lived mainly on curry and rice, but the food was good—fresh fish from the sea, sometimes curried chickens (which ran about the decks until it was time for conversion into curry), good unleavened bread, plenty of tea and coffee.

Our seven passengers included three taciturn young fishermen named Moosa, Mahmood, and Ali Manikee, who had been blown away from their island in a storm eight months earlier. Their boat capsized. The sail was lost. The oars washed out. Their water pot went overboard. They righted the boat but could not retrieve the gear. They drifted for ten days, blown before the southwest monsoon towards the Malabar coast of India. They could not catch a fish, because their lines were gone. Finally they drifted ashore, more dead than alive. Now they were returning to their atoll, to fish again.

I asked them about their experience, which they seemed to take for granted. It was "tough", they said. I could believe that. The captain said many fishermen were blown away. He knew one who was picked up and taken on in a big oil-tanker to Africa. He spoke only Maldivian, which no one understood, and it was a long time before the officials could discover to which country to send him back. The 90,000 people of the Maldive Islands speak a language of their own.

The *buggalow* sailed to the Maldives in three days, and the captain came into the big lagoon of Malé after midnight on a moonlit night. Here he was in waters which he had known since childhood. We could hear the breakers roaring on the reefs outside and passed so close to some of the atoll beaches that I heard the monsoon sighing in the coconut palms. There were no lights. The water was deep in the broad lagoon, and our captain knew very well where the reefs were. In the morning I saw that we had come to anchorage in a group of three *buggalows* and one other vessel, a rigged-down old sailing ship with a lovely hull. Even rigged down, she was still beautiful. Could this be the *Attiyathur-Rahman,* at last? I hurried across in the *buggalow's* longboat, but I knew the answer. No other surviving sailing ship could have a hull like that.

As the longboat rounded the shapely counter I read

BRIG ATTIYATHUR RAHMAN
MALÉ, MALDIVES

This was in bold lettering, including the word "brig," which was really her type and not her name. There was no sign of hog or sag in the graceful hull, which was coppered to the waterline, though the iron fastenings in the bulwarks and upper planking were weeping rust. Her topsides were rotten, I was told, and her masts and yards lay beached on the waterfront of Malé, where she would follow them on the next high tide.

We climbed aboard. Except for the absence of rigging, she was like a ship still in commission. The serang and a few hands were still aboard, and the deckhouse galley was in commission. The quarters, fore and aft, were immaculate, ready for immediate use. The afterguard had lived in a raised deckhouse aft, which was spacious and airy. There was an indoor bathroom and W.C., and I saw a telltale compass above the master's bunk, slung where he could watch it with half an eye even while he rested. The teak decks, the deckhouses, the old-fashioned windlass, the wheel and the bell, and all the quarters were in good order. The crew had slept in bunks below the low fo'c'sle head, apparently, where there were bunks for half of them only, the rest stretching out where they could, and there was no headroom at all. There was headroom aft, for the admiral of the government's fleet, I gathered, had handled the brig on her annual visits to Colombo on the nominal tribute voyages, before Ceylon was granted independence.

I liked the look of the beautiful brig and was sorry I was too late to sail in her. But there it was. She was finished, and the Sultan and his prime minister, I soon gathered, were most anxious to replace her with a small motor ship or steamer at the earliest possible moment.

Neither the *Attiyathur-Rahman,* nor any other brig, would sail again.

CHAPTER

8

LIFE AT MALÉ

WELL, here I was in the Maldive Islands anyway, so I might as well have a look at them before the fever caught up with me—if it ever did.

From the lagoon—one of twenty similar great lagoons in the twenty atolls which comprise the Maldive Islands, lying in a long double line on a subterranean shelf which to the north sprouts another atoll group called the Lacca-dives (which are Indian) and, to the south, the Chagos Archipelago—Malé (or Sultan's Island) looked a fascinat-ing place. The long gray walls of ancient fortifications fronted the blue lagoon where the fishing craft skimmed before the morning breeze at speed, their white sails mak-ing a perfect picture and the Viking hulls of their high-prowed, broad-beamed, and shapely craft looked almost incredible. There was not a powered vessel anywhere in sight. No factory chimney belched smoke to pollute the soft air. There were, indeed, no factories and no chimneys. A row of godowns fronted the lagoon where the Borah merchants did their business. A white minaret rose near the flagstaff by the Sultan's palace. Schools of great fish broke the surface of the lagoon here and there—bonita, albacore, marlin—and the fishing craft ran down towards them, brown-skinned mariners throwing out live bait to attract the schools and then, once among the big fish, all hands piling aft with short lines on stout bamboo poles, hauling the striking fish out of the water in such profusion and at such speed that all I saw was the flash of silvery bodies as the astonished fish were flung inboard. A moment or two of this, and the fish were gone, while the boat skimmed away again towards another school.

One of the boats passed close and I saw that it was all but waterlogged. The fishermen kept their bait alive by the simple means of opening a plug and filling the bottom of their vessel with sea water, in which the fish were swimming round. The idea was that the bait fish became so used to swimming in tight circles that when they were thrown overboard they still swam that way, and so stayed in the same spot and attracted the big fish.

Malé lagoon was a fisherman's paradise. The big fish leapt in all directions. But it was very hot, and ashore the mosquitoes were a plague. The residents did not seem to be bothered by them, but they bothered me a little. I took all the precautions I could against those mosquitoes, for I suspected that they might carry the germs which caused Maldivian fever. I had a mosquito net and repellents of several sorts, and used the lot.

I lived ashore in a broad-fronted bungalow which the Prime Minister, Mr. Ibrahim Ali Didi, kindly made available for me, with staff. It stood in a street called Orchid Lane, among spacious gardens full of mangoes, breadfruit, pawpaw, and plantains, and the low stone walls were festooned with bright red flowers. It had five bedrooms and two bathrooms and was a fine place with a wide veranda all round, where there was room for fifty men to sit. Apparently I was the only European just then in all the 2,000 islands, islets, atolls, and atollons which comprise the Maldives, and all the children walking down Orchid Lane stopped at the open gateway and peered in, quietly and respectfully, to have a look at the stranger. When I walked in the streets crowds collected, and the children, whenever I stopped, formed a dense group to within two feet of me and stared. It was a strange experience for both of us. They were nice little children with fine, tranquil faces, and they had bundles of schoolbooks under their arms. I looked in the books. They were writing books in Arabic and in the Maldivian script, and books of arithmetic lessons and geography, just as one might find among a group of children in Oxford.

Malé more than lived up to the bright promise held out by its pleasant aspect from the sea. It was the sort of island we dream about and look for in vain among the fabled South Seas—the unspoiled, lovely, warm, and languid land, "away from it all" and yet offering something besides sunshine and a golden beach and the waving coconut palms. Malé is an island-city of 8,000 inhabitants, fronting a wide, deep, and lovely lagoon which is more than twenty miles long and ten miles broad. It has a thriving bazaar, where

most of the larger shops are kept by so-called "Borah" merchants from India. All the goods for these shops came in
sailing ships, but one could buy almost anything. Several
shops specialized in the kind of tailless kite which Maldivians love to fly—well-made kites, sometimes six feet
high, made skillfully of colored paper and decorated with
pictures and tinsel, stuck on. All these kites were fitted with
noisemakers, some of which I saw were shaped like small
bows with rubber stretched on them as taut as violin strings,
and when the kites were flown the rubber vibrated and the
bows gave out a sound like a distant jet fighter, or a noisy
sawmill.

This was the only noise I heard—this and the rowdy caw-
ing of a thousand crows. Crows were the most numerous
birds. There were often more kites aloft than crows, and
the Maldivian children and grown men alike were expert
at making their kites perform complicated aerobatics. Kite
flying was more than the island's principal diversion. It was
part of Maldivian life. One morning I walked to the post
office, beside the waterfront, and there was the happy clerk
sitting on a bench doing his accounts with one hand while
with the other he held the string of a cavorting bright-blue
kite about 500 feet aloft, outside his window. Nobody
seemed to think there was anything incongruous about this.
He gave me my stamps, and the kite still flew. A group of
sailors, waiting for a longboat to take them out to their
buggalow, watched its capers with informed and critical
eyes.

Kite making was an industry, but the kites were fragile
and could not be exported. Malé's chief industry was the
preparation of dried fish, though the fish were smoked and

dried on other islands and in other atolls. All trade for export came to Malé, which was the only port of entry. Other trades were making copra from the million coconuts that grew on every island, twisting coir rope (from the husks of coconuts), catching turtles and drying the beautifully figured tortoise shell which was sent to Ceylon to be worked, collecting the famous cowrie shells (Cypraea Monita) which are so beautiful that they were once used as currency and are still valued highly, weaving mats, coloring and carving graceful vases in the delicate lacquer for which some of the atolls have long been famed. In the garden of the bungalow on Orchid Lane, a group of lacquer workers was doing exquisite work, using a primitive hand-turned lathe which was set in the earth and a few sharp chisels and knives.

There was one other strange industry in these extraordinary islands, and that was collecting ambergris. I had been a whaleman once, in a big Norwegian expedition to the Ross Sea in Antarctica. We took hundreds of whales down there but I had never seen any ambergris. There was a lot of the stuff in the Maldives. It was found, they told me, cast up on the fringing reefs, and sometimes on the sand in various islands. But I saw no whales. There must be some mysterious spot round the Maldive Islands where the sick sperm whales come to die and throw up their ambergris. The grayish-white, unattractive substance is a product of sick sperm whales. It used to be the base of fine perfumes and, though chemical substitutes have long been produced, it is still of value.

I asked where was this mysterious place where the sperm whales came to die, but nobody knew. Once, in the *buggalow*, I had seen some sperms blowing, but that was a hundred miles from the islands. In the old days, Yankee whalemen out of New Bedford and Old Salem used to roam the Indian Ocean. Probably they knew, but they kept the knowledge to themselves. Today the islanders know only where to pick up their ambergris, and it is exported through Malé. A friend gave me a piece. It looked the kind of stuff one would pass by on the beach, even if one tripped over a couple of hundredweight of it. They told me it was still worth thousands of rupees.

The Maldives are 100 per cent Moslem, converted from Buddhism in the twelfth century. Their central position in the rich, monsoon-blown waters of the Indian Ocean attracted the navigators of the past, and the Arabs came early—and Chinese in junks, Persians, pirates from the Malabar coast, then the Portuguese, after Vasco da Gama. Of the Europeans, only the Portuguese occupied the islands, and that briefly. Some of their bronze cannon still poke their ancient muzzles from the thick stone walls of the bastions, and much of their fortifications still stood when I was there.

But it was the Arabs who left an abiding mark among the islands, and the Maldivians reminded me strongly of the sailing Arabs of the Persian Gulf. Tough, law-abiding, conservative in outlook, quiet, independent, they lead lives of great simplicity, finding their wants (except for rice) among their own islands, asking little or nothing of the outside world, which has passed them by. Once they stood athwart the great sailing routes in the Indian Ocean, and the riches of Ceylon and the Malabar coast are close to them. Their myriad fringing reefs trapped many a spice-laden galleon, and some girls I saw in Malé even now wear ornaments made from gold which came originally in a treasure ship cast away on their shores. But the steamer lanes cut past the Maldives in the north, by the island of Minikoy, which shows their only light (and is now administered from India, being considered part of the Laccadives, though the people speak and are Maldivian). All other traffic leaves the Maldives alone. And so they remain unspoiled, and the islanders like it that way. Who can blame them?

There are some odd survivals among them, such as sorcery. In Colombo I was warned that there were powerful sorcerers in the islands, who—among other things—knew how to cast spells. If they could do that, perhaps they could do other things. While I was at Malé the local newspaper, in its monthly edition, published a list of thirty-nine approved medical practitioners of one sort and another, ranging from herbalists and bonesetters to qualified sorcerers. There were six of these, most of them qualified in sorcery only, but a few also as bonesetters. What did the sorcerers accomplish in these days? I asked my new friends at Malé.

"There are many *jinns* in our islands," a Ceylon-educated young man explained. "Many of our people believe in them, although I do not. If they believe in *jinns*, they believe illnesses can be caused by them. If they believe that illnesses can be so caused, then they will also believe they can be cured by people with the ability to cast out the *jinns*. So you see our "sorcerers" are really useful practitioners like your psychoanalysts, who sometimes cast out your *jinns*. It is the same thing."

It was as easy as that. After all, I reflected, my young friend was quite right. We call our *jinns* by long names. The number of our inexplicable ailments and temporary aberrations steadily increases. Maybe we could do with honest *jinn* removers, too. Their usefulness depends upon belief in them.

I was very interested to meet some of these sorcerers and, if it could possibly be arranged, to meet some of the *jinns* too, or at any rate to watch a *jinn* remover at his work. So it was arranged that one of the chief sorcerers come to the bungalow. His name was Hajara Mohammed Didi, and he was a tall man with a striking face. His headgear was a gray fez, and he was dressed in a well-pressed white jacket which he wore over an immaculate white shirt, with, instead of trousers, the more suitable and better-ventilated long sarong. This was standard dress for professional men among the islands. The shirt was worn outside the sarong, and his brown feet were protected by leather sandals of Maldivian make. He had fine features, and his complexion was that of a Syrian. The most striking thing about him was his eyes. These were piercing, direct, and challenging.

It was early morning when he came and he arrived depressed, saying that a patient in a delirium the previous evening had warned him that there were a thousand *jinns* waiting for him on Wirigili Island, which is very close to Malé. Apparently they were waiting for a chance to "get" him, because they were tired of having him undo their work. He brought no *jinns* with him that I could see, and it was explained that this was not his work. His function was to get rid of *jinns*, not to use them. Had he been a bad sorcerer who conjured up evil-doing *jinns*, or pretended to do so, he would never have been given official approval.

He looked round the bungalow and called for a few simple

utensils such as an ordinary white soup plate, a small glass, a jar of black ink of the type used locally, and a bit of a pointed twig to write with. Then he sat down beneath an orchid bush and, taking the plate in his left hand, began at once to draw a sort of diagram inside the bottom. This, I was told, was a magic diagram, but it looked very straightforward to me. He got on quickly with the job, without any "business." It looked like a set of crossed straight lines such as children might use to play the game of noughts and crosses. He wrote something beside the drawing in what looked like Arabic, put various hieroglyphs and twirly pieces in some of the squares, and then promptly poured the glass of water over the lot. He swilled the water round the bottom of the plate until the diagram was all dissolved in it, and I wondered how such goings on could possibly affect *jinns* or anything else.

"This is the moment," my friends whispered. "See what he does now!"

The sorcerer took the glass of water, which had gone a gray and clouded color, held it to his lips, mumbled something over it which I could not hear, and then his face began to work and his piercing eyes—always odd—looked strange and frightening. Then he looked once very fiercely about the garden, got up, and left. The demonstration was over. He didn't say whether he had seen any *jinns* or not: apparently not—but that night none of us could sleep. The bungalow seemed to be haunted, and I for one tossed and turned all night long, though the nights were cool (after 11 P.M. or so) and good for sleeping.

Maybe the sorcerer had stirred up some *jinns*.

Hajara Mohammed Didi was a well-respected practitioner

who was said to have cured many men. If he could not cure
the ills he was summoned to treat, he announced at once
that they were not caused by *jinns* and other methods must
be tried. He had, I was told, never cured a woman. Apparently *jinns* could not be exorcised from women, being with
them always.

Women had a special place in the Islands and did not go
about veiled, as in many other Moslem communities. Indeed,
they did not go about at all by day, except for the small
girls who went to morning school. High school for girls was
in the evenings, when women were allowed to walk abroad
taking some exercise with their close relatives or with their
husbands or brothers. I noticed in many houses curious
structures overlooking part of the walls, a sort of iron-barred
cell which could act as a lookout post on occasion. Some of
the bigger homes had these cells built up in two or even
three stories, and there was a fine lookout post over the
Sultan's lawns and gardens, by the waterfront.

These lookout posts were for the women, I learned. From
these vantage points they could see and not be seen. Such
places were provided also by the sports grounds (where
cricket, hockey, and football were played, just as in Ceylon).
The women were segregated in these, but they were free to
attend any function. They did not go to the bazaar or do
the shopping. Men did that. When I was invited to the high
school to take some photographs of the classes there, I noticed that the girls were beautiful, and even their teachers,
though one of them was a married woman, looked like fresh-
faced girls of thirteen or fourteen years old. The girls in
school were from twelve to sixteen, and they all looked

about eight or ten to me. Maldivian women must know the secret of eternal youth, but they keep it to themselves. I found it impossible to guess their ages. Up to forty or so they all looked like children.

The younger women and girls were all dressed in the same styles, though not alike. Each wore an ankle-length frock, high in the waist with a full-gathered skirt, a large Peter Pan collar, and long sleeves. On their well-kept, shining black hair they pinned short veils of gossamer stuff of various colors, which fell down behind them, over their shoulders. On their feet were colored sandals of an attractive shape, usually red. Some simple golden jewelry set off the ensemble and, with a wide variety of colorful materials to choose from, they managed to make this national costume both individual and attractive. Many older women still wore the old-style national costume such as the French castaway Pyrard de Laval had noted when he was five years in the Maldives after shipwreck, from 1602 to 1607.

This costume consists of a chocolate-colored or dark-blue waist cloth made of homespun and always having two or three horizontal stripes in white near the bottom, with the upper part of the body covered by a sort of knee-length chemise, always in blue or terra-cotta. The waist cloth or skirt droops nearly to the ground, and the general effect is that the lady is wearing a short dress over a curiously old-fashioned ankle-length garment in a material both too hot and wrongly colored for the intense heat. The hair is always done beautifully, and generally kept in place with a dozen or more large combs of exquisite tortoise shell, the older style being that the hair was gathered into a bun at the side and a veil was wrapped closely round this. How the veil was kept there I don't know. I saw many older women dressed in this fashion, but I never discovered how they kept the veil knotted to their bun of hair.

Weddings are dull, by any standards. I saw something of one or two, but I saw no brides. The bride is not at her wedding—at any rate, not at any function attended by male guests. Nor does she go to the court or to the mosque, for there is no ceremony for her at either place. The Maldivian Moslems are monogamous, and they choose their brides with care. The bride must sign a certificate that she agrees to her marriage and has not been compelled to accept it, and this certificate is produced to the court before the bridegroom is allowed to go to her home to claim her. Both parties must sign a further agreement on the manner in which they accept and will treat one another, and the bride has just as much right as the bridegroom in all this. Both agree to lead good lives, to be faithful to one another and never to separate except for grave and insoluble difficulties. Without proving such difficulties to the satisfaction of the court, there can be no divorce.

The bridegroom must sign the Maldivian Seven Rules of Marriage, in the presence of the court, and these rules may be summarized as follows:

1. He must clothe his wife.

2. The wife must obey the husband, so long as he keeps the laws of God.

3. So long as she remains obedient, the wife must be housed, fed, lodged, and given the means of cleanliness. She must also be given proper housekeeping money.

15. The old brig — last of her kind. She will sail no more.

16. Brig's cook in his galley, currying fish.

17. Sorcerer.

18. They were lost, but then found — the three shipwrecked fishermen.

19. In the inner harbor of Malé, Maldive Islands.

20. *Below,* kite shop, Malé.

21. The *Mayflower* took shape very slowly in the Brixham yard.

4. Neither may abuse nor harm the other, mentally or physically.

5. If in disobedience of these Rules one party does cause harm to the other, there must be no revenge. The matter must be referred to the court for settlement.

6. Unless the husband proves his wife's misdeeds, he must support her.

7. The Rules must be kept on pain of punishment by the court for any infringement.

When the bridegroom, having signed this document, takes it to her home, the bride also signs, and that is her wedding ceremony. There is no going away for a honeymoon. There is nowhere to go from Malé, and Malé is the best of the islands. It is usual for the young couple to make some sailing trips on the lagoon, and here and there on the nearer islets there are guest houses. But mostly they stay home, where the bride soon settles into the well-knit family group. The family is a real unit, and she must belong to it. That her training and her background make her well fit to do. The excellence of Maldivian wives was attested by Ibn Batuta, who had four of them. The sailors in the *buggalow* declared that Maldivian women were the most passionate in the world, and one was enough for any man.

If the rules for brides and bridegrooms are of interest, so also are the ancient Rules for Rulers, and some of these could be taken to heart in places far removed from the Maldive Islands. The four essentials for Sultans were defined by a learned Maldivian to be: (1) A well-filled treasury; (2) a fighting army; (3) unity in the army; and (4) a righteous and generous rule, free from injustice.

The object of the well-filled treasury, it was explained, was to ensure peace among the subjects and to make *them* affluent, not the ruler. To preserve the treasure it was necessary to maintain an army, "but an army to treasure is like unto flies that swarm round sugar." So there must be full friendship and trust between ruler and army. A man fit to be Sultan must be able to "instill fear and inspire confidence, while exercising justice and fair dealing. It is unthinkable that the people will be contented with rulers who do not possess these two qualities."

This good advice went unheeded often, not only in the Maldive Islands.

Today's Sultan is elected, and government is by a parliament of members drawn from all the big atolls. There is a prime minister who exercises the executive rule. There are no foreign advisers, no agents, not even a single consular representative of another race, from anywhere. The Maldivians are under a measure of British protection in their external affairs, but they govern themselves entirely. It is they who made a garden city out of Malé. It is they who made their 12000 islands (215 only are inhabited) the abode of a happy, healthy, and carefree populace, and keep the Maldive Islands a zone of sunlit peace and prosperity, a nation of simple content and real happiness, in a changing world. But now there is a proposal to make a landing field on their island of Gan, at Addu Atoll in the south. There was some flying there during the Second World War, and in 1956 a war-surplus radio station acquired from the Royal Air Force was still Malé's only means of communication with the outside world.

I left the Maldives on a sunny morning in March, and I

walked along the wide, sanded, and flower-lined streets with
some regret. Each citizen is required to sweep the roadway
before his property twice weekly, but they sweep it twice a
day. All the rectangular island of Malé—about a mile long
by a half mile wide with 8,000 people—was hospital-clean
and orderly, as if it were a naval gunnery school, but the
only admiral was the Amir-al-Bahr of the government's fleet
of half a dozen sailing ships. The only guns were those
muzzle-loaders in the ancient fortress, and a few on the
walls. Most of these guns had been removed and upended
in the coral sand to support the city-island's lampposts
which were thrust down their muzzles. The fact that only the
Sultan—His Highness Mohammed Farid Didi—is allowed
to have an automobile (and that a small one) helps to keep
things clean. Others ride bicycles, which are licensed, and
each citizen must ride his own.

The little children were hurrying to school, clutching
their books with them, and, as always, they stopped and
stared with a sort of kindly wonder as I passed by. Over the
Sultan's palace, where the thick stone walls keep out too
much of the fresh sea breezes, the Maldivian flag was flying, and the three signaling guns up there were being un-
covered to fire a salute later in the morning. The usual
orderly crowd of citizens padded quietly along the paths
among the lawns and flower beds, and the usual collection
of kites was buzzing and diving in the clear air.

By the waterfront, I saw one of the qualified bonesetters
—a Mr. Hajan Bakoy—at work on a boy who had broken
an arm while playing football. The child stood near the
water's edge, and the bonesetter was massaging the good
part of the arm with handfuls of wet sand, and setting the

whole arm again to mend. The lad's mother stood miserably by, watching, and the lad himself was quietly accepting the treatment given him though it must have hurt. He would soon be well again, I was told, and everyone seemed to accept that without doubt, although the methods of the bonesetter looked a little odd to me. Further along the waterfront where the little shapely ships from other atolls were moored closely together, happy throngs of brown children and some adults were playing in and out of the thatched houses built on their vessels. These were their homes.

For a moment, a graceful lugger sailed framed in the arch at the entrance to the gardens, and I could hear the stevedores singing and dancing while they worked, unloading rice. How they worked, and how they danced! For a few pence a day, a hundred men bustled along with heavy sacks of rice and bags of Australian flour, cases of textiles and stuff from Japan, which they manhandled along that hot and dusty waterfront as if it was fun. Three of them were dancing a wild African dance to their own great delight and the entertainment of the others, writhing and making grotesque faces while they pranced and stamped, and the singing stevedores vied with one another to see who could carry not one but two 200-pound sacks of rice at the fastest pace!

A small German motor ship had come in with rice from Colombo and was going back to Ceylon with a cargo of dried Maldivian fish, and I took the opportunity to sail with her. It might be weeks or months before there was another such chance, and the few *buggalows* could take a month to beat back against the light northeast monsoon. There were only eight *buggalows* and the one brigantine left, with no possibility of replacements since no more such vessels were

being built in India—the only source of supply. Old—or
new—Arab dhows would not do, even if they were available, for the Maldivian sailors put to sea the year round and
Arab vessels were built only to sail in the good-weather season, the northeast monsoon. To keep the seas in the southwest monsoon, a stout and able ship was needed, like the
Indian-built *Fath-ur-Rahman* I had come in. This *buggalow*
was lying in the lagoon after discharge of her cargo (done
by the cheerful crew) under some repair, and the sailors
waved to me as I boarded the German. It was because the
government, through the shortage of *buggalows* and the
wearing out of the brig, found it had to charter expensive
motor ships that it was anxious to acquire one of its own—
preferably with capital advanced by Britain. The Prime
Minister, Mr. Ibrahim Ali Didi, had asked me to use such
influence as I might have to hasten this acquisition. I came
to sail in the brig and returned to speed the purchase of a
motor ship. Well, it was necessary: I could see that. There
was no timber in the Maldives to build another brig.

The motor ship weighed anchor, blew a salute on her
siren, thrashed the blue water white while she maneuvered
to turn, and was outward bound towards the passage
through the barrier reefs of Malé Atoll. We passed by
Hulule and Dunidu, islets in the great lagoon which I had
visited, and in the distance was Wirigilli, where the thousand *jinns* were alleged to be waiting for Mr. Hajara Mohammed Didi. The Viking-hulled fishing boats skimmed
about the broad lagoon, their lateen sails pictures of grace
and quiet power, and I reflected that it would be a long
time before they were mechanized, even if a small steamer
or a motor ship must replace the brig.

The *Hugo Arlt* hurried on, and soon the islands and all the atolls, more sea than land and none of them six feet above sea level, had sunk below the horizon, where the coconuts and the breadfruit trees—the last things I saw—rose like prairie grass growing mysteriously out of the sea. Soon they were gone, too, and only the lonely sea—four hundred miles of it—stretched away towards the coast of Ceylon.

THE *MAYFLOWER* STORY

CHAPTER

9

LAUNCHED, FLOATED, AND
ALL BUT CAPSIZED

THE dock gates opened with obvious reluctance, for they had been shut for months, ever since the ship was launched from the ways in the September of the previous year, and it was now the first of April. I say the "ship" had been launched, but in fact it was less than the half of her. She was built on the ways only to the main strength deck, the 'tween-decks of a modern vessel. The weather deck, all the towering upper works of great cabin and aftercastle, the forecastle, the rudder and the masts and all the rest were added afterwards, when the shell of her was floated into the dry dock, the gates closed, and the water pumped out. It took a high tide in Devon to get her into the dock, and it would take a higher to get her out again. Held back by the fresh wind that had been blowing all day, the tide was not going to reach the height predicted: it was no use waiting, for there would be less on the morrow. The gates must open and she must come out now, or stay there for another fortnight. And now there was not water enough to lift her and she refused to budge.

The neighborhood of the dry dock and indeed the whole shipyard and the fish wharf across the harbor were crowded with people of all sorts. Every roof, every window in the Upham store, every possible vantage point sprouted photographers, still and cinema. Determined and industrious men, leather-throated and loquacious, barked unnautical commentaries into microphones which their engineers had perched precariously on the tops of tin roofs and presumably connected by cable to some power point which was passing on the discourse to such listeners as cared to hear it or had not bothered to switch their radios off. The little ship looked complete, with all her yards and running rigging up, and very brave in a gay coat of new paint. The painted Mayflower on her extraordinary high transom was over thirty feet from her keel, though she was not ninety feet long, and her unstayed bowsprit end was nearly in the second-story window of the Upham store.

Mr. Upham the builder, Mr. Baker the designer, Warwick Charlton who had been throughout the principal promoter of the venture, the blacksmith who had made the ironwork, the rigger who had erected the complicated fantasy of Elizabethan rigging, the sawmiller who had shaped the planks, the foreman shipwright and all his brother shipwrights, apprentices, and aids, the ship chandler who was to provide the stores, all watched with interest, as also did a considerable contingent of dignitaries, civic and social, from Plimoth Plantation, the organization in Plymouth, Massachusetts, which had dreamt about this ship for the past decade and now had been promised her ownership—if she ever reached America, which many doubted and some said loudly was impossible. Among those watching was Henry Hornblower II, of Boston and Plymouth, who with his father Ralph had been an enthusiastic supporter, and had no doubts about the ship's arrival at all. There were other good friends in the large crowd—Felix Fenston, of London, who had helped considerably, and Bill Brewster of Plymouth among them.

A little more water came in, and the level in the dock was equal to that of the harbor outside. There was obviously no way to increase it further. It was the predicted moment of maximum level for the day—indeed, for many days. Under the builder's keen eye and the foreman shipwright's direction, the baulks of timber which had been holding the ship upright in the dock were knocked away, to allow her to be pulled out by a little tug which stood waiting just beyond the gates. No sooner were the baulks removed than the ship took a horrible lurch to starboard. Her total capsize right there in the dock seemed imminent, bringing her heavy yards crashing into a crowd of onlookers, and there was a wild rush to get out of the way. Several who had been aboard now experienced a desire to remove themselves hastily ashore, for their presence, they realized, was not really necessary, and they leapt over the rail and onto the stone sides of the dock while there was time.

There was, after all, some precedent for "replicas" to fall over on such occasions, for the alleged *Santa Maria* had done just that when coming down the ways in Spain some years earlier, and had then sunk. The Erikson bark *Penang*, not a replica at all but a twentieth-century Cape Horner, had fallen on her side in a dry dock in London, and it was not at all unknown for the most modern steamships, on rare occasions, to do likewise. There was a lot of weight in the new *Mayflower's* rigging, squat as it was by Cape Horn standards, and more than enough in her inordinately high upper works.

For the moment, however, she hung there, somewhat drunkenly, at an angle of between fifteen and twenty degrees —listed heavily but not capsized. The diesel tug belonging to Mr. Ernie Lister, taciturn and competent as a good Devon man should be, worked manfully to get the ship out of the dock, dragging her heavy oak keel along the bottom if needs be. It was obvious to a seaman that the new ship was in a condition of critical stability but, since she had not gone right over with the first lurch, it was reasonable to hope that if she came out of the dock at all on that tide, she would emerge with a list but not on her side. For the moment she stood stubbornly, resisting all Ernie's stout efforts, which might have been more effective if he had had a slightly more powerful tug.

At last she began to move when I had almost given up hope: out she came, very slowly at first but picking up way as she scraped past the sill and was properly afloat. Then she took a nasty sheer, and Ernie's efforts to straighten her seemed likely to pull her right over, a feat which might not have been very difficult just then when the wind was on her beam. She flopped over this way, then that, and the crowd watched spellbound, waiting for the final capsize. My two lads Christopher and Peter were on the high poop with me, and I showed them where to clamber up the rigging if indeed the ship did go right over. There was not water enough just there in the harbor to drown the lot of her, and at least some of the rigging would remain above the surface. I caught a quick glimpse of my wife's white face in the crowd ashore. A couple of shipwrights who were aboard walked to the rail, and she listed a little further. It was all rather alarming. As soon as she was clear of the wires and posts and things round the dock, I ordered the course and the lateen yards to be lowered to the rail, to take at least some of the heavy weight aloft from the ship and, the moment the buoy rope was secured, the competent Ernie hurried off to bring out a lighter full of additional ballast.

Legally, I had no right to order anything, though I was the master-designate of the vessel. She was not yet handed over and was entirely the responsibility of her builder until such time as she passed her trials satisfactorily and was paid for and accepted. The builder had no pilot or crew aboard for what was expected to be the simple business of moving the ship a cable or so from dry dock to buoy inside the harbor, but I had already assembled the mates and half a dozen other sailing-ship sailors who were to make the Atlantic passage. They were helping with the rigging and general preparations, and it was they who got the yards down and, when Ernie was back with the additional ballast, got on with hoisting that inboard and stowing it in the bottom of the ship for the night, as quickly as possible. There was not enough of this ballast, which consisted of sawn lengths of old steel rails, properly to correct the vessel's appalling lack of stability, but for the moment it sufficed. We got the ship on an even keel, and she stayed that way for the night.

The additional ballast could not have been put into her while she was still in the dry dock for the very obvious reason that then she would have drawn too much water to come out at all; but in truth the critical state of her stability

had not been foreseen. There was no real need for those
heavy yards to be aloft. They hoisted on halyards called
jeers and could have been left down, while the topmasts
and their yards could have been housed very easily.

Well, there she was, afloat at any rate, a tight and staunch
little ship looking incredibly romantic there in Brixham
Harbor, with the riding light shining from halfway up the
hempen forestay, and the tracery of her unusual rig showing faintly against the stars. Her ballasting could be put
right later. The Ministry of Transport experts in Berkeley
Square would see to that. Indeed they arrived hotfoot in
the morning to carry out inclining tests for that very purpose. There was not, indeed, much data on which a naval
architect or a ship surveyor could base his calculations for
the stability curves of such a ship, since none had been built
for over 250 years, and the data on those which were built
could hardly be expected to be adequate. In those days
shipwrights built good merchant ships by eye and their traditional knowledge handed down from father to son, and
academic calculation did not enter much into it, if at all.
The Ministry experts, who had given a great deal of thought
and study to the subject (like the skilled naval architect
who drew the plans after years of burning midnight oil, and
Stuart Upham the builder), declared that another fifty tons
of ballast must go below, and called a conference in their
offices in Berkeley Square to discuss the matter and others
affecting the vessel.

With considerably over a hundred tons of old railway
iron secured in the bottom of her deep hold, the vessel might
be stable but she would also be what sailors know as "stiff"
in the sea. She would roll like a pendulum, and this severe

rolling would throw stresses on her masts and rigging which might strain them. This had to be accepted at that late stage, but I wondered what Elizabethan seamen had done about the problem. I knew that they would never have built a ship so cranky. From the start, we all knew that this "replica" was proportionately higher in hull form than an early-seventeenth-century ship had been, for the designer had perforce to put headroom under the beams of the 'tween-decks and in the great cabin. His designs were for a ship to lie permanently in Plymouth harbor, in New England, in the safety of the Eel River, where a million ardent Pilgrim followers might board her each year and climb all over her, but none would go to sea. The Pilgrim Fathers, and the mariners who sailed their ship, had to accept low decks. Headroom in ships, like running water and inboard lavatories and such things, is entirely a modern idea, and to build it into the ship seriously affected her stability. I suspect too—thought I am no expert on the subject—that the upper works in this new *Mayflower* were far more substantially built than those of the old, which we know worked alarmingly in the sea. Light upper works mean less weight, and so do low decks, and I don't doubt the original ship had stood up all right with a bit of shingle thrown into the hold, if it were empty, and her course yards and topmasts run down. I would like to have seen our ship a foot or so beamier than she was, too, to help offset her extra top weight, but I am no naval architect. I had nothing to do with the ship's design, nor the overseeing of her building, nor anything else not strictly relevant to her sailing.

As for that, what was I doing there anyway, on the poop

of this vessel, master-designate to take her across to America? The answer to that was simple enough. If the ship were built and seaworthy, then obviously to sail her to America or anywhere else was just about the most interesting piece of practical nautical research of the century, and that was my field. All that sailing with the Arabs, the long haul to the Maldives, the Cape Horners, the circumnavigation in the full-rigged ship *Joseph Conrad*, the school-ships experience, led to this. I was first asked by my good friends of the National Geographic Society in Washington, D.C., to take a direct interest in the ship, for they wrote that there was a great and growing interest in the project in America.

They were not the only American friends who expected that I should know all about it.

I did not, and so I sought the promoters, Warwick Charlton and John Lowe in the London office where they were to be found—there were only the two of them, apparently, with a third in the offing who later withdrew. Charlton did the talking. He explained that the preliminary promotion was private—but nonprofit—for the good reason that it was likely to succeed that way, and when sufficient funds had been raised from industry, from the sale of rights, from exhibitions, and in every other legitimate manner the promoters could think up to ensure that the ship would be paid for, then a public trust would be formed to take the project over. This was their planned manner of procedure. It was all arranged down to the last detail and, on that basis, the project had an imposing list of illustrious patrons, supporters, and other sponsors ranging from the Dollar Exports Council to the Lord Mayor of London. Distinguished members of the House of Commons noted for their interest in the furtherance of good Anglo-American relations, a noble Duke in Scotland, generals with household names, an Earl, several Knights, clerics, and a sprinkling of hardheaded businessmen headed the list.

Mr. Charlton further explained that a general public appeal for funds for the object they had in mind would probably fail, which would do Anglo-American relations more harm than good, for there were other appeals—there always are—of greater and more obvious immediate need. The project had the support of a considerable section of British industry, and their exhibition in one of the sheds alongside the building ship down at Brixham had been a great success. They intended to exhibit her in other ports when she was ready, notably at Southampton and London, where they were sure of her success and a good deal of further income. There was revenue from the film, still-picture, book, and magazine-story rights, and their project was indeed going quite well.

They looked forward anxiously to the time when they could form the Trust with a reasonable prospect of its success, and the whole of the framework for the Trust—the legal formalities, the selection of some of the trustees, and everything else—had been prepared already. The sooner the Trust was formed the better, for they were finding that the unpaid work of promoting the new *Mayflower's* construction was far more than they had ever imagined. Because of it, they were unable to get on with their other affairs at all. All of this appeared very reasonable. Though they knew nothing of ships (nor claimed to know anything), these men were experts in the strange world of public relations, in which Charlton had something of a reputation. It appeared that they also had a real feeling for the idea of the *Mayflower* venture as an abiding gesture of good relations between Britain and the U.S.A. They had begun quite an undertaking, more so perhaps than they knew, but they meant to see it through.

Privately promoted or not, across the Atlantic this project was already looked upon as a British achievement. More than that, there was considerable excitement about it. Plimoth Plantation was a philanthropic organization of the highest repute, and its officials were all prominent citizens in New England. The Plantation had a file of correspondence dating back at least ten years on the general idea of building a *Mayflower* replica, and had planned such a project in detail long before the London venture was begun. Now they were excited at the prospect of at least being *given* a ship. The cost of building such a vessel themselves in America or in England had daunted even them, for they had also to raise large sums for other purposes. Their objective was, in short, to create a sort of Williamsburg near Plymouth, and so provide all America with a worthy memorial to the Pilgrim Fathers.

I knew some of these New Englanders associated with Plimoth Plantation, and it was indeed the fact that such an organization existed which made sound sense of the whole *Mayflower* project. There had been other "replicas," such as the entire Columbus fleet which somehow turned up in the Great Lakes in time for the great Chicago Exhibition of the early 1890's, and a Norwegian Viking boat which sailed to the same destination, to say nothing of a reconstruction of Henry Hudson's *Half Moon* which had burned out in the River Hudson, through neglect. All these ships had disappeared (except the Norwegian, which was small enough to put in shelter ashore and may now be seen at Lincoln Park in Chicago), and the same fate would certainly overtake any new *Mayflower*, were there no influential organization to look properly after her. Many of my American friends had written to me enthusiastically on the subject of sailing the ship across long before I had anything to do with the project, and had assumed (since to them it was a national affair from the start), that I would be there. Most of them wanted to be in the crew.

"We are delighted to hear of your interest in the *Mayflower* replica," they wrote from New England, "and we very much hope that, when she is ready, you will sail her over for us. There is great excitement about her over here already, and we have already spent a lot of money to be ready for her. The Commonwealth of Massachusetts has voted $287,000 to dredge the harbor, and the town of Plymouth will spend thousands more, erecting grandstands and so on. We want her to arrive."

I required little persuasion to have a "bash" at so fascinating a sailing proposition. Here was a real galleon (well, more or less) to be sailed to the west'ard over the Western Ocean, without power or modern aids to help her. Here was a venture which (by the uninformed, who were legion) was considered to be impossible, derided in some sections of the British press. ("The ship with the 50-50 chance," they screamed. "She'll never make it!" after a long campaign about the impossibility of getting a British master or a British crew, if the ship were ever completed. They declared, almost unanimously, that it would prove impossible to find British shipwrights, ropemakers, sailmakers, riggers, and tradesmen generally to do the job.) All this nonsense passed me by.

"Who is going to sail the ship for you, when she is ready?" I asked the promoters, who obviously had undertaken quite enough in trying to bring her into being at all, without worrying over the problem of sailing her.

"Why," they answered, "we were thinking of you."

"You may consider that arranged," I said. "You build the ship, and I will do my best to get a British crew and sail her across."

I volunteered to sail the ship, without any question of payment for my services. I was not paid. In that decision, I was not unmindful of the moving story of the Pilgrim Fathers and how much their love of freedom and their magnificent pioneering meant in America. I wanted, as the promoters said they did, to see the voyage made in a manner properly in keeping with the Pilgrim spirit, although to her crew this would be primarily a ship-delivery job, a piece of sailing—perhaps difficult, perhaps not, but at any rate once begun to be carried through, under God.

We had learned much about the spirit of the Pilgrims in my own Australia, too, and found great inspiration in it. In no sense did I see my crew or myself following in the footsteps of the Pilgrim Fathers, except that we were to have a tolerable copy of their ship insofar as that was possible. We were not Pilgrims. Above all to any sailor, the new *Mayflower* was a ship to sail, and a most intriguing one.

The keel had been laid in Messrs. Upham's shipyard at Brixham in July, 1955, and the shell of some half the hull was launched on September 22, 1956. Upham's yard had

been building wooden ships for 160 years, under five genera-
tions of the same family, and had not only the right tradition but also most of the right tools—the actual tools, not
copies of them—and these were used to a considerable
extent in the construction. The ship was designed by Mr.
William A. Baker, a professional naval architect employed
by a large shipbuilding corporation at Quincy, Massachusetts, which specializes in very big steel ships of modern
construction.

Mr. Baker had made a study of sixteenth- and seventeenth-century ships in general and the *Mayflower* in
particular, as a personal hobby, over a period of some years,
well aware that there exists no precise information about a
vessel which, after all, did not come much to historians'
attention until a century or more after she had been broken
up quietly in her home port, a worn-out, unhonored, and
unnoticed hulk. There were many ships called *Mayflower*
in her period, and the fact that one of them had once carried
an impecunious collection of strong-minded nonconformists
from England to somewhere in the new land across the
Atlantic excited her contemporaries not at all. At best, the
"replica" could be no more than a reconstruction of a typical
English merchant ship of some nine-score Elizabethan tons,
but Mr. Baker had been most thorough in arriving at his
conception of just what such a ship was like. He had followed, very largely, the formula laid down by his Elizabethan namesake, Matthew Baker, and had worked out
plans for a sturdy, chunky little ship, 183 tons by the rule of
1582, some 220 tons net by modern measurement and 365
tons displacement, about 90 feet long by 25 feet beam and
drawing, deep-loaded, approximately 12½ feet of water.

With 135 tons of inside ballast, the ship would have a G.M. of 2.5 feet and a freeboard of 6.8 feet to the weather deck, which was a lot of freeboard—considerably more, indeed, than we had in the 3,000-ton Cape Horners.

The problem of what the *Mayflower* may have looked like had been tackled by other scholars, notably by Dr. R. C. Anderson, president of the Society for Nautical Research and a trustee of the National Maritime Museum. Dr. Anderson had devoted some years to the subject and had produced a beautifully constructed model of a ship of the *Mayflower's* size and period. This model is in a large glass case in the Pilgrim Hall at Plymouth, Massachusetts, where I had studied it, and as it had made no compromises with historical accuracy in the matter of headroom or anything else, it had a few differences from Mr. Baker's seagoing vessel.

Just how Plimoth Plantation was going to explain that *both* ships were the *Mayflower* I could not see, but that was not my problem. The model, after all, stayed inside its glass case and had neither to be lived in nor sailed: but for my part, I would have suffered the lack of headroom for the sake of increased stability and better motion in the Baker ship. There was no headroom in the minute cabin I was to occupy, anyway. This was right at the top of the high after-castle, where all the motion would be felt. This cabin was left as it must have been in the original ship, to show visitors just how they should have found the 'tween-decks.

Mr. Baker, Mr. Upham, the experts of the Gourock Rope-work Company in Scotland who made the cordage (there were twelve tons of it), and everyone else concerned went to infinite pains to produce the best ship possible, and the most authentic. Mr. Baker, for example, drew the lines with the instruments of the period—a scale, a straightedge, and a pair of compasses. In the dry dock where one could get a good look at her, the underwater lines looked pretty good to me, and the manner in which the little shell had first slipped through the water when she went down the ways was a delight to see. Mr. Upham had selected her Devon oak timbers with the greatest of patience and care. To be authentic, the ship had to be built of most solid timbers, most of them hewn individually from whole trees, and it was necessary to select trees which conformed as near as possible to the timbers desired (in order to avoid cross grain, and so retain the full strength of the wood), then bring in the trunks and go to work on them in the yard. As Mr. Upham said, she was all shape, with hardly a straight plank in her. This meant a lot of work.

Built in this way, the ship grew slowly. Though the birds must have been singing in some of her timbers not long before they were built into the ship, apparently this bothered no one, except me, for it seemed that the old custom was to build the ship from growing oak and let her season herself on the ways. As for that, it looked as if this new ship would have time enough to season before she began her voyage. She was fastened in the old manner, with wooden trenails or treenails, long, narrow, double-ended spikes of the best dry old oak. Wood for these was found, after some searching, in the large casks of an ancient cider-making plant at Totnes, not far from Brixham, but the art of fastening a ship with treenails was almost dead and only a very few shipwrights could be found who still knew how to do it. This sort of work was a time-wasting and expensive way of doing things, but it was thorough. The ship *had* to be good.

Masts and yards were made from pine brought from Canada and, except for the course and lateen yards, I would have liked to see these stouter sticks. Their dimensions were calculated from tables in contemporary books, I was told, but I distrusted those books. I remembered the six-foot circumference of the Maldivian *Fath-ur-Rahman's* mainmast and the immense strength of her stoutly fished lateen yards, to say nothing of the heavy spars that Chinese sailors like to put in their seagoing junks. With cordage rigging, I considered that the most solid lower masts practicable were required, but I had no books to support my view. It was too late to bring forward new ideas, anyway.

As for the cordage, I had no doubts about that. Laid up especially by the Gourock Ropework Company at Port Glasgow, it was made from the best Italian hemp and was wholly faultless and magnificent. This company had two and a quarter centuries of ropemaking experience, with its own records dating back to 1740, and spared no pains to provide authentic, stout, and long-lived cordage, ranging from the great hempen cable for the awkward anchors to the light stuff for the ratlines (steps in the rigging). Some of this cordage, such as the tapered main tacks, was most difficult to manufacture, and the Gourock company had to revive techniques which had not been in use for 150 years. Another excellent Scots company, Francis Websters of Arbroath, provided the flax canvas for the sails. I knew their canvas well. We always used it exclusively in the *Parma,* and most of the sails in the Cape Horners was sewn of it. It was splendid stuff. Websters ought to know how to weave good canvas, for they had been doing the job since 1795. The very name of Webster means weaver, or maker of webs. Using this stout material from Scotland, Harold Bridge the Brixham sailmaker had sewn an excellent suit of sails, cut much better and setting much more efficiently than most Elizabethan sails could have done, to judge from the paintings one sees of them and the multiplicity of awkward running rigging which seamen in those days judged to be necessary to get an efficient set to their baggy sails—bowlines to haul the leaches taut, and all the rest of it. Indeed, the new *Mayflower's* sails required no bowlines at all, which was historically incorrect but very helpful to us mariners.

Copies of navigational instruments of the right authenticity were provided by the English firm of Kelvin Hughes, which also had over two centuries of experience. Nobody knew what navigational instruments were aboard the original *Mayflower*, of course, but knowledge of the more or less standard instruments then in use was sufficient to provide good replicas. A copy was made in pearwood of a beautiful ivory cross-staff (a forerunner of the sextant) preserved in the National Maritime Museum, and a traverse board—a simple device of holes and pegs to record a sailing ship's day's work, so foolproof that it could be used by the illiterate—and an Elizabethan dry-card compass, mounted in a wooden binnacle which was lit by a candle lanthorn, were provided, but I was glad to see that the firm had also furnished several of their modern instruments for daily use—a good standard compass and a first-class sextant. Another firm provided a chronometer of British make, and the mate had a second. Altogether, the ship would be well fitted out.

The Ministry of Transport, being the responsible authority for the control of ships in the United Kingdom, had taken a benevolent and helpful interest in the construction of the new *Mayflower* from the start. In the 1950's she was a highly unorthodox little ship, and it could scarcely be expected that she could be built to comply with the multiplicity of regulations which had grown up since her predecessor's day, for the safety of ships at sea. How could she be fitted with such things as davits, for example, and modern lifeboats, and remain authentic? Yet the Ministry could not allow her to go to sea without adequate lifesaving gear of some sort.

These problems were solved by methods of typical and efficient British compromise. It was settled by conferences at the Ministry—held long before I had anything to do with the vessel—that she would avoid the more awkward regulations by being classed as a "yacht" and, for the lifesaving, the Ministry would accept a sufficiency of inflatable rubber rafts (this sufficiency to be twice the number needed to accommodate all persons on board). A raised hatch coaming here, better waterways there, steering by wheel instead of the Elizabethan whipstaff (which, as rigged up through the too-high decks from the tiller below the great cabin, would not easily apply helm enough), stout hide coverings for the opening where the tiller was attached to the rudderhead outside the transom, a boat with a diesel engine (supplied very kindly by Messrs. Lister, and a first-rate job) stowed above the main hatch, stout hatches instead of the gratings which served to ventilate the stuffy 'tween-decks of the authentic *Mayflower*—all these things, and a two-way radio, were required. In return, the ship was exempted from Rule 20 of the Merchant Shipping (Life

Saving Appliances) Rules, 1952, and her classification as a yacht was approved.

A yacht? Such a classification was a helpful piece of fiction, a nice exercise of the privilege of experienced and practical compromise at which the British civil service so usefully excels. "Yacht," indeed! Those Ministry officials knew as well as I did that she was no yacht, and this was going to be no yachting voyage.

CHAPTER

10

HISTORICALLY CORRECT!

THE ship was afloat, rigged, and—in due course—properly
ballasted, but she was far from ready for sea. She had sailed
no trials, and was not ready for them. The business of securing 135 tons of old iron in the bottom of the hold and then
building a stout deck over it took several days, and there
were all sorts of finishing jobs to be done. There always are,
in a new ship. The date I had suggested as the best sailing
day was April 2, from Plymouth and not from Brixham, because that is a good time to look for easterlies. In the first
part of April the Channel easterlies often blow for two
weeks, to the considerable chagrin of the city dwellers but
offering good value to square-rigged ships seeking an offing
towards the west.

The easterlies blew very nicely, just as I had hoped they
might, setting in on April 2 and continuing steadily until

the 15th, but during the whole of this time the ship was compelled to remain at her buoy in Brixham harbor. All hope of taking her to Southampton and London had long since been abandoned, to the dismay of the school children of both cities and the considerable loss of revenue to the promoters. This could not be helped. Having, in their enthusiasm, gone to such lengths to prepare for their promised *Mayflower,* and brought the politicians and national leaders in, it was necessary for the various reception committees in New England to have some idea of when they might expect the vessel. For their part, the sooner the better. For mine, the matter (as in all sailing ships) was under God and, not being in His confidence nor indeed able to do much about guessing the probable rate of progress of the completely untried vessel, nor even certain that she could be trusted to arrive in one piece at all, I was reluctant to make any forecasts or to commit myself to anything. It would be sufficient to sail, and to try to arrive.

Nonetheless, some optimist had selected an arrival date, more or less arbitrarily. This was declared to be May 25. There were, I was told, a great many important persons who were planning to be on hand to welcome the ship, and these included the President of the United States and the British Ambassador at Washington, to say nothing of the Governors of Massachusetts and all the other New England states, and a tribe of Indians from Oklahoma. These had to have a date, for their busy lives were geared to such things. The date being set, it was necessary to do one's best to try to keep it. Had we been able to sail on April 2 and bounded away before those good easterlies we stood a fair chance, but by the middle of April it was manifestly impossible to bash across the North Atlantic in something like forty days.

By that time, another thirty or forty tons of exhibition goods, packed in chests, had been stowed and timbered off in the hold, and some five tons of stores and ten tons of fresh water were aboard (the water was in steel tanks and not in barrels), and the ship was drawing a lot of water. The way that big transom sat down in the sea indicated a lot of "drag," and I thought we would be lucky if we ever had eight knots out of her, loaded like that. The designer said she might do twelve but he must have meant when she was empty. I had earlier made a flying visit to Plymouth, to meet the reception committee and the other dignitaries there. I knew their problems and was determined to make the best passage I could. I pointed out that it was impossible to keep any promised arrival date and, if the ship reached America by May 25, I would be surprised. But I would do my best.

In the meantime day after day hurried by and the easterly blew, cold and strong. My crew was assembled and the sails were all bent but, beyond testing their set and the gear on them while the ship lay at the buoy, we could not even begin to learn anything about them.

Sir Alan Moore, Bart., an eminent scholar in the field of sixteenth- and seventeenth-century shipping, kindly came to help us and was of great assistance. But there were some awkwardnesses in that rig with which none of us could know how to cope, without real sailing trials. That lateen mizzen, for example: what did you do about that? How did you swing the long yard and have the sail flowing nicely to leeward at all times? I knew how the Arabs did it, of course, and the Indians and the Maldivians. But the *Mayflower,* like her model in the Pilgrim Hall, had *standing* rigging on the mizzen. The Asian sailors overcame the problem by letting all the rigging go every time they swung the lateen yard. That was no answer for us, obviously: what was? And that spritsail, stuck away out on the unsupported bowsprit: what did you do with that? How trim the thing for the ship to go to windward, when its tack came down in the empty air? How good was the bowsprit anyway, with no rigging to support it? It could have no standing rigging and carry the big spritsail. What about those hoisting course yards, with their jeers, and the catharpins and all the rest, and the strain that would come on the cordage standing rigging from what seemed to us the bad Elizabethan habit of leading the braces to the stays?

We could correct these things, of course, and that easily, from our knowledge of latter-day sailing ships. We could contrive some jibs to do the work of the spritsail, and a jib-headed trysail for the mizzen. We could give better leads to the braces, fix the course yards aloft, modify the rigging in all sorts of useful ways. But where would modifications of this sort end? Carried to their logical conclusion, it would be more practical to sail the ship across with a modern rig, as a three-masted schooner or maybe a barkentine. That granted, there would be little point in sailing her, anyway: she might as well have been given an auxiliary engine.

For this reason, we left things as they were. We must learn how to use them but, as long as she remained at that too familiar buoy, we did not know even whether she would steer. There had been no lack of "experts" to point out that she would not, for—they declared—the rudder was too small. Perhaps it was, but I doubted it. It *looked* very small for the work it had to do, and I was dubious about the windage of all that towering aftercastle and its effect on the balance of the ship. There was scarcely a fisherman in the port who expected the ship to sail successfully, though what most of them (apart from a few old-timers) knew of handling a ship under sail was very little. Several of my crew had served also in the lugubrious *Pequod*: if *she* could be induced to move under sail, then we knew that we could overcome whatever problems this new *Mayflower* might have ready to throw at us.

It was, however, essential to get on with the job, and it was most frustrating to be kept at the buoy. Until the builder was ready for acceptance trials, she could not be moved and I had no real control of her. All this time, the ship was beset by a horde of newspaper reporters, press photographers, and the like. The world demanded news of the *Mayflower* because she had captured the phenomenon of world-wide interest. Therefore the newspaper people had to be there, doing their job of serving the people with such news as there might be.

News is one thing and news stories may be quite another, and a ship lying day after day at a buoy offered little if anything of real news value. Therefore there had to be recourse to stories, and although on the whole press treatment of the venture continued to be kindly, all sorts of rumors flew about. One newspaperman from Fleet Street inquired was it true that Scotland Yard was conducting an investigation into the finances of the promoting company? There had been no word yet of the formation of the promised Trust, and that for the sadly sufficient reason that, lacking income from the further exhibition of the vessel, the promoters were still trying desperately to raise the finishing money to complete payment for her. They had raised a lot, but not enough. She had cost far more than the sum estimated, and there was little time left.

There was no truth, as far as I ever discovered, in the Scotland Yard financial "inquiry." What *was* true was that the ship, now rapidly approaching completion, stood at the buoy under legal notice of arrest unless the builder's claims were met, and that in full and immediately. This was not my worry, and I thanked the Lord for that, but it was my worry to get time for some real sailing trials. The builder's final bill was queried by the project, which pointed out that no records were produced to substantiate a considerable item for timber (of which the Lord knows the ship had used enough). Money to clear the account and get the ship to sea was put up by a London financier, Mr. Felix Fenston, who was president of the project but, apparently, not a director of it nor even a shareholder. His contribution, which was substantial, was simply a gesture of good will. Mr. Fenston had an international reputation as an enterprising sportsman in many fields, and although he had only one leg (the other having been lost in the war) he intended to ship as a greenhorn crew member for the voyage and that was all he hoped to get out of the *Mayflower*.

Putting up the money apparently was not enough of itself to clear the ship. The proposal was that the project would pay the builder's firm a certain amount in cash forthwith and put up the balance in a guaranteed check against arbitration and an agreed settlement, in the early future. On this basis, which seemed very reasonable, the ship could sail. But the problem as I heard it was to agree on the method of arbitration. I was summoned to a meeting of the directors of the shipyard, for Mr. Upham had a partner, and solemnly issued with notice of their intention to serve a writ to hold the vessel. I was informed that, pending satisfaction of their claims, she must in no circumstances be taken from the buoy, not even for trials.

As these should legally have been the builder's trials anyway, he could scarcely have a case for final payment until it was proved that the ship *could* sail. I had no connection with the promoting project nor any facet of the promotion, and I did not follow what such threatened legal formalities meant to me personally, nor to what extent any writ, libel, or legal service whatever, served on myself, could have any effect or status in law. I was not an officer, nor in any sense, a salaried employee of the project, or of the Trust, or whatever body was then or might ever be concerned with the ownership of the vessel. Nor was I legally the master until the ship was handed over, and therefore writs or notice of writs served on me could scarcely have much real legality. That was hardly the point just then, which was to find out how to sail the ship. There was no one else in Brixham to serve such things on, I suppose, for there were only the two officers of the Project Mayflower, and, apparently, a sort of secretary-accountant who, I thought, was acting in an honorary capacity. These were all in London. It must be remembered, too, that throughout all this time these gentlemen had other business to attend to. They were not wealthy, and they had to make a living.

The real problem was that until the builder agreed to hand over the completed ship, she could not be given her certificate of British registry. This document was vital. At any rate, it was obvious that the ship would have to stay where she was for the time being, and how long the fact that she was under virtual arrest might be kept from the news-hungry horde from Fleet Street, Times Square, West 43rd Street, and points west, I did not know. Not for long, anyway!

Here was a story for them, but they did not get it. Publicity of that sort, when the money to pay all known claims was already put up, would serve the good-will gesture no useful purpose at all. The press photographers were the most anxious of the newspapermen, but they wanted pictures of the ship under sail and not a story. These were so numerous, by that time, that they had formed themselves into an orderly and democratic organization, with a president and secretary who kept in close touch with the situation. When could they have sailing pictures? The refrain dinned in my ears all day long and half the night.

By the fifteenth of April, when the shipwrights were done with their work and put to scraping the decks, it was beginning to be obvious that something must be wrong. There were some minor difficulties about formalities, we said. Large numbers of kind persons arrived daily with gifts for the ship—Bibles for the crew (three apiece); some silver for the ship from the English Elks, and another piece from one of the chapters of the Daughters of the American Revolution; a handsome bell rope from the Torquay Naval Association; an enormous book, provided by the Brixham Corporation, full of names of citizens and school children who wished us well; a handsome silver drinking cup from a well-wisher in Edinburgh; a complete library from Dr. Ronald Hope and the excellent Seafarers' Education Service (this was a most valued gift) in London; a bronze of the

Red Indian Chief Massasoit who had befriended the Pilgrims in 1620, and a small piece of the famous Plymouth Rock (where the Pilgrims landed) mounted on silver which had been suitably inscribed. I received all these gifts, on the ship's behalf, with real pleasure; but my crew were all there and the ship was rubbing at the buoy, itching to be gone.

This threat of a writ, though somewhat cavalier, was perhaps understandable and I suppose a proper enough procedure on the part of the builders, for why should they accept any imagined risk that the ship they had built might sail away, leaving some debts behind her, to another flag? But it was much too historically correct for my liking. The original *Mayflower*, I remembered, had been held in Southampton for the nonpayment, or alleged nonpayment, of some item of the Pilgrims' indebtedness to her owners. They had disputed some of the claims, too, but they had to meet them. This they managed by selling a deal of their butter to raise the necessary funds. We were prevented from following this precedent, I discovered, for the butter had not been paid for either. The supplying ship chandler—a *Mayflower* supporter named Burnyeat who was always most helpful—had agreed with the promoters to wait for settlement of his account until later, and had already foregone some of it, by his own offer.

The aggravating thing was that the money to clear the ship was available. A quarrel among the legal gentlemen in London on that arbitration issue was holding us up. I began to get cables from the reception committee in Massachusetts asking when I would sail. Sail? What about trials? The Ministry had asked that these be thorough and include bad-weather tests. Without any request from the Ministry, this was obviously good seamanship. The photographers, still amazingly patient about the whole thing (though it was costing their offices a great deal of money to keep them waiting at Brixham), began to be really worried. I received a cablegram from some merchandising corporation in America asking when they were to expect their "treasure chests" of exhibition goods. Treasure chests? How a ship classed as a yacht could be carrying anything of the kind I didn't understand anyway, and it was only by good tolerance and cooperation on the part of the authorities on both sides of the Atlantic that our "yacht" was allowed to be a cargo vessel. In plain English, that was what she was.

A few more days dragged by. The easterly wind blew itself out, to my disgust. It was that nonsensical "arrival" date of May 25 which caused the real worry. Unrealistic as that might be, it was necessary to get the ship on her way, for a good many friendly transatlantic reputations were at stake at least in the matter of her arrival within a reasonable time.

The Lord Mayor of Plymouth, Devon, and the Mayor of Dartmouth were on the telephone to know when the ship might be expected at their ports? For they were arranging receptions, and so forth, and they must have firm dates. And, writ or no writ, I had to manage at least some semblance of sailing trials. At last, on April 16, by signing an undertaking to bring back the ship to her moorings in Brixham harbor immediately the trial was over, I obtained permission to make at least a bit of a show in Tor Bay. I got the ship under way, Ernie Lister giving her a bit of a pluck beyond the breakwater, and was able to handle her under sail for a few hours.

As for a real sailing trial, this was a press photographers' exercise. The forty photographers had hired a fast launch, which they had had standing by for some days. From this they had a field day. The local yacht club gave us a salute of guns as we passed out on trials, but we were back in again a couple of hours later, with no gunnery at all.

I had been able to find out a lot, even in that brief run. The ship steered and handled quite well; the sails set and drew beautifully; we could manhandle the lateen yard with a minimum of trouble, and the spritsail, far from being a problem, looked like developing into the best little maneuvering sail any of us had ever been along with, as soon as we could master the practical problem of setting and handling it properly with its rather intricate and cumbersome gear. It was further demonstrated that the ship had an excellent crew, but I was aware of that. It was not going to take them long to settle down. I had a big crew, because of that complicated rigging, but it looked as if I was going to need all of them. The promoters had given me carte blanche on crew matters, of course. In practical matters of this sort they were wholly cooperative, and I sympathized with them in their troubles. They had to keep public interest at the highest possible pitch to promote the venture at all. I was told that they were expert at this business, and indeed they seemed to be.

Our return to the Brixham buoy caused some mystification not only to the locals (most of whom never had expected to see the ship under sail at all), and I was fully extended, in a diplomatic way, keeping the news of the ship's threatened arrest from the inquisitive pressmen. The promoters were still busy with their own problems, in London, and this was left to me. This I did in good faith, for it would never have done to allow an erroneous impression about this good-will gift to cross the Atlantic. The whole situation was extremely anomalous. The ship was already cleared outwards, with customs clearance for Plymouth, Massachusetts, by way of Dartmouth and Plymouth, Devon, but I was without her Certificate of Registration, which is a ship's passport without which she cannot sail. As far as I know, there never was any formal acceptance from the builders. I hoisted the Red Ensign when I went out on trials, and that was that. Yacht or not, she was a plain Red Ensign ship, in no sense officially sponsored nor entitled to any sort of special consideration. There could be no official sponsorship for a private venture.

For yet another night, and I had no way of telling for how many nights afterwards, she must stay at the buoy. There were some difficulties about the formalities, I explained again, and indeed there were. The newsmen wrote pleasant stories about the sailing trials, which in truth had been both brief and far from thrilling and, for the moment, they were satisfied. But I breathed a great sigh of relief, and so did Mr. Upham and everybody else concerned, when towards midmorning of the following day it was announced that the formalities were settled. All was well at last, and I could go.

I went, forthwith, standing not on the order of my going. The faithful Ernie Lister towed us to sea and, for that night, I went only round the corner of Berry Head and into Dartmouth. It was enough. We were off. Once round Tor Bay and then off for America! It was no way to go to sea on a Western Ocean's westward crossing, in a ship of a type so thoroughly unusual. It was plain bad seamanship, but it was forced on me by that overoptimistic arrangement for the arrival date.

There was a freshening wind from west-southwest in the Channel, with the promise of worsening visibility and a lot more wind to come. There were even more depressions on the weather plot of the North Atlantic than usual, and there was more awkward ice on the chart than there had been since plotting icebergs and drift ice had been begun, after the loss of the unfortunate *Titanic*. It was my intention to try to go the direct route, the way that Captain Jones must have gone with the original ship, and I had charts for no other. I did not expect the ship to sail so fast that she might knock an iceberg over, but a succession of westerly gales— why, that could be another matter.

First we had to make brief courtesy calls both at Dartmouth and Plymouth, for Captain Jones had been at both places. Some of the vessel's activities of late had been much too historically correct altogether, but here was an occasion where an historical thread or two might be picked up with harm to no one. We were at Dartmouth for twenty-four hours, and the ship and all hands were very pleasantly received there. On Good Friday I went on towards Plymouth, towing behind the enormous tug *Englishman,* of Hull, which had once towed us in the *Parma.* The wind had blown out, leaving a calm with a lumpy sea, and I could not continue with further sailing trials. This was a pity: it looked as if the voyage itself would have to be our trial.

That it was pretty sure to be, prehaps in more ways than one.

CHAPTER

11

THE CREW

BUILDER Stuart Upham had every interest in getting the little ship on her way. Not only was she a credit to his yard and to himself, but he had volunteered to serve in her crew. So had Edgar Mugridge, of Sweet Briar Cottage in Knicknack Lane, Brixham, one of the Devon shipwrights who had worked steadily on the ship since the keel was laid. Edgar Mugridge was signed as carpenter and Mr. Upham in the traditional role of caulker. I was delighted to see these good Devon men come forward in this way. It showed unbounded confidence not only in their work, but in the whole venture. There had probably been some Devon men in the original ship (not that anyone could check that, for there was no crew list in existence from her), and it was proper that some of their descendants should be in the new one.

There were also two direct descendants of Pilgrims who

had made the original passage, who had likewise volunteered, and that gladly. These were young John Winslow, descendant of Governor Winslow and now a sub-lieutenant in the Air Arm of the Royal Navy, to whom My Lords had given a few months' leave to serve in the vessel; and Chief Petty Officer Charles Church, R.C.N., to whom the Canadian Navy had given as much leave as he required and his passage across the Atlantic to join us. Young Winslow was a bright and cheerful lad who obviously was an asset to the vessel. He could fly jet aircraft very skillfully, and that from the pitching decks of aircraft carriers. A job on the jumping tops'l yards of the new *Mayflower* he could take in his stride. C.P.O. Church was a shipwright, a skilful helmsman in racing yachts, and a first-rate shipmate from the start. He had been selected especially from many applicants from the R.C.N.'s sailing association, and we were very glad to have him.

Stuart Upham, Edgar Mugridge, John Winslow, and Charles Church were dedicated men and would obviously be most useful crew members, but they were not deep-water square-rigged sailing-ship sailors. Like most of their generation, they had had no chance to serve in any such ships. A sufficient nucleus of the *Mayflower's* crew must know their business from long prior experience, to lead the others. The thread of tradition and personal skill in such matters must be continuous and, by 1957, it had worn extremely thin not only in Great Britain. Above all, the ship's officers must be sailing-ship men with watchkeeping experience, and no doubt about it. The officers must know how to handle the sails and the ship too, in emergency. The master must be expert at handling the ship and have the confidence both of his officers and crew. As for my part, I would take a chance on that: but a sailing ship—any sailing ship—can ask a dreadful lot of her crew, and go on demanding it to the limits of their endurance. None of us was playing with this ship. We had a fair idea of what we were trying. Nor did we care for those (to our eyes) spindly topmasts and the cordage rigging, no matter how good we knew it to be. We were used to steel masts and iron-wire rigging which stayed rigidly where it was at sea. To work aloft in a jumping, leaping little thing like this new *Mayflower*, almost rolling her sticks out in the Atlantic swell, with hempen footropes (according to some academics there should have been no footropes at all; such academics are welcome to sail a ship rigged to their specifications), could be much more dangerous than the normal activities aloft even in an undermanned Cape Horner. As for that class of ship, we were used enough to them.

I found the crew myself (apart from a few inexperienced but very useful chaps suggested by the "ideas" man of the project; he could be a brilliant ideas man, and these were excellent suggestions) and I found them because I knew where to look for them. They had to be Britishers, if possible, for this was a British venture, but it was years since there had been a British sailing ship, and it was of no use to dig out a group of old-timers who once had known their stuff and now were past it. They had to be fit, agile, competent, and determined seamen. I knew that I could not hope to find more than half a dozen who were of the real stuff—the mates, and three others. This would be enough; the rest could be any good youngsters. We had never hesitated to sail the grain ships in that way, with a nucleus of six or eight experienced

seamen and the rest boys. The average age of our usual
Parma crews was seventeen. Oddly enough, it was only the
well-manned ships with over-large crews which had gone
missing on the Cape Horn run, in our time—ships like the
German *Admiral Karpfanger* and the Danish *København*.
I was not afraid of a well-led crew of young men and boys,
with the more boys the better.

Ever since the *Parma* and the *Joseph Conrad* days, I had
kept a file on sailing-ship seamen, and one of the first things
I did was to look this out. I had had trouble to man the
Conrad even in 1934, but the boys who made her circumnavigation became good sailing-ship men. I knew where
they were (those who survived the war), but the trouble
was to have them released from their present employments.
One was master of the ice ship *Magga Dan*, where his special skills were also unique, for he had become one of the
most experienced Arctic and Antarctic ice pilots in the
world. Another was a captain with an international airline,
who had long become more accustomed to flying four-
engined aircraft across the North Atlantic than sailing the
seas in ships, though he had kept his hand in with a seagoing yacht. Neither of these was British and neither was
available, anyway. A third, an excellent English able seaman, was barred because he had once been a member of a
Communist trade union (in order to get a ship), and this
made it impossible for him to be granted a visa to land in
the United States, as he would have to do if he came with us
in the *Mayflower*. This was absurd, but there it was. Though
in a sense the Pilgrims must have been regarded as the
"Reds" of their day—at any rate in England, which had
thrown them out and sent them penniless to Holland—no

faintest smear of pink could be accepted on the crew list of the new vessel. This was American law.

There was a good Britisher who had helped me in the *Conrad* days and had been a shipmate in a hungry big Limejuice four-poster not long after the First World War. This was Godfrey Wicksteed, an extra master, and an experienced watchkeeper in square-rigged ships. I looked him up and found that, fed up long since with the sea of powered vessels, he had turned to schoolmastering and was then teaching school somewhere in Cambridgeshire. I needed him as mate. Like most of us, however, he was no longer the carefree, world-wandering sailor of his youth. He had long had a wife and family. He was devoted to his shore career, in which he then had twenty years experience. More than that, he owed his home, his pension rights, and his hope of anything like a settled future to it. He was fifty-seven years old. If he sought leave from his schoolmastering, he must give up his home. What then? Where would his wife and children go? If he sought leave, would it be granted? Experienced schoolmasters were in short supply, not only in Cambridgeshire. Well, I put the proposition to my old shipmate, and he jumped at it. His education authority granted leave, all hands moved out of the schoolhouse, and Godfrey Wicksteed was at Brixham by the very next train thereafter. It was a considerable sacrifice, for he would get nothing from the *Mayflower* beyond his bare mate's pay. He, too, was a dedicated man, and I was most thankful to have him.

The second mate, Mr. Adrian Small, was one of those adventurous seafarers who, determined to serve properly in sail, had spent years in the big Finnish four-masters belong-

ing to the late Captain Gustaf Erikson. Mr. Small had been
with me as second mate of the *Pequod,* and I knew him as a
competent and determined seaman. The boatswain of the
Pequod, Mr. Isaac Marsh from Barry Dock, signed as boat-
wain—bos'n, we call it—of the new *Mayflower.* For third
mate I had a gem of a sailor, very well known to me. This
was Danish Captain Jan Junker, Eskimo-speaking ice pilot
from the Greenland trade. I hoped, of course, that we would
not need the services of an ice pilot, nor did I plan to go so
far north that we might require an Eskimo-speaking inter-
preter. But Captain Jan had been a sailor with me in the
Joseph Conrad and, with years of such sailing behind him,
had gone on to become a master in sail. He had been a
watchkeeping officer in the *Georg Stage* and the *Danmark,*
both full-rigged ships. I knew him well as a steadfast and
supremely competent sailing-ship seaman both before the
mast and abaft it, and I regarded his presence aboard as a
major asset to the vessel. Captain Jan got leave from the
Royal Greenland Company to come with us, although they
could ill spare an ice pilot, and I don't know what happened
to the Eskimo crew of the stout ship *Kaskelot* without him.

Another grand seaman, an old Cardiff Cape Horner
named Ted Howard, who was rigger as well as good bos'n,
should have been aboard, but he died while the ship was
building, and we regretted that the Lord had not spared
him for at least another twelvemonth. I signed Joe Lacey
and Joe Powell as able seamen, both from the *Pequod,* and
Harry Sowerby, who had experience in the *Conrad* and the
big *Moshulu.* All these were men with some sailing-ship
experience, though Harry Sowerby was a man of independent means who *chose* that sort of adventurous life and not a

professional seaman, and Joe Powell was by calling a film "stunt man." Joe had been in other ships beside the *Pequod,* and I knew him as a quiet shipmate and an excellent chap.

It had been ruled (though loosely) that American nationals could have no place in the *Mayflower's* crew on grounds of their obvious historical inaccuracy, but some of my best boys in the *Conrad* had been young Yankees. One of these turned up in Devon on a hired bicycle which he had ridden down from London, with his sea bag on the back, after coming over at his own expense from some lovely port in Maine. He had turned to with a will aboard, quite voluntarily and unpaid, for he knew the ruling. He proved to get on so well with the others that they came aft and asked if it could possibly be arranged to give him a berth for the voyage. I knew Andy Lindsay as a first-rate seaman, quietly competent and completely reliable. All right, I said, he can be a pierhead jump (a man who ships at the last moment, and in the old days often literally jumped down into the waist of outward-bound Cape Horners as they passed the pierhead), and his wages will be one shilling monthly.

Several others signed for this unprincely sum which, like pierhead jumping and the like, was an old custom of sailing-ship days, meant to cover supernumeraries and passage-workers. The wage of a shilling a month though nominal was legally binding, when signed for on the ship's articles. Another good seaman and fine shipmate, John Goddard, had signed for the same thing, though "Jumbo" Goddard was no pierhead jump. Jumbo had served in the tough *Herzogin Cecilie* in the grain trade round Cape Horn, and knew what he was doing. More than that, he had served a full apprenticeship with Rolls Royce, in the north of Eng-

land, and was a competent engineer. As we were required
to have two-way radio, the ship also must have some sort
of small generator to provide power for the thing, and
Messrs. Lister had furnished one of their good diesels for
this purpose. Since we had it, it must be looked after, and
Jumbo's shilling a month covered also his extensive duties
in this department. Immediately before joining, Jumbo had
been prospecting for uranium ore in Central Australia. He
flew to England at his own expense and entirely of his own
volition. This was the sort of real fellow that the venture
attracted.

These, then, were my sailing-ship men—three of the
mates, the bos'n, and five seamen. Some of these could
scarcely rate as real professional sailors, for they had gone
in the grain ships from a spirit of adventure which led them
later into other fields. But I had a grand nucleus. For the
others, besides Church and Winslow, I had a couple of
young fellows from the Oxford University Yacht Club, Mike
Ford from University College and David Thorpe from
Corpus Christi, both yachtsmen of international status and
the right spirit; Jack Scarr, a teacher by profession, from St.
Edward's School in Oxford; Peter Padfield, an officer from
the P. and O. Company(which had given him leave); and
two young officers from Mr. Holt's well-run Blue Funnel
Line of cargo liners, Messrs. Fred Edwards and David
Cauvin. Cauvin was a South African who, always interested
in sail, had served aboard another "replica" in his own Table
Bay, a reconstruction at half-size of the famous *Dromedary*,
which had been sailed for pageantry.

The *Mayflower* could have been manned with these young
Merchant Navy officers, a good many of whom—like Ed-

wards and Cauvin—had experience enough to whet their
appetites at the Outward Bound Sea School at Aberdovey,
in Wales. Jack Scarr, too, had been a seaman, specializing
in the delivery of awkward small vessels round the coasts of
Britain during the war. His Head, Warden Fisher of St.
Edward's, granted him a term's leave to help sail the *Mayflower*, but—naturally enough—Jack had to provide a substitute master to carry on his schoolwork. I don't know
whether it was the excellence of the work he had been
doing or whether he could only find qualified masters on a
part-time basis, but it took *two* competent men to carry on
at St. Edward's while Jack was with us. Since his absence
was the cause of their employment, naturally he had to meet
their salaries, too, which meant that Jack sacrificed a good
deal for the pleasure of sailing with us. This bothered him
not at all. Indeed, he was delighted. Such was the type of
man I had to back up my Cape Horning nucleus.

Beric Watson, whose family had a printing business in
Leeds and whose previous sailing experience had been a
delivery passage with an ancient yacht called the *Catalina*
from Liverpool round to the English Channel with the mate
(the mate reported that young Beric had done well throughout a particularly unpleasant run); Andrew Anderson-Bell,
our Scot (who had come, also at his own expense and entirely of his own volition, from his appointment as a town-
planner in Addis Ababa); our surgeon-seaman John Stevens,
from South Africa; second cook Dick Brennan, from his
club in Fleet Street; Jim Horrocks, a volunteer radio operator from the Marconi Company; and a couple of boys
selected one by the British and the other by the American
boys' clubs, just about completed the crew.

Dr. Stevens, like Anderson-Bell, had originally intended to follow the sea professionally, and, as a young R.N.R. lieutenant, had been executive officer of one of H.M. submarines during the war. Afterwards taking up medicine, he had done very well, but he left his family and his prospects (temporarily, at least) and everything else for the sake of helping on the voyage. For his skill as surgeon he received an additional £5 a month over the union rate for an able seaman, which was little more than the twopence a month apiece the first *Mayflower's* mariners were required to subscribe for their "chirurgeon and apothecary," who also cut their hair.

One crew member I have left to last. This was the cook-steward. It was difficult to get a competent cook-steward for a ship like the *Mayflower*, where there was no refrigeration and the provisions were perforce those of the old sailing-ship days. The cook-steward was responsible for storing the ship in his department, for baking fresh bread, for keeping thirty-three able-bodied men adequately nourished on three square meals a day, all prepared and dished up in the one minute galley underneath the quarter-deck. The historically correct brick oven forward had been officially ruled out as too great a fire risk, but there were times when we would have preferred it to the more modern contraption which we had. As cook of the *Mayflower* I needed an old-timer who knew how to turn out real sea pie, and make something of pease pudding with salt horse and no fresh vegetables. He was just about the last man I found, though there was no lack of volunteers willing, they wrote, to be "cook or anything." "Cooks or anything" are of no use aboard a seagoing vessel, for a sea cook is something and

Somebody. He is a petty officer of importance and, indeed, as a sailing ship's voyage progresses, he may well become the very keystone of her hope of harmony. So I chose my cook-steward with the greatest of care, and the assistance of the National Seamen's Union. I was delighted when they found Mr. Walter Godfrey for me, at the G.S.N.—the General Steam Navigation Company, in London. Mr. Godfrey was elderly, wiry, resolute, and competent, with a lifetime of experience at sea dating well back to the days before refrigeration. He was nearly sixty—perhaps more—but I did not worry over that. The G.S.N. granted him the necessary leave, and I signed him on with alacrity, and sent him along to the American Embassy to be duly fingerprinted and visaed.

All in all, whatever else might have worried me, I had no qualms about the crew.

There were no passengers as such. A temporary cargo carrier the "yacht" *Mayflower II* might be, but a passenger vessel she certainly was not. Not that there was any scarcity of offers to buy passage in her—far from it. There were thousands. The promoters had wisely laid down the ruling that no one could pay for a passage in the *Mayflower* except with services which were required aboard. Representatives of an American magazine which had bought the magazine-story rights and of a film concern which had acquired the film rights (whatever these might amount to) joined the ship, but they were not passengers. It was planned that Felix Fenston should be there, not as a passenger either, and at least one of the promoters always intended to come along. Everyone who came was signed on the ship's articles in some capacity or other, which meant, among other things, that whoever they were, they were subject to the authority of the master.

There were no pilgrims, no family groups, and no women. There was no official ruling against these, and any latter-day Pilgrim Father who chanced also to be a Cape Horn seaman would have been welcome. As for family groups and women, they would have been in the way. The original ship had had them aboard by the hundred. We knew that well enough, but the first *Mayflower* sailed entirely under God, and we were also under the temporal jurisdiction of the Ministry of Transport and Civil Aviation. The officials of the Ministry had at no time said that the ship must not carry passengers, for as a yacht she could at least have had some owner's guests. What the Ministry had laid down was that there must be 200 per cent lifesaving gear aboard, and that is expensive and bulky stuff aboard a small vessel.

After all, the new *Mayflower* was small—incredibly so, at first sight. Even with thirty-three persons as her complement, she seemed crowded. The washing and toilet arrangements aboard were so primitive as to be nonexistent by modern standards. She would be extremely uncomfortable. The passage from Brixham had shown how wet the 'tween-decks could be, for they had to be bailed out. Her "heads" were just that—a grating in the beak, below the bowsprit. This was a cold and windy spot where the spray, and perhaps the sea as well, could be guaranteed to concentrate in a blow, or whenever the ship was on the wind in fresh conditions. There was no fresh water to spare for washing. If they were to keep clean and to attend to their personal needs with any slight degree of comfort, it was plain common sense to restrict the ship's company to men.

There was a bit of a howl at this from both sides of the Atlantic, but on this point I was adamant.

I was also determined that there would be no young women stowaways, or men. In this matter, the ship could be vulnerable. Not even the most ardent pursuer of *Mayflower* publicity cared for the idea of news stories about successful stowaways in the vessel, and it behoved us all to be careful indeed. There was, for instance, room in any of those chests down below for quite a large female, or male: many of them were under bond and could not be examined until we were at sea and, even then, the manner of their stowage in the small hold would make them extremely difficult to get at. I hoped they would be difficult for stowaways too. We wanted no stunts aboard the *Mayflower*.

I set a double gangway watch, had my boys make a daily search of every smallest nook and cranny while the ship was in coastal waters, and hoped for the best in this, as in other matters.

CHAPTER

12

WILL SHE MAKE IT?

WHILE the ship was towing through a race off Salcombe at
nine knots behind the strong tug *Englishman,* the working
of the foremast and the bowsprit worried me a lot. The
cordage shrouds on the foremast, which had little spread
because the mast was stepped so far forward—standing almost in the bows, with the step actually in the curve of the
cutwater—went slap, slap, with a great wrenching at the
lanyards and the chain-plates and the channels themselves,
as the vessel was hauled along willy-nilly against the short
and jumpy sea. She jumped, too, and that more than enough,
and I thought the fore-topmast might jump out of her.
However, everything stood, and the little ship presented a
brave sight to the vast crowds on Plymouth Hoe as she
came towing in. The Hoe was black with people. I wished
that I could sail in, and not to provide a spectacle, but it

was flat calm then. The Queen's Harbormaster allotted us a destroyer buoy off Drake's Island and the Lord Mayor came aboard, with the Mayor of Plymouth, Massachusetts, and many other dignitaries. The Lord Mayor had been in the Navy himself, knew a thing or two about ships, and had long been waiting to welcome this one.

Officially, lesser visitors were forbidden, for we had the bonded chests to load, water, bread, and stores to top up, the rigging to set up again, and all sorts of other things to do. But the ship was immediately crowded with all sorts of persons all of whom when asked appeared to have real reason for being there, and it was most difficult to get on with our essential work. There were invitations of all sorts to which I could unfortunately give no heed, being busier than enough, and with no secretary. The captain of the Navy's emergency destroyer came aboard to discuss methods of securing a towline to the vessel if he were suddenly called upon to dash out with his destroyer and bring us in from a Channel gale in the near future, which he appeared to expect. Arrangements for towing had been foreseen, though not the drill for summoning destroyers in a Channel gale, or any other foreseeable conditions. It was my intention *not* to do any such thing, and every possible plan had been most carefully made against any such contingency. However, the destroyer man's foresight was appreciated and I was pleased to know the Navy was so interested in us, but when shortly afterwards there came three handle-barred officers from the Royal Air Force Air-Sea Rescue Service, licking their chops at what they obviously regarded as the prospect of an imminent and most interesting job, I thought the rescue business was being taken a little too far and all this pessimism was uncalled for.

An emissary from the Mayor of Provincetown, Massachusetts, came out to put in a plea for a call at his good harbor, if only for twenty minutes. It was to Provincetown, he pointed out, that the original *Mayflower* first went. Just how historically correct was this venture? he went on to ask, surveying the decks crowded with everything but Pilgrims and a large chest labeled Plymouth Gin which was just then being swung over the rail, nearly knocking him down. I answered that in these days all ships must go to the ports of entry to which they were cleared officially: that was international law and the *Mayflower* must abide by it. I saw a glint come into his eye and suspected that, while we were on passage, the fair port of Provincetown would be declared a port of entry, too. In this matter of the Pilgrim heritage, apparently, there was some rivalry between the citizens of Provincetown and the larger port across Cape Cod Bay. This was happily no affair of mine, but no one wanted any quarrels on the matter.

My attention was distracted by a pleasant Swiss gentleman with a case of gold wrist watches, which he wished to see nailed by their wristbands at difficult spots in the rigging of the vessel, and I set the bos'n to this task forthwith, to the bos'n's great astonishment. A moment or so later, there was another smiling Swiss gentleman with another wooden box of beautiful watches which he wanted secured to vantage points round the waterline and beneath it, if possible, and the bos'n, with even greater astonishment, was put to work organizing that task too. For a moment, I wondered whether the idea was to have the crew racing aloft or jumping overboard whenever they wanted to know the time, but on reflection it seemed that this must be some variation of the treasure-chest idea. Each watch carried a legend, carved into its reverse side, that it was shockproof, waterproof, anti-magnetic, and so on, and I suppose the idea of carrying them across the North Atlantic secured about the vessel was to bring these features to the public notice in a way that would be understood and—it was hoped—sufficiently publicized, into the bargain. If this sort of thing helped to clear the little ship's load of debt, it had to be accepted, and the Swiss gentlemen were very nice fellows.

While their handsome watches were being so wantonly fastened here and there, a man arrived from the post office with 30,000 letters all addressed and stamped, but not a single one postmarked in any manner. It was an awfully large parcel of mail: maybe there were 50,000 letters. The official brought half a dozen canceling bangers—those hand-held stamping things that clerks bang so viciously behind postal counters at everything you give them,—with which instruments, apparently, the crew were expected to cancel these thousands of envelopes on the way across. That is, if the sea did not get at them first, for where was there a dry place aboard to stow all this stuff which could be guaranteed to stay dry?

These envelopes, which contained nothing but a printed copy of the *Mayflower* compact, were, apparently, what is known as "first voyage covers," much sought after in the philatelic world. Some merchant had obviously bought the rights in this matter—another way of helping to finance the vessel. It seemed that no possible avenue had been overlooked, for very shortly there were six more men bringing cartons of what looked like 100,000 more envelopes, apparently not even stamped.

These were put in the hold to take their chance, for it was time to hurry ashore for a rehearsal of the civic ceremony at the Barbican Steps on the morrow. The pilgrims had left England finally from those same steps, in 1620, and we must be seen to leave from there too, but I was so busy with all these activities that there was no time to get on with the ship's real business. Affairs of visaed crew lists, and manifests, the necessary bill of health, and so on, had to wait. There was also a man who appeared to be an official of some sort, wanting to know where was our escort.

Escort? I asked, taken aback at that one, for we wanted no such fuss.

Yes, he said, the tug that is to accompany you.

My dear fellow, I said, there is no tug and there will be no tug nor any other kind of "escort." We sail alone, and that is final.

A Ministry of Transport official, making an exhaustive last-minute check that all those modifications required for the ship's seaworthiness had in fact been properly carried out, nodded his head to that, and I found that the tug seeker was a newspaperman. Apparently, in the early days of the venture, there had been some talk of an escort, but that was before any sailor had anything to say in the matter.

One of our inflatable life rafts chose that moment to inflate itself, with a hiss of gas and an alarming swelling under its cover. These were sensitive things which once inflated had to be returned to their makers for a new gas cylinder and fresh stowage. Perforce now the bloated thing had to be replaced, but it was the Easter holiday, and there was not another such life raft in the port or anywhere within a hundred miles of it. In this emergency, the aircraft carrier H.M.C.S. *Magnificent* came to our aid. She was decommissioning at Devonport close by and offered all assistance but, unfortunately, she had no inflatable rubber life rafts of the approved style either. After telephoning for half the night, eventually one was located in a shipyard at Appledore, and a motor lorry set out with it towards Plymouth. Whatever else we lacked, the lifesaving equipment must be aboard, although in fact we should have had sufficient life rafts even if another blew up.

I barely had time to attend at the ancient Customs House to clear the ship on the following morning before having to hurry back to the ship to land formally at the Barbican Steps, and depart from them again in a gig rowed by four of the mariners attired in their Elizabethan seamen's clothes, in the meantime having given a brief speech and listened to several long ones. There were 10,000 people there, together with more cameramen, newsmen, and TV recorders than we had seen before, even when we left the dry dock, though it was a rainy, blustery morning. It was a pleasant ceremony, and very good of the Lord Mayor to arrange it. When we rowed away in the gig, the Lord Mayor aboard with us still in his stately chain of office and full robes, we rowed only as far as the first corner of the dock wall. Here we transferred smartly to a motor launch which had been waiting, hurried aboard, and got the ship ready for immediate departure to sea. The new life raft had arrived, and I could go.

But in the meantime Mr. Fenston had perforce decided that, much as he wished to make the passage to which he had been looking forward for years, the tangled skein of the ship's financial situation (in which he had a considerable stake) was such that he would have to remain in England to look after things. Mr. Fenston was to be one of the trustees of the *Mayflower* Foundation, the public trust. If he came with us, he would certainly be cut off from the management of any affairs, and no one could say for how long.

In his place, the ship accepted a special photographer from the project, one Leon Israel, whose name had then to be attached to the crew list. Photographer Israel was an American and so, fortunately, there was no need for him to waste time being fingerprinted, visaed, and so forth. He came aboard with a cheerful smile and a great interest in the vessel for which, indeed, he began at once to work so hard and so constantly and continued to do so throughout the voyage that I wondered how he found time to take his photographs. But he did that too, and very well.

Now I could sail. The wind had dropped and I had to get a tow out of the port, beyond the breakwater. Out there the wind was from the southwest, very light, and the strong tide was against us. No matter, we were under sail and free of the land, and the next stop—we hoped—would be America.

In the meantime, as a result of a last and most comprehensive search, a stowaway was discovered. He was found by the mate, hiding in the 'tween-decks where he must have climbed almost at the last moment, for the place had been thoroughly searched several times earlier. There was some suspicion that he had been "planted" there by a certain London newspaper, not noted for its scruples, and when the fellow was bundled over the side there was a press boat there, which seemed to expect him. Perhaps not: perhaps, by that time, the pressmen, who are blamed for much, were merely prepared for anything.

I was told later that the stowaway had some excuse for his action, for he had been "promised" a passage in the *Mayflower* for winning a singing contest on an independent television program in London, and he saw no evidence that the alleged promise would be kept. This may have been so and it may not, for I had no knowledge of any such prize, nor of the stowaway. Aboard a deepwater ship, stowing away is a crime and stowaways are common criminals. They seek to steal a passage, which is thieving, like purloining anything, and stowaways can also get ships into serious trouble. Authority ashore invariably takes the view that the stowaway is the ship's responsibility (the ship brought him, didn't it?) and ships can find themselves compulsory hosts for an indefinite and expensive period to obnoxious persons, frequently unemployables and stateless to boot. What state might claim this fellow I don't know, but we found him before quitting English territorial waters, and bundled him back into the said waters without further formality.

The following morning, after a peaceful night during which the ship creaked a lot but made no progress whatever, we were nearer to Brixham again than we were to America. This day or so of fine weather was much appreciated, for it gave us a further chance to learn the ropes properly and to experiment with the set of the sails. The day was Sunday, Easter Day, and there were morning prayers on the quarter-deck, followed by the reading of a chapter from Bradford and some discourse on the Pilgrim Fathers. I wanted the mariners to be familiar with the great venture of the first *Mayflower*. It was all there in Bradford's classic, *Of Plimoth Plantation*.

These activities were rudely interrupted by the arrival, in mid-Channel, of another press launch, with a fellow aboard apparently from yet another London daily, determined to get a last story. He was allowed to stand on the weather main channels and look inboard. This seemed sufficient for his purposes and he left, after a while, promising to be back on the morrow in an aircraft. Then an aircraft flew over so closely that I could see my wife inside, surrounded by newsmen busily scribbling. The machine circled twice and my wife threw out a message, which we picked up in our pram.

The Eddystone lighthouse was in full view, and the ship seemed reluctant to leave its neighborhood. We did not worry over that. We had sea room and were all right for the moment: the forecast spoke of west-southwest gales. I was anxious to get out of the Channel before anything like that blew up on us, both to be off the too-crowded shipping routes and to have the necessary offing from the land. The ship showed that she could ghost easily, slipping along at up to four knots or so with very light airs, but how well she might perform in a gale of wind was quite another matter.

The breeze increased and the sea got up, when the wind was against the tide, and again I hated to see the way the masts were working, and the bowsprit. The fore-topmast looked little better than a knotty broomstick and the main topmast was not much stouter, nor was there anything like an adequate supply of spare spars aboard, if the ship were even partially dismasted. Only a sufficiency of pine to mast the ship once had been bought from Canada, for this was expensive stuff. Watching it from the vantage point of my small cabin, I could see the mainmast-head move laterally a foot or so with each roll of the ship, following it across my small rectangular bulkhead window. The heavy main-yard was jumping, and its wooden saddle dug viciously into the pine lower mast with the ship's motion (which was al-ready considerable), while the whole foremast seemed to stumble and jerk violently at its supporting rigging with every pitch, like a hard-mouthed steeplechaser jerking at the reins as it came to a fence. Soon there were "fences" enough there in the chops of the Channel, and I wondered how long the topmasts might stay with us.

The after gun ports, cut into the transom, were leaking, and so were some of the gun ports in the 'tween-decks, though none seriously. These gun ports ought not to have been cut into the hull before the ship reached her final haven in America, but there they were, and it proved impos-sible to prevent the sea seeping through several of them. There was some leakage in the starboard side, in the way of the main chains, which we could not put to rights. There were leaks in the main deck too, and in the quarter-deck. None was serious, and there never were more than twenty inches in the well. The ship drew 13' 8" aft and 11' 10" for'ard as she left Plymouth, and this was a lot of water. I don't think it had been foreseen that there might be so much of her below sea level, although that should have made no difference to the amount of leakage. There was a great deal of chafe aloft—chafe on the huge tops where the roaches of the topsails came in too frequent contact with them, chafe of cordage rubbing on cordage, and canvas against wood or shroud. All hands, divided into the proper watches, were put at once to fighting this chafe, making mats of canvas and the stranded rope called "baggywrinkle" to fix at the worst places, and baggywrinkle by the score of fathoms to wrap wherever it was most needed. The bowsprit, too, waved like a wand when a strain came on it from the big spritsail, and the spritsail could not be reefed. There was not a reefpoint in a single sail aboard, for there were none in 1620 and we had to be historically correct.

Again, I reflected as I walked the reeling quarter-deck and kept a wary eye on all these things, I wished that those lower masts and that bowsprit had been stouter spars. The lateen yard was heavier than the mast which carried it, and the mainmast would have been acceptable only aboard a rather small dhow. I don't doubt that the dimensions of the spars had been most meticulously worked out according to formulae, and a great deal of research had gone into the problem. I knew it had, but it was the formulae I distrusted. These were my personal views, but they were shared by the mates. We had had no part in the specifications for those spars. Well, now we were stuck with them, and the fact was worrying.

What if those pessimists in Brixham and in London had been even half right? Just what real chance *did* the little ship have of safely completing her passage? Our task was to induce this vessel somehow to move herself across the North Atlantic Ocean, preferably intact and, in any event, without serious accident. The machinery to accomplish this was her rig—her rig against the ocean winds and the sea and the storms. I began to wonder how well her rigging might stand up to a succession of gales. She could run before very heavy winds, I was sure, but to stand up to a series of gales in her face could be another matter. If she could not hold her ground, she could be lost. I did not see how she could hope to hold her ground when it looked as if I would be able to keep no sail on her, in anything like a gale of wind.

Those big topsails would have to come in first (we moderns were used to holding at least the lower topsails, or a close-reefed main topsail in a ship like the *Joseph Conrad*, until the last) and the mainsail was too big to stand in a gale. I could only reduce its area effectively by taking it in altogether. The foresail was small: I could not see the ship making anything to wind'ard with only that small fores'l and the bonnetless lateen mizzen set. What then? Where would we get, beating about the wild ocean that is the North Atlantic? She was a short and chunky ship, and her action in a big sea would be alarming. It would also throw great stresses on those over-light spars if I held a press of sail which they might not be able to stand; if I held no press of sail she would drive away to leeward, like a sea-borne stack of hay.

These problems might not have worried the good Captain Christopher Jones of the first *Mayflower*, 337 years before, but they worried us. Captain Jones knew better what he could do with his ship, from long experience, and really what she could stand. He knew, moreover, that she *was* masted adequately. (We might be, too: I just could not know.) Presumably he had a crew who knew their ship and her style of rigging, and no other. I had studied old journals from Elizabethan ships, and I had read how shipmasters then had sometimes half-lowered their course yards in heavy winds, to carry out the maneuver which they knew, apparently, as "lying a-try," converting the course temporarily into a trysail by securing the weather leach and canting the yard by brace, tack, and lift, until it was virtually a lateen. But we could not quite figure how to do that with the new *Mayflower's* yards. I wished that I had been able to manage adequate sailing trials before being committed to the voyage! Then we could have worked out all these problems and tested the spars, if necessary to destruction, in a gale of wind.

Well here I was, committed, and soon the gale would test us, for the wind and sea were increasing. The eyes of the world were upon this ship and this voyage, and very few of them could be knowledgeable eyes. Whatever else might happen, for us there could be no fiasco greater than preventable disaster at sea, whether it showed by an ignominious return to port partially dismasted or just, much later on, in a simple failure to arrive. These were fates to be avoided at all costs. Well, I would go back to no port and, under God, we would arrive.

There were four types of accident which could bring the ship to ruin, and all had been predicted. She could open up and founder (but she was too stoutly built for that); she could be blown over and founder (but she was now too stiff for that); she could show herself so unweatherly in a succession of strong head winds that she could not claw her way offshore, and so she might be cast up on a coast somewhere and destroyed (those east winds of spring, which I had begged that the ship be ready for—she could have been—would have given us offing enough to wipe out all risk of this, at least on the British side of the Atlantic; on the other side, she could have the assistance of a tug at the last moment, without disgrace); or she could be dismasted and left a useless hulk, to yelp for a tug and be towed in somewhere, if she were lucky, to the jeers of the maritime world. She could also, like any other vessel under sail, be lost by collision with some powered vessel not keeping lookout for the colored side lights which are all that a ship under sail may show, under the international rules. As for that risk, I could do something about it, and had done so. We had a good supply of flares to scare away steamers. It was risks three and four which were the serious hazards.

The wind piped up from west-northwest. The tops'ls were made fast. The big sprits'l was tugging at its sheets and at the bowsprit as if it wanted nothing better than to tear it bodily from the ship, yet I must keep the sprits'l set to counterbalance the high poop. The gammonings lashing the bowsprit to the solid beak were beginning to work a little loose. The topmasts, even without their sails, were over at an angle from the vertical. My mariners reported her to be a difficult ship to stow tops'ls in, for up there she was throwing her rigging about in bights with the shrouds alternately slackening and jumping taut, though the catharpins were tended and everything possible done to keep the whole fabric properly set up. The motion of the vessel was violent, ceaseless, and thoroughly trying, in a way none of us had known before, not even in an empty LCI(L) in an Atlantic gale. The glass was dropping, and the visibility closing in. The longer I beat about in the chops of the Channel trying to fight out the northern way, the greater the risk of the worst danger of all—collision with a steamer in the narrow seas. By this time, I was to windward of Ushant, thanks to the northing in the wind.

The wind backed a point or so more to the north, rising.

My decision was made.

"Put the helm up," I said, above the ship's noises. "Let her fall off two points. Mr. Mate, the weather main brace."

I fell off before the wind, to go the southern way—the trade-wind way, the "safe" way, down to the tropic's edge and then westwards in the wake of Columbus. It was the long way round, and it might take some time, for it would add another 2,000 miles to the passage. But we had a better chance that way, and I wanted to arrive.

The mate checked in the braces and trimmed the yards, as was his duty. Then, seeing all well, I went to the great cabin and had the radio operator send messages to Plymouth and to London telling them of my decision. Although this meant the end of all hope of coming in during May at all and possibly even in June, there was no answering moan from Plymouth.

They were sensible people, and they wanted their ship to arrive, too.

CHAPTER

13

ACROSS THE BAY
AND HEADED WEST

It seemed that the Lord approved the decision to take the ship westwards by the southern route, for the wind stayed north of west and then went to north, and we bounded along. Ideally, this route can offer the advantage of fair wind the whole way across, for the wind system of the Atlantic there roughly corresponds to the currents—blowing from somewhere north on the European side (once a ship is away from the tempestuous chops of the Channel and all the Bay of Biscay), then northeast and east-northeast by the tropic's edge to give a square-rigged ship good westing, and finally sweeping up from the south'ard inside the Gulf Stream's northerly swing, off the eastern seaboard of America.

There were difficulties about the route, of course. The first was to get away from the Channel (we had managed that) and across the Bay without being driven in on that lee shore by a violent westerly, but, once a ship was south of Cape Finisterre, she should have an assurance of northerly weather to bring her to the trades. In the spring, however, the trade winds could be light and even nonexistent, and it was because of that fact that I had not considered sailing by the southern way when planning the voyage. I could not afford to dawdle too long looking for wind, or we might find ourselves uncomfortably close to the onset of the West Indies hurricane season. We had to approach the West Indies, at the end of the run from somewhere near the Canaries. Freak hurricanes seem to be more frequent in the Atlantic nowadays than they used to be, as also do poor trade winds. (A particularly vicious hurricane, curving unpredictably, was to destroy the powerful German four-masted bark *Pamir* later in the year, and drown thirty crewmen and fifty-five boys.) A sailing-ship master has to weigh all these considerations and decide to do what he thinks best. The decision made, he must keep to it.

Our routine was set and the ship's company was already working as a well-knit team. They were splendid, and the rapidity with which all hands settled into that curious ship's uncomfortable stride—the inexperienced with the experienced, the two ship's boys and the yachtsmen, the surgeon-seaman, the schoolmaster mariner, and the architect-seaman, the cargo-liner officers, the fifty-eight-year-old bos'n and the fifty-nine-year-old cook and all the rest—really was phenomenal. For this I had to thank their own good spirit and the excellence of my watchkeeping officers. How handsomely it paid that these were sailing-ship officers! From eight bells to eight bells, struck on the mellow old church bell (dating from the early 1600's, which was a gift

from Brixham), whatever might happen or however the
ship might jump and pitch and lurch and roll, the routine
went on, helm-turn and lookout, an hour at each, seven men
in a watch all alert and ready, by day employed in the
ship's work, by night standing by.

The two boys took turn about in the great cabin, tending the mess in there (with eleven members it was as big
as it could be) while the mariners took their meals in the
tiller-flat, which was wet but had at least the merit of considerably less violence of motion. The great cabin was the
only good one in the ship. It was rough, and unpaneled, but
it had three picturesque stern windows and good oak
beams, and something could be made of it. At the moment,
and for most of the voyage, it was inevitably cluttered with
radio sets, large cameras and tripods, cases of film, a box of
books by Sir Winston Churchill, and the bodies of several
of our extraneous persons, the non-crew members. The only
good piece of furniture in it (or in the ship) was a handsome oak table, made and presented by some school children in Boston, Lincolnshire. It housed also the library from
the Searfarers' Education Service, which was much appreciated. In due course, we could make something of that
great cabin, for it could be impressive.

When not acting as cabin boys, the lads were on deck,
and this they greatly preferred. Joe Meany, the boy-of-the-
year from Boys' Clubs of America, soon showed himself
to be an excellent lad. Until his selection which carried
with it in '57 an automatic place as ship's boy in the new
Mayflower, Joe had shown no great interest in sailing. He
told me that he had been out fishing one day on a river in
New England, and that was his previous seafaring. Like
many others, he was severely seasick. The life, the food,

and the sea language were alike all new to him, but he came up smiling. He was good aloft, and anxious to become better, and he spent his spare time learning all he could. Graham Nunn, the British boy, had been at sea and intended to make seafaring in some form his lifetime profession. But he was judged colorblind by today's severe tests (nobody bothered about such defects in the original ship, for color-blindness then was quite unimportant) and was barred from deck duty. He had perforce to serve in the catering department, and had been a bellhop for a voyage to Australia in the P. and O. liner *Arcadia*. Bellhopping was not to his taste at all, and he thrived aboard the *Mayflower*, whose only bell was the ship's bell, where the hours were struck, at the break of the poop.

He, too, took naturally to the work aloft and the intricacies of square-rigger "sailorizing," and proved himself a cheerful, willing, and competent young seaman.

Looking at the good the ship was doing for these boys, I regretted that we had not twenty of them, and that the ship could not spend five or ten years taking boys like that to sea, giving them a real taste of what so many youngsters crave—a little red-blooded adventure—and, for lack of it, sometimes get themselves into trouble. After that, it would be time enough to think of "enshrining" her, and she might be more worthy of it.

I take up the story from my private Journal:

WEDNESDAY, APRIL 24   *Noon position: 46.46N. 10.12W.*
Day's run: 147 miles

Wind still north and north by west. Vessel rolling along about six knots, the sound of the wake gurgling and bubbling in the open great cabin window, but my cabin, high in the over-high poop, so violent in its motion that it is a strenuous exercise to stay in it asleep or awake, at work or reading. Mr. Godfrey, the old cook, does wonders in the stuffy galley: the mates' cabins on the main deck practically awash, and the carpenter, Edgar Mugridge, rushing everywhere to deal with freshly reported small leaks: the fight against the chafe aloft going on day and night: the ship not steering (or perhaps not being steered) very well. In the night watches, the mates exercise the hands at finding their way about the rigging at stations for taking in sail, etc. Some of the younger hands very seasick.

Appoint three boatmen, one emergency boatman for each watch. We have only an eight-foot pram given to the ship by Stuart Upham: fit this with buoyancy tanks in the shape of old tins and a couple of old life jackets, for it has little freeboard and could easily be swamped in the sea. I hope it will not have to be used.

THURSDAY, APRIL 25   *Noon position: 44.39N. 12.02W.*
Day's run: 148 miles

Freshening northeast winds, but she will not do better than seven knots. At nightfall make the two tops'ls fast (the masts and slender yards bending with the increasing weight of wind) but she keeps her speed. The tops'ls secure quite well along the small yards, without too big a bunt and no need to lash an untidy bundle in the commodious, circular tops. Take the lateen off her, too, to help the steering: she runs along free in a boiling of foam, leaping and rolling with the most rapid motion I ever knew. It is hazy today: we see no shipping. A high following sea and the wind to Force 7: she does well under the fores'l, mains'l, and spritsail.

Inspect the cargo hold every day—all secure. Watch and listen for stowaways among the chests, for there could still be a body

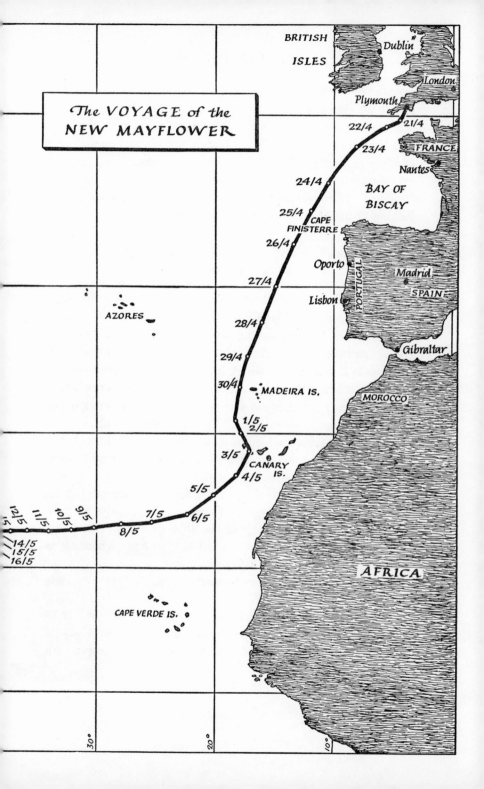

The VOYAGE of the
NEW MAYFLOWER

in some of the more inaccessible: no sign or sound of any. She has about eighteen inches of water in the well in the mornings.

Some of the stuff in these chests is valuable. Each day the mate and I inspect independently the leaden customs seal on the chest of silver and gold, which is in the 'tween-decks, in full view of everyone. I never imagined that some day I would be sailing a "treasure" galleon towards the Spanish Main, when I was a boy looking at the old Cape Horners in Melbourne!

FRIDAY, APRIL 26   *Noon: 42°21N. 13°35W.*
             Day's run: 154 miles

Begins with fresh northeast wind and high sea with some northwest swell, the ship laboring but not shipping water, apart from the leaks. Run on, making about seven knots, under the two courses and the spritsail: these tops'ls are about the equivalent of gaff tops'ls in a schooner, which is odd to us from large modern sailing ships where the tops'ls are of stouter stuff, and likewise the masts. The tops'ls here are of very light canvas, and the topmasts and tops'l yards are very slender. The doublings are short; nor are there any backstays to help support the mast—nothing but a couple of preventer tackles. There is still a horrible play in both topmasts. The ship does well under her lowers. Set up the catharpins (lines like frapping tackles across the shrouds) again the better to tauten the rigging. Water in the 'tween-decks again, and still coming through one of the after gunports. This being declared irreparable, the water is led to the bilges, whence it is pumped out without much difficulty.

The cook doing us extremely well, in spite of the appalling motion.

A lot of silly radio messages come in: instruct the operator to accept only those which are really on ship's business. Many of these messages are stupid and bombastic stuff, from people with no business sending them. No answers. We make the daily position report via Portishead to Plymouth and London, as promised, and a brief news story of our progress once weekly, for all the press, with no discrimination or special stories. This was the agreed arrangement and I see that it is kept. A newspaper tries to call the ship tonight by radio telephone under the pretense that the call is from my wife, but Portishead tells us the real origin. No answer.

SATURDAY, APRIL 27   *Noon: 39.58N. 14.56W.*
Run: 154 miles

Same conditions—a good north wind pushes us steadily towards the trade-wind zone (between Madeira and the Canary Islands, we hope, at this time of year) but the ship makes a disappointing run. We have to accept the fact that, loaded like this, she is slow. Instead of the twelve knots which it was estimated that she could make, the fact is that she will do little more than seven. She might do more if less of her great towering stern were in the water. She is difficult to steer running before the wind, which is no help. Some of the helmsmen sometimes swing a couple of points either side of course.

In the afternoon, wind freshening again, with rain squalls: reduce to the lowers for the night, because I do not trust these topmasts, and she sails very well on her lowers.

A balk of timber falls from the main hatch on the bos'n's foot: laid up briefly. It is the week end anyway. Put him to day work. I need him in the rigging.

SUNDAY, APRIL 28   *Noon: 37.36N. 16.06W.*
Run: 153 miles

Same northerly conditions, rolling heavily, most uncomfortably, and slowly along in a welter of foam, with the whitecaps racing. She makes wake and fuss enough for a ship doing twelve knots, but it is all from the bluff bows and the drag. The sea boils astern almost as if she were twin-screwed, and her white wake stretches back for a mile and more. The *Conrad* at this speed would leave no discernible wake at all, a ship's length astern of her. But every mile (more or less) is on course: we are lucky to carry this northerly wind. The weather forecasts speak of wild conditions elsewhere in the Atlantic, particularly in the area where we would be now, had we gone by the other route. I shudder to think of her up there! As it is, we make a lurching six and a half knots on our way—the *long* way round, but it should get us there.

At 10 A.M., prayers for all hands, followed by some further discourse on the Pilgrim Fathers and reading a chapter from Bradford. I want these fellows really to know something about the *Mayflower* story, not the *Mayflower* myth.

MONDAY, APRIL 29   *Noon: 35.13N. 17.02W.*
Run: 150 miles

As yesterday, rolling handsomely along—but such rolling! The motion is frequently most violent. Putting up chafing gear aloft (big baggywrinkle pads round the tops, wrapped baggywrinkle on the stays, etc. etc.) but she has already chafed a hole in the fore-tops'l and another in the lateen. The fight against chafe is redoubled: indeed, it is the principal activity of the watch on deck. The ship now on the three-watch system, with six in a watch: will change this in the trade winds by the selection of daymen and get more work done that way.

Boat drill today: each watch has its own life raft, with a fourth for the supernumeraries. Organise the motorboat (an old thing which does duty for our longboat) with water and provisions, etc. for all the rafts, and fit it with the emergency radio as required by the Ministry. Abandon-ship drill is for the motorboat to keep the rafts together and tend their wants: but it is no lifeboat. The ship is well supplied with fire-fighting equipment, which is also exercised on Mondays.

Wind inclined to shift west of north.

TUESDAY, APRIL 30   *Noon: 32.56N. 18.13W.*
Run: 149 miles

The northerly continued, now north-northwest. Pass the island of Madeira about forty miles to windward but see nothing, the visibility not good. I do not need nor wish to touch anywhere: to go too close to these places means delay, for high islands spoil the wind. Continue course to pass to windward of all the Canaries and then to make westing in the assured trade wind. See one old tramp bound west, in ballast: pay no attention to him, nor he to us. He looks as if no one is on deck and he is going along without human aid. Probably all hands are chipping and scrapping down below.

Open the main hatch, no sea coming over there now, to bring in light and air to the 'tween-decks, where most of the ship's company live in rough cabins with old iron cots, discarded by some old hospital ship, by the look of them. They can go over the side again when we reach America.

Break out the salt-meat casks, one of pork and one of beef, and stow them on deck. Cook Godfrey has been doing wonders to keep the fresh meat going, and dishing it up generously too. Likewise the shore-baked wrapped bread, which is still good. Cook Godfrey is altogether a pretty remarkable fellow, and a considerable asset to the vessel.

Yarning in the night watch on the quarter-deck with Jan Junker about his year or more in concentration camps, when he was picked up by the Gestapo after being dropped by a Polish crew flying a R.A.F. bomber over Denmark during the war. Once he was one of a party of ten imprisoned Danes. The other nine were shot, but the Germans had mislaid his papers. Always thorough, they marched him back to prison until the missing papers were found. They never were.

WEDNESDAY, MAY 1   *Noon: 31.11N. 18.36W.*
                    Run: 107 miles

So we are come to May, and the wind is dropping, and well west of north—not so good for progress. It cannot be perfect all the time: we have been very fortunate. Now the ship is being slowly forced towards the westernmost of the Canary Islands. There are many of the sail-driven jellyfish called Portuguese men-o'-war about. Being the eleventh day at sea, begin the daily issue of lime juice, which is of much better quality than the sad, poor liquid which used to be dished out in so-called limejuice ships. The hands seem to like the stuff and none is left: in the old days it was often scorned. Felix, our cat, won't have any, preferring the scurvy. Felix settled down aboard faster than anyone, though he joined the ship when only a few days old.

A large whale blows near by, after looking deceptively like a sea serpent for some time: a balasted oil tanker passes on the northern horizon, purposeful and plodding. The main yard is hoisted a little to allow the mainsail to set and point up better (but the bonnet is rather too big for it and when it is set, we cannot see for'ard from the quarter-deck). Carpenter Mugridge works in my cabin where I can see the side planking opening up to let the daylight in, and there are many leaks in the deckhead: all of which is far too historically accurate. Even a 16th-century-ship, surely, should keep the rain out.

The sea is quieter, and a comet is in view in the first night watch, with a new moon. A beautiful night, but we still head towards the Canary Islands.

THURSDAY, MAY 2   *Noon: 30.08N. 18.18W.*

Run: 65 miles

Almost calm in the middle watch, though she goes along. The flap of her sails gives her steerage way, for she is an admirable "ghoster." The wind then comes from west-southwest, forcing us towards Tenerife (for I will not go north on the other tack: it is southing we want, south for the trades). See the high island of Palma to wind'ard, some eighty miles away, and make slowly on a southerly course, the wind heading. Oil down the masts and yards, which they greatly need (for some of them are tending to split a little): the hands still fighting the chafe so abundantly in evidence aloft, but we seem to be winning that fight.

Caught aback once, and let her come round on her heel. She responds pretty well. The spritsail is a grand maneuvering sail.

This morning the wireless operator reports that some Argentinian vessel is asking urgently for a doctor, not far from Las Palmas. We answer, prepared to help: so do six other vessels, all with doctors, and all much nearer. A Dutch steamer takes care of him: it would have been odd if we had been nearest.

At midnight wind strong southwest: take the tops'ls in.

FRIDAY, MAY 3   *Noon: 28.47N. 17.11W.*

Run: 100 miles

A jumpy, bumpy, trying day with the ship's motion excessive as she bounces, lurches, and rolls violently down the passage between Palma and Hiero (or Fero) on the western hand, and Tenerife and Gomera on the other, with a good wind just favorable enough for the ship to lie the necessary course. We pass closest to Gomera, some twelve to fifteen miles to windward, seeing houses distantly and, though clouds cover it heavily most of the day, we are treated to some lovely views of the peak of Tenerife. The wind stays good: before midnight we are clear of all the Canary Islands. We pass fairly close by Hiero.

The whitecaps run bravely all day long, and we make about seven knots.

SATURDAY, MAY 4   *Noon: 26.54N. 18.40W.*
              Run: 138 miles

A beautiful day of northerly wind and steady (though slow) progress under all plain sail, and I wish that I could set some more, particularly on the foremast. The big spritsail pulls well but at times gives the bowsprit a vicious jerk: we have put two extra gammonings on, which should take care of it. Hiero is still in sight far astern until early afternoon, when it must be seventy miles away: see nothing else except a few flying fish.

This is the northeast trade now, though it is northerly at first. Splice the main brace with rum in the lime juice at four o'clock to welcome the trade wind. Much appreciated by the older hands, and the youngsters get none of it.

Despite the good trade-wind conditions, several cabins in the 'tween-decks are still very wet, especially that occupied by the two guitarists, Winslow and Watson. Carpenter is working at the main deck but some leaks persist. These are all minor leaks, but annoying. The only cabin aboard which doesn't leak somewhere is that chosen by the builder, but it is also the worst ventilated.

The little kitten continues to do very well, and has as good sea legs as anybody. He is living with the two boys, and eating everywhere and everything.

At night we roll along well, and the high poop below the lateen looks incredibly romantic.

SUNDAY, MAY 5 *Noon: 25.18N. 20.02W.*

Run: 121 miles

Trade wind and going well, but the day's run disappointing. She could be doing a steady 180 a day here. However, it is her capacity to move along in light airs that is saving her: for a seven-knot ship, she is really getting along pretty famously. I recall reading somewhere that a sailing replica of the *Santa Maria* could do only six knots.

At 10 A.M., prayers, the crew assembling in their seventeenth-century clothing, which blends well with the ship: whereafter more discourse on Bradford and the Pilgrims on the old *Mayflower* voyage. All the crew have good costumes, well made of real stuff by Berman's, the theatrical costumiers, in London, some very colorful, but all very warm. They are intended mainly for use in America. Most are seaman's dress of the period, with a sprinkling of Pilgrim suits, stockings, silver-buckled shoes, and high hats. I am told the buckled shoes are wrong anyway, but I am not worrying about things like that.

Appoint daymen, reducing the watches to four men each. Begin canceling the special philatelists' covers which the ship is carrying in such vast quantities.

MONDAY, MAY 6 *Noon: 23.46N. 22.13W.*

Run: 150 miles

A good trade-wind day of tolerable progress, but as one is in the beak watching the spritsail skim the sea and pulling bravely, and listening to all the fuss of foam singing at the bow, she seems to be doing a good ten knots. That she isn't! Nor anything like it. The sea is a beautiful blue, the sky is flecked with the trade-wind clouds, the flying fish rise and fly with wide-eyed alarm from the roll of foaming water at the bows. The bos'n's gang, with daymen to assist, set up the rigging, a job which at least is simplified in this ship by the provision of permanent tackles in the shrouds for the purpose: they do all the fore and main shrouds both sides, and the fore-and-aft stays as well, which is good going. Peter Padfield of the P. and O., in charge of the postal gang, canceling the stamps sent aboard by the dealer in Southampton. This is a job that no one cares for, and it takes some time to acquire dexterity. Many bruised and date-canceled fingers today.

At night doing seven knots under a good moon—fine conditions.

TUESDAY, MAY 7 *Noon: 23.17N. 25.05W.*

Run: 160 miles

Begins the kind of northeast trade-wind day that sailors really like, and stays that way—warm, but not too warm, good sailing breeze, neither too strong nor too weak, dry decks, and the clear good sunshine on the flowing sails all day long. She jumps and rolls a lot, this stiff little ship, and my cabin is impossible (I have to clutch everything in an encircling sort of a bearlike hug, in order to write). But she averaged almost seven knots noon to noon, despite some indifferent steering, and the sunlight dances on the sea astern in the morning and on all the sea ahead all afternoon.

Bos'n Ike Marsh and his assistant Joe Lacey set up the mizzen rigging; the carpenter's gang again caulking decks; an Oxford lad oils the fore spars high aloft; and the doctor comes to me with news that the cook should lay up a day or so, and his medical history is appalling, abounding in strokes, large abdominal operations and such. His stomach is stitch-scarred as if his cradle had been a barbed-wire fence. Change his cabin, take him some medical comforts, and do not doubt the good old war horse will recover. I had medical clearances for the others but I forgot about Cook Godfrey, being so pleased to find him. Dick Brennan carrying on.

It is a considerable relief to have Dr. Stevens in the crew.

At night rolling heavily and jerkily: a little fearful for the masts again.

WEDNESDAY, MAY 8   *Noon: 23.00N. 28.08W.*
Run: 164 miles (average 6.78 knots)

The best day's run to date: she logged thirty in one four-hour watch. Yet she does not keep up an average seven. The wake sings in the stern windows, the foam boils at the bow: she rolls and lurches along with as much fuss as if she were making twenty. Postal gang, rigging gang, caulking gang all busily at work all day long in this good trade-wind weather. Cook Godfrey improved, but not back in the galley. Felix the kitten playing on a coir fender on the main hatch, in the sun.

At night the trade wind gone more to the east, and dropping. These North Atlantic trades are never wholly reliable. I remember some very quiet days, sailing the *Joseph Conrad* from Madeira to the Bahamas, and some roaring fine days of good sailing too when she kept up better than a steady ten knots for twenty-four hours. Jan Junker says that when he was second mate of the ship *Danmark* in 1947 on a passage from Oporto to Balboa, she met no trade winds at all.

The foreyard creaking horribly, in spite of rolling tackles etc. and the expenditure of much tallow.

THURSDAY, MAY 9   *Noon: 23.00N. 30.08W.*
Run: 116 miles

Begins gray, dull, with no whitecaps racing, the trade wind easterly and too quiet. She logged little better than three knots in the middle watch: with daylight she does better, but it is a poor run all day. However, one must expect some patchiness in the trade winds. At least the sea is quieter and she does not roll so much. The postal work continues to absorb the energies of half a dozen men all day, which is a nuisance when they could be doing more important things. Canceling letters by the 100,000 is a terrific business for the uninitiated: and I have a new and somewhat raw ship to lick into shape here, without that sort of employment.

Cook Godfrey appears to be fully recovered and is back on his job. The routine of the ship flows pleasantly along.

We are nineteen days at sea and the second mate, who is navigator, reckons we have another 1900 miles to do on this course and, after that, at least a further 1,000 to landfall. The mate remarks that it isn't so much the fact that we are sailing here in a late-sixteenth-century ship that he finds so remarkable, as to find himself at sea again in an engineless square-rigged ship at all.

We do not sail so well at night; the trade wind far too quiet.

FRIDAY, MAY 10   *Noon: 22.47N. 31.50W.*
                 Run: 95 miles

Begins almost becalmed: then a breeze at daylight, dropped by seven again, and back about eight when we do a little better than four knots in a very quiet sea beneath a heavily overcast sky. Rig a studding sail on the weather side of the fore, out of a spare tops'l yard and the storm trysail: perhaps it may help. At any rate it makes all hands feel better. There are as many camera men photographing the operation as sailors working at it—the industrious photographer from American *Life*, seaman-photographer Israel, our movie cameraman, and half the watch below, who seem to have at least two still cameras apiece and a movie camera to each three of them.

At midday, speak a westbound oil tanker, in ballast, which

came up over the eastern horizon: asked him by the international code flags to report us to Lloyd's, the radio being temporarily defective. I want to give no fool the chance to say this ship is "missing," or in any form of trouble whatever. The tanker alters course, hoists an ensign which we cannot make out, and puts up a hoist of flags saying that he will report us. Then, leaving a great track of oily bilge water for miles upon the sea, he waddles slowly towards the western horizon. Could not read his port of registry.

SATURDAY, MAY 11   *Noon: 22.04N. 34.00W.*
Run: 120 miles

Begins with good trade wind, east by north, ship rolling a lot but going better with the trysail disguised as studding sail doing its best, and the weather clew of the mainsail hauled up to allow the smaller foresail to draw and so the ship to steer better.

The whitecaps race merrily all day and the splashing of the wake gurgles very pleasantly through the stern windows. But the wind is right aft and she just won't shift much—and there's nothing I can do about it. By midafternoon, the breeze quieter: one can hear every little crest turning over on the sea as one walks the high poop, and a pretty uphill walk it is. She may be a slow and somewhat uncomfortable ship: but so far she is a lucky one. She keeps on going. For a ship which never yet has managed to log a steady seven throughout a whole day, she keeps her average up well and is getting the miles behind her. Today we are about halfway between the two Plymouths.

At night the breeze dropping quiet again.

And so it went, day after sunlit day, and I often thanked the Lord I had gone that way when we heard the weather reports for the Atlantic further to the north. Up there was nothing but storm after storm, all of which would have been directly against us. One afternoon our fore-topsail yard broke quietly in two pieces, for no good reason, and I wondered how the other yards might have fared had we gone by the route of my original intention.

Not only was the ship safer on the southern route. It was possible to get to real grips with the tremendous job of getting her into first-rate order—caring for the rigging, scraping the decks (an abominable job), cleaning, painting, perfecting everything—and, so far at any rate, we were making quite a tolerable passage.

22. She was a plain Red Ensign ship — the new *Mayflower* at Brixham, ballasted and almost ready for sea.

23. The stern was very high and rather narrow. It carried no name, only a painted Mayflower.

24. Joe Meany helps to set up the main rigging.

25. Prayers on the quarter-deck.

26. Ship's Boys Nunn (on bunk) and Meany.

27. Cook-steward Walter Godfrey was a grand sea-cook.

28. Setting the fore topsail.

29. Man the halyards!

31. Bos'n Marsh could do without footropes.

30. The *Ark Roy*
streaks past.

32.
Bowling
along
towards
Cape Cod.

33. The Plymouth shallop, designed by William A. Baker and built at Plymouth.

CHAPTER

14

COLUMBUS DID BETTER

As THE ship slowly drew nearer to the area of the West Indies, we realized with surprise that Christopher Columbus had made better time of the run from the Canaries on his first voyage than we looked like making. His journal showed that fact. He had the advantage of passing through the trade winds at a better time of the year, when they were both fresher and steadier, but he had three ships. Three ships are much, much more difficult to keep together, and sailing in company inevitably retards the speed of advance to that of the slowest vessel. Columbus' ships must have been all right for that kind of passage, anyway.

We often thought of the illustrious pioneers, for we sailed in their tracks almost precisely, in the same type of vessel. Drake, Hawkins, and the rest knew that sea road. All the West Indies voyages and a good many of the early

Virginian had been made that way, the Roanoke ships and the little Jamestown ships, the *Susan Constant*, *Godspeed*, and *Discovery*, leading the American van. Their way west was the way we came, and the way home again was to the north, with the help of the Gulf Stream drift. Columbus seems to have known of the North Atlantic's circulatory movements of air and water to help westbound and eastbound ships, but if he were the true pioneer how *could* he know such things? This was a seafaring mystery, and we wondered often about it, walking the poop in the mooncast shadow of the lateen mizzen discussing the problem and the many other mysteries about this most baffling of all the great navigators.

Those early transatlantic seamen had many hardships which we avoided, no matter how honest our replica. The sailors of those days threw themselves down in their cloaks to sleep where they might, for there were no quarters for them as we know such luxuries, taken for granted today. They lived on such unpalatable stuff as pease soup, boiled and reboiled, burgoo, the toughest of salt meat, and the hardest of hard biscuits. Any fats that might have been in the food the cook did his best to bake or boil out of it, for all slush or grease was his perquisite and he could find good market for it. We had a wide variety of the best of canned goods, plenty of potatoes, and fresh bread thrice weekly. As for fresh water, it used frequently to become quite rotten and was often loathsome and disease-filled stuff when first barreled. Ours was in cool steel tanks, well down below, and Seaman-Surgeon Stevens watched its high standard of purity. The old-timers had ale, and we had that too—a hundred cases of Truman's special *Mayflower* brew, bottled in London. What the sixteenth-century mariners called ale I don't know, but ours was excellent stuff and well suited to the tropics. The boys saved theirs to take home for their parents, but the mariners quaffed their daily issue at once.

I read in my Journal of a day—our twenty-third at sea, with indifferent progress of eighty miles noon-to-noon— which set us to thinking further about the trials of Columbus:

MONDAY, MAY 13   *Noon: 22.22N. 37.07W.*

Run: 80 miles

Begins quiet, dull, close, heavily overcast, the ship making about three knots on a westerly course before a very light east-southeast air. A frigate bird about and one Mother Carey's chicken: this part of the ocean seems very empty and we see little life—today not as much as a Portuguese man-o'-war. Sometimes we go for days without seeing even a flying fish.

After variable conditions all afternoon, more like the so-called Horse Latitudes than the trade winds, there is a sunset of the melancholy, almost satanic, threatening kind that must so have alarmed Columbus' crews. The distant roll of thunder, the strange display of the clouds—here piled up in dark and threatening overcast, there a roll of fluffy cumulus touched a brief red in the setting but unseen sun, there a mass of white cloud flung high, pure white, in the east, hung against a pale blue patch of sky— and then the overcast grows, with rain, and the wind comes from the east, fresh, so that she boils and hurries along in the quiet, black sea, for once with perfect conditions. But these don't last: nothing lasts. By midnight, after three hours of excellent sailing, the wind is light again and well south of east. A lot of lightning about, silhouetting the ship suddenly against the dark sea, and then all is darkness again. It is eerie, and we can imagine that such conditions could be alarming to the superstitious seamen-pioneers.

And again the following day:

TUESDAY, MAY 14   *Noon: 22.20N. 38.47W.*
               Run: 93 miles

Begins quiet, overcast, dull, the wind southeast, the ship full-and-by on the port tack just lying a westerly course. A small flying fish dead in the weather main channels, found by the mate and given to Felix the cat.

Wind dropping very light at noon: becalmed in the afternoon with real doldrums conditions and the ship without steerage way for the first time since leaving the Channel. This will never do: we must make an average of 100 miles a day to have anything of a passage at all. But the trade wind is quiet with the weariness of time, and sleeps this day. The courses are hauled up, the sails and the rigging slap about, and I fear for the fore-topmast. But it stands—so far. There is rain, but not enough to catch, though sundry mariners take showers in it, washing off the soap with salt water.

In the first night watch, with an incredible moon of almost day's brightness, there comes a light air from north-northeast and she steers. But it doesn't grow.

Day after day at this stage of the voyage, we met good, quiet weather. Sometimes our progress was very poor. As for example, as this day:

WEDNESDAY, MAY 15   *Noon: 22.25N. 39.11W.*
Run: 25 miles

Flat, glassy calm from midnight, the kind that looks permanent, as if the sea's oily face would never again be ruffled by a passing breeze. At noon, making perhaps half a knot, hands over the side to swim, but have to throw the cook the end of the main-tops'l halyards pretty lively to get him back when she increases to a couple of knots or so with a breath of hot, southerly air. Remember that this was the way John Howland, a passenger aboard, was got back when he fell overboard on the original passage, but the tops'l halyard was trailing over the side then and he grabbed it. This southerly air doesn't last long: but she keeps steerage way all day. It is very hot, and the easterly swell keeps her jumping—an activity at which she is far too expert.

After serving out the lime juice at eight bells at the end of the afternoon watch, send all hands out in turns in the boat in order that they may have a look at the ship in an Atlantic swell, under sail. The ship looks her part, but she does seem to have an enormously high hull out of the water even though she is so deep beneath the surface, too. The sails are nicely cut and her appearance is most interesting, as she dips and rolls and plunges along like an old galleon of Spain. Everyone back aboard, very pleased to be serving in such a vessel. It is extraordinary how a look from outboard at one's ship under sail at sea can be such a stimulating and thoroughly rewarding experience, and the effect is permanent.

The spirit of the crew is extremely good, and much laughter rings about the decks.

THURSDAY, MAY 16   *Noon: 21.50N. 39.45W.*
Run: 49 miles

From midnight to 4 A.M., second mate's watch, it rained a lot and some of it leaked into the ship's upperworks. More water was caught in a water-sail stretched over the poop—a dozen buckets or so, and plenty for a good bath for the watch. The dawn is a doldrums dawn, with rain clouds darkening the sea in all directions and a long greasy swell pock-marked both by rain-drops and catspaws of wind, which do little if any good. By seven she has lost steerage way and the sails slat and bang.

She *is* having a job of it to get past longitude 40° W., almost as if the road were uphill. This morning everything is wet, gray, clammy; but at least the water has stopped coming into the ship now the rain has cleared. Rain seeped into my cabin through the sides, despite recent caulking, and through the stern, in large quantities, but at least it had the grace to keep out of most of my bunk, which is more than it did for the unfortunate mates. However, the opportunity for a bath is much appreciated, and this afternoon there is a different look to all hands. They have been washing assiduously in salt water, but there must be some-thing about the fresh that is different. It *feels* different: we know that. We don't mind a bit of rain coming into the ship's cabins. It is warm here, and not unpleasant. We wonder just how it must have been for the Pilgrim families to keep warm, or dry, or even clean in a ship like this, and how hellish her cold and much more constant leakiness must have been for them.

The rain clears later. But we don't get back the trade wind, and we don't get across 40° W. today.

FRIDAY, MAY 17   *Noon: 21.45N. 40.05W.*
           Run: 19 miles

Begins very quietly: during the morning the Italian liner *Lucania* of Naples comes tearing over, ripping up the sea, to exchange salutations. She zoomed round us at a great speed, making us lurch and stagger. We were doing two knots at the time. There were many *"Vivas"* and *"Bravos"* from the Italian, and a voice from the bridge shouted "Good Voyage." It was a beautiful sunny morning. After circling us once, the *Lucania* went off lickety-split for the horizon.

At noon very quiet: hands to swim again. John Winslow sent to examine the rudder pintles, there being a horrible thump at this end of the ship, the cause of which is most elusive. He finds all in order.

SATURDAY, MAY 18 *Noon: 21.49N. 40.35W.*

Run: 27 miles (at an average 1.13 kn.)

(2950 miles sailed, 2300 to go)

Begins quiet but with a light easterly which I hope will grow, but a confusing swell mainly from northwest is making the ship lurch enough to roll one's teeth out. All one can do is hang on. I write this standing at the chart table, legs wide astraddle, one hand clinging to the side of the chart table, and frequently both, for dear life. The sunshine streams in the small leaded windows. The sea is a deep and brilliant blue: an oily, high swell picks the stiff little ship up every now and again and shakes her like a pup while everything aboard falls over, even the kitten where it is asleep in the shade underneath the boat. But the kitten doesn't wake up. Perhaps it has the right idea! Fore and aft comes the sound not of sailors singing at their work or the wind in the rigging (it is some days since we heard that) but the clack-clacking of the special canceling dies stamping our first voyage covers full of unwritten letters. Gangs of stamp cancelers work on the fo'c'sle head, in the great cabin, in the 'tween-decks. Every mariner (being promised a bonus to finish the unwanted job) is putting in at least two hours of extra work each day, in his watch below.

Simultaneously with the canceling of the last stamp, a sailing breeze comes from the south. A burst of cheering celebrates the last letter, and Peter Padfield, Postmaster, is chaired.

The sailing breeze is soon assailed by rain which brings variables, but it doesn't quite stop again, and we go along.

SUNDAY, MAY 19   *Noon: 21.41N. 41.31W.*

Run: 54 miles

The breeze stays, swinging between east-southeast and east-northeast: it is very pleasant to hear the life in the sea again, and feel the wind coming through the stern windows. All day we go along—very quietly; but we go. The sea is quieter, the glass high, the sky a beautiful cloud-flecked trade-wind sky, almost everywhere.

We have sailed over 3,000 miles in four weeks, despite these recent very poor runs. I hope we will get the chance to do the remaining 2,000-odd in three weeks.

At 10 A.M. prayers, as usual, followed by some discourse on the voyage of Columbus. We see quite a bit of old Gulf weed in the sea today: one imagines Columbus' crews looking at such stuff, and probably thinking that it indicated the proximity of land, which it does not. Any land other than the sea's bottom is still hundreds and hundreds of miles away.

In the first night watch, a very small whale playing phosphorescently round the ship, as if he wanted to have a good look at her.

The arrangements for this voyage, and the routine for the crew have worked very well, though there have been some handicaps caused by coming this southern route. The galley (extremely well designed by Cook Godfrey as it is) is insufferably hot and poorly ventilated for these warm conditions, and so are the cabins. The lavatory arrangements work excellently, the "heads" in the beak being airy, foolproof, and hygienic. It would be a very different thing in cold, wet weather, with a bad-tempered head sea. Again, one wonders how the poor Pilgrims fared.

MONDAY, MAY 20   *Noon: 21.30N. 43.00W.*

Run: 83 miles

Begins with a beautiful dawn and the quiet trade continuing, the ship slipping along under all sail including the studding sail but without the lateen, which interferes with the steering when the wind is as far aft as it is now. Bos'n's gang setting up the rigging again—a job which is frequently necessary because of stretch in the lanyards. Daymen and watch members painting overside in the good weather, for this is the first day for some time in which there has been no rain.

Considerable Sargasso weed about this morning, which increases very much about noon, with long lines of the stuff indicating that there has not been much wind in these parts. Some weed is hauled aboard and found to be inhabited by minute fish and little crabs, and a sort of legged mollusc which writhes about. Suddenly we are out of the area of greatest weed and, after that, there is very little.

Yarn with Third Mate Jan Junker (who much appreciates the sunshine here as a change from the cold and gloomy Arctic Trade) in his watch about his experiences in the war. Escaping from Copenhagen by small boat, he was arrested in Sweden (and would have been sent back forthwith if he had not taken the precaution of reporting to the British authorities first, for the Swedes he encountered were then very pro-German), was flown to Scotland in a small aircraft piloted by Norwegians and the aircraft was chased by fighters several times, was trained as a saboteur and trainer of other saboteur-agents, the course including burglary, arson, etc., and how to deal with various sorts of

watchdogs and to stand up to Gestapo methods of investigation
—all most useful information. The courses were given in part
near Mallaig in Scotland and in part in Fairford and in a large
house near Oxford. Then, being a trained parachutist as well, he
was dropped from a R.A.F. Wellington bomber pretending to be
returning up the Great Belt from a raid on Berlin. His equipment canisters fell among roadside telephone wires and could
not be cleared before morning. He was picked up by the Gestapo
within the week, from a watched house in Aarhus. Then hell.

TUESDAY, MAY 21　　*Noon: 21.22N. 44.48W.*
Run: 101 miles

We barely scrape over the 100-mile mark for the twenty-four
hours, for the first time in ten days. When the little whitecaps
break it is lively enough, and it is always lovely, with the dawn
sky moved westwards for the night and back to the east again
in the morning, and the blue sea golden-weed dotted and the
blue sky patterned with the fleecy trade-wind clouds. But our
progress isn't what one would like, in this part of the ocean,
where a square-rigger should be romping on with a great bone
rolling in her mouth day after day.

WEDNESDAY, MAY 22　　*Noon: 21.16N. 46.11W.*
Run: 78 miles

Begins as yesterday, with practically the same dawn, and the
trade wind even more reluctant to get started. When it does, the
pattern changes, with rain squalls and the wind jumping from
northeast to south and back again, always freshening before the
rain and then dropping again, so that at times we do six or seven
knots and then drop again to two or three. We do not even get
100 miles for the twenty-four hours—this will never do. A lot of
Sargasso weed about.

Restaurateur Dick Brennan of Fleet Street (second cook here, and always good and cheerful at the job) celebrates his forty-eighth birthday, and there is a party in the evening on the main deck, with strumming of guitar and banjo and considerable song, the mate (off watch) singing lustily with the mariners.

THURSDAY, MAY 23   *Noon: 21.05N. 47.16W.*
Run: 61 miles

Begins even quieter than usual, but the sea is a sparkling blue, the golden weed drifts past, and the lilt of laughter is heard about the clean decks and in the well-kept rigging.

A few porpoise came close (the first we have seen by day on this voyage), a lone whale blows distantly and his spout is in sight for some time; there is a lot of weed; we bend the small bonnet on the fore (and it completely blankets the view ahead and smothers the side lights).

The bonnet seems to pull quite well, and the spritsail pulls as much as it ever did, which is not at all badly. The lookout moves aloft to the foreyard, for now he can see nothing past the deep bonnet from the fo'c'sle head, and we are ready to pull the bonnet off (it comes off very easily) and clew the spritsail up if we need to show our side lights. They burn brightly, but they are reflected only on the after side of the spritsail. We see no shipping. I always have flares ready, anyway, and we keep vigilant lookout. At least, we are very unlikely to encounter another ship which has the same difficulties!

FRIDAY, MAY 24   *Noon: 21.06N. 48.38W.*
Run: 77 miles

Begins with the blue sea flat and almost weedless, the wind gentle in the east, and the weather forecast speaking of gales near Newfoundland where we ought to be. Break out the bonnet for the lateen and set it. There is a lot of weed about at midday, and also a beautiful white frigate bird which we have seen before. This bird rarely approaches the ship. Where it can live I don't know, for we are a thousand miles and more from the nearest land, which is the Windward Isles of the West Indies.

Talk with the mates about how Captain Jones probably handled his *Mayflower,* which could not have been so sluggard to get across the Atlantic in the autumn in sixty-seven days, during several of which she was hove to. And she must have been a very old ship at the time. It is difficult to understand how all the family parties could have been crowded into her, with their stores and food and bits of household equipment with them. They must have bedded down the best way they could, in crowded family groups, all over the wet 'tween-decks, where many of them could never have been properly warm or dry at all. It may be that Jones took the ship across much of the way in the latitude of the Azores and was lucky with his winds. If he did that (which he well could have done), things would have been better. However he went, those Pilgrims were tough citizens!

SATURDAY, MAY 25   *Noon: 21.04N. 50.00W.*

Run: 75 miles

This was once considered the day that the ship should arrive at Plymouth. Instead, we still have 1800 miles to go. The dawn comes with rain and a light north wind shifting to the eastward, and at midmorning a school of beautifully colored dolphin swim close alongside, with their golden tails and magnificent rainbow designs in clear view. One of them, a great bullheaded fellow all red-gold in color, appears to be the head fish. Two others have nasty scars on them, one scar being obviously from the bite of a great fish. How the dolphin survived such a bite, or escaped from the fish close enough to make it, I cannot think.

At noon, without headway in a great surly swell from the north and the golden weed stopped on the sea all round us, with the same "speed" that we have. But by four o'clock we are logging 5½ knots: at sunset it still blows though quieter. Let us have at least a consistent watch, a day, a week!

Later: Our wish is granted, at least in part. For the first time in two weeks we run several watches logging more than twenty miles. Her motion is frightful again and there is a mysterious thump-thump somewhere down below which we cannot trace. It is a considerable thump, as if the rudder was jumping on its pintles (it isn't). It doesn't seem to be the rudder, or the masts. We don't know what it can be after the most careful search and listening down below, but, whatever it is *shouldn't* be and I don't like it.

SUNDAY, MAY 26   *Noon: 20.55N. 52.01W.*
                        Run: 117 miles

Begins well, the northeast wind still with us, though quieter now. In the morning, an unusual number of sea birds about. I count four swooping about together, and one can imagine that such a sight might have cheered Columbus and his crew, though we are still 800 miles from the nearest islands of the Lesser Antilles. Forenoon, the wind drops a lot, with a couple of minor rain showers: by noon, we watch the Sargasso weed again to make sure it is going past. Just what sort of trade wind is this?

This tedium is relieved by speaking the Belgian oil tanker *Belgian Pride*, bound light from Antwerp toward Venezuela—a huge black-and-red, wall-sided thing with towering white upper-works of bridge and after accommodation which stand up higher than any aftercastle on any galleon ever did. She is flying a lot of flags, which are seen to be her signal flags drying: she swings close round our stern and circles us once, and the voice of the captain shouts across that he is dropping a parcel for us, which he did. At once back the mainyard, come up to the wind, out pram with Surgeon Stevens, and recover parcel, which is secured in an old lifebuoy marked *Belgian Pride,* Antwerpen, and an old lifejacket. A screwed-down watertight tin proves to contain a dozen cigars, some packets of cigarettes, thirty-six bars of chocolate, a bottle of Belgian cognac, and a bottle of eau de Cologne. It was a pleasant meeting, and all hands greatly appreciated the present from the sea.

We saw a good many vessels about that time, and many of them hurried out of their way for a better look—the French liner *Colombie,* for instance, which came bounding along, a great stack-surmounted and shapely white hull, one noon, passing very close. She dips, blows on her siren, shouts and signals greetings, steams off, turns and swings back *very* close along our weather side, with shouts and cheers again from her passenger- and crew-crowded decks. She takes the wind out of our sails as she goes past and, swinging ahead of us, seems reluctant to return to her course. The sun was bright and our little ship sailing nicely.

Later the same afternoon, the British fleet tanker *Olna* also passed, bound from Malta towards Venezuela for naval oil—a big black ship with gray upperworks and enormous derricks, and decks full of boats, booms, etc. She slowed down on our quarter and signaled a lot, as is the naval manner, with lights and flags and semaphore: we have no signaling lamp here.

"You look like a beautiful old painting," she signals, almost with envy (for we cannot return the compliment); white uniformed figures on the bridge wave and the crew

break into a burst of British cheers, which is warmly returned as we dip our Red Ensign to his Blue.

The French liner *Antilles,* the fleet tanker *Tide Austral,*
the motor ship *Tennyson* of London were among many
passing ships which greeted us.

So we came to June, still dribbling westwards. Columbus
was by then ahead of our time by two or three days. The
ship just seemed reluctant to come in from sea; or perhaps
the trade winds, not having seen her like for several centuries, were loath to let the little ship go. Well, she was
coming to no harm, although the passage could scarcely be
called adventurous. High on my list was the need to avoid
"adventure" if at all possible, and I had taken all practicable steps to abide by this seamanlike, but perhaps un-
newsworthy, requirement.

CHAPTER

15

GULF STREAM SQUALL

So, in due course, the little ship reached the western turning point of 65 West longitude, 25 North latitude—the last
turning point, where she wheeled on her tracks (more or
less) and stood directly towards her landfall on the Nantucket lightship. So far her passage had been more like
that made by Christopher Columbus than by Christopher
Jones, but the main thing was that we were now on the
American side of the North Atlantic, without accident, with
the ship in first-rate order and all hands in good heart. Even
if some Gulf Stream gale or dirty great squall were to throw
serious trouble at us, at this late stage, at least we could
contrive somehow to get a jury rig up again (if we had to)
and bring the little ship into some port on the proper seaboard. The month was June, and the weather ought to be
reasonable. I meant to swing to the north well inside the

248

island of Bermuda, taking care not to be set to the east-
wards of the Nantucket lightship, in case westing might be
difficult to make again against the Gulf Stream.

The northeast trade wind never had been much good in
all the month or so that we had been sailing in the area
where it was supposed to be found. Now, as we swung towards the north, it was superseded by squalls and calms,
and our progress dropped. There was still an enormous
quantity of weed about: at one time the ship sailed through
about a solid acre of it, and the black shadows of her sails
fell on the golden weed. Time and time again, weed fouled
the rotator of the patent log. In the first night watch of the
forty-second day at sea, squalls of puffy wind and driving
rain alternated with calms and it was difficult to know
where the next squall was coming from, in the dark. The
mates and I kept watch most vigilantly lest the weak masts
be taken by the lee. The ship must make all possible progress, yet keep the masts aboard.

Black clouds rise up to wind'ard and to leeward. Squall
fights squall. Which shall win? Which reaches the ship
first? How shall the sails be trimmed? The aim is always
to keep the wind on the driving side of all the canvas,
naturally, and never to allow it to jump ahead and strike the
sails on the wrong side, for the masts are rigged to accept
stresses only from their sides and behind them. But just
what way may the fresh squall strike the ship? Which of
several competing puffs (or more than puffs), whose presence is shown by the cloud and sea movements, may reach
the ship first? Here the experienced sailing-ship watchkeeping officer is most necessary. He may guess, but it has
to be an informed guess and it had better be right. In bad

conditions a wrong judgment may cause the loss of the ship.

We run this way and that, to keep her going in safety, now bearing away before a vicious puff from the west-southwest, now just avoiding being taken by the lee by another, full of wind and rain—but mostly rain—from the southeast. It is haul up port side of the mains'l, sheet the starboard, around head and spritsail yards, then haul up starboard side, around the yards again, with the white water streaking past upon the black sea in the rain. That is what we want to see! Never mind the price in effort and ceaseless vigilance. We were on the home run now, and landfall was just under a thousand miles away.

My Journal continues the story.

Sunday, June 2   *Noon: 26.00N. 65.33W.*
          Run: 84 miles

Begins squally, as last night, the wind jumping with rain squalls, then blowing fresh for a tantalizing little while before dropping away almost—sometimes quite—to nothing, then to come again swinging from quarter to quarter, frequently with heavy and sometimes blinding rain. But always (and for this the Lord be praised) the squalls come from some point in the south, from southeast to southwest; and every mile we are able to sail her through the water is another mile towards her destination. Compared with what this voyage might have been, we have no complaint whatever.

Save some rain water, the mariners bathing and washing clothes industriously. They are the cleanest lot of mariners I ever saw, and their high standards would have amazed Captain Jones' crew. To them, even a piece of decent soap was a luxury. Here we have it by the case, and detergents as well.

MONDAY, JUNE 3   *Noon: 27.36N. 66.51W.*

Run: 120 miles

Begins handsomely, a good breeze from east-southeast blowing constantly since midnight, logging six and a half knots after daybreak. Make the main bonnet ready to bend, but we cannot bend it without hauling up the mains'l, which is our main driving sail. Therefore do not haul the main up, for the foresail is a very small sail. The lateen has its bonnet set, the fores'l has its bonnet and its stuns'l, and we do our best. The sun shines brightly, the golden weed (frequently in large and numerous pieces) bounces in the somewhat confused but never high sea, the mariners get on with cleaning and scraping and polishing, and we bowl along merrily with the good wind well abaft the starboard beam, making a course to pass some 150 miles to the west'ard of Bermuda.

A U.S. Navy flying boat, a heavy twin-engined monoplane with retracted wing floats and a high, single fin on which the large tail plane is mounted, flies round us for about an hour, apparently taking photographs, and then makes off in good time to be back in daylight wherever it was going—maybe Bermuda, or some mainland U.S. base. It is good to be in U.S.N. care this way, but the aircraft was such an ugly, noisy thing that all hands were quickly bored with it and (except for our jet pilot) wished it would go away. It made a large number of very close passes, and was sometimes signaling with some sort of lamp, as if it were using us for practice bombing runs.

We are threatened with visits from two more flying boats tomorrow, one from Bermuda, with photographers, the other said to intend a landing. If he does put down near us, it is to be hoped that he has his own boat.

Going well all day and to midnight, the new and growing moon making the first night watch beautiful. We are very fortunate to be slipping through the Horse Latitudes like this.

Tuesday, June 4   *Noon: 29.35N. 67.54W.*

Run: 131 miles

Begins well with easterly wind, sometimes southeast and a little uncertain, with the wind dropping in the early morning watch and the backwind of a bit of a squall in the forenoon. But the glass is high, the weather near perfect, the sea generally flecked with at least a few whitecaps, and the ship slipping along at from four to six knots under all sail that can be set, including the main bonnet. This fills the decks and completely obscures the for'ard view, but it pulls well and she can wear it—at least in this fine weather. It must come in if we are to see our way across steamer lanes, or anyone is to see our lights at all.

Another flying boat approaches us midmorning and circles us at about 200 feet for the best part of an hour, sundry assorted photographers peering from an open doorway in the fuselage, industriously clicking cameras, which they do with such absorption that they do not appear ever to look at the ship herself. Yet another flying boat drops a canister containing a copy of yesterday's *New York Times* and a couple of news magazines, all of which make depressing reading. Had to back the mainyard and put out Beric Watson in the pram to recover the canister, and lost half an hour—meantime the southeast wind steadily dropping. All hands except Sub-Lieutenant Winslow of the Fleet Air Arm agree that three large aircraft are too many. None tries to land—too much sea. An oil tanker passes, southbound (the *Oilfield* from New York towards Venezuela), while we are hove-to and salutes the ship, which we return.

At sunset we still go along with a fair wind, but with patience-consuming slowness. The main bonnet pulls pretty well.

At night, still going very quietly. But we *go*, and that's the thing.

WEDNESDAY, JUNE 5   *Noon: 31.00N. 68.29W.*
Run: 91 miles

Begins quietly, with gentle southeast wind and the ship slipping along at three or three and a half knots under every sail we can set, including all the bonnets; the sea flat, the night clear, the conditions excellent. About 2:30 A.M. sight the lights of two warships; at first light, about 4 A.M., make them out to be two light cruisers, not American; at 5 A.M. they form station on us, one at either quarter; at 6 A.M., having manned ship, they dash splendidly ahead and pass us, one on either beam, cheering us resoundingly in the proper naval manner as they rush by. They are the Italian cruisers *San Giorgio* and *San Marco,* bound towards the Jamestown festival in Virginia—a splendid pair of well-kept and well-run ships. We dip our ensign—rarely is the old Red Ensign so honored!—and cheer lustily in return: the *San Giorgio* drops a boat, very smartly; a commander comes aboard with photographers, signalmen, etc., and presents of fruit and wine and a letter from his admiral, and a miniature standard from the cruiser. He is full of felicitations and enthusiasm, throwing his arms wide open as his boat approached and shouting his delight—"Magnificent! She is magnificent!"—a very nice fellow. He soon returns to his ship, which then passes us ahead *very* close, as if reluctant to pass us at all.

The *San Marco* boat comes with presents of more fruit and wine—splendid. Then they steam past again, and are off towards the horizon and the rendezvous in Virginia. It was a splendid gesture. The commander had served in the Italian naval school ships *Amerigo Vespucci* and *Cristoforo Colombo,* full-rigged ships.

Long before the Italians are gone, another flotilla of warships shows up and alters course towards us. These prove to be the U.S.S. *Ault* and three consorts, large destroyers, come by order from Washington for the *Life* pictures and story. The *Life* writer, M̃aitland Edey, is a fine fellow and has been a most useful crewman aboard here.

We cheer the *Ault* and then, in a gathering rain squall which breaks with very heavy rain and the ship scudding at her best speed, foaming along, the four U.S. destroyers man ship and race by in line—a magnificent sight in the black rain and spume. Out of the rain comes a brave south-southwest wind, which stays with us all day, freshening, and we bound along, at last logging watch after watch of more than twenty miles.

At night, squally: but the wind continues south-southwest and the Bermuda Race veterans aboard say that this is the settled June wind.

THURSDAY, JUNE 6   *Noon: 33.20N. 69.36W.*

Run: 152 miles

A Gulf Stream day, though by all the books we ought not to be in the Gulf Stream area yet—a night and early morning of good sailing before a fresh south-southwest wind develops into a midmorning of hard squalls with rain and thunder, culminating in a snorter which puts her over, a driving rain squall of nearly gale force, which fortunately eases very quickly. The two tops'ls come in at once. She was logging 7   knots before the hard squall, but what speed she touched just then we will never know. She logged only 30 for the four-hour watch and 152 for the day, but whether she made much more than this cannot be said, for the heaviest rain and wind came at noon and lasted forty minutes, so there were no reliable noon observations. It has been overcast, squally, bumpy, humid, and frequently raining, throughout the day, with often a squall coming up and the wind jumping ahead, sometimes to northwest, then dropping, but always going back to south-southwest, southwest, and west-southwest again, for which the Lord be praised. We must be very little over 400 miles from our landfall at the Nantucket lightship at noon—a very few days of tolerable and accident-free sailing should bring us there.

The boys very good aloft and on deck this morning, but some still not too good at the wheel. Either a fellow has the knack of steering a sailing ship, or he has not.

Unbend the main bonnet, which blinds the quarter-deck like the side of a circus tent, and send it below. Send down the studding-sail gear on the fore.

In the very heavy rain this morning, posted a lookout on the foreyard and have the foghorn going. But we sight no ships.

All day going along splendidly sometimes logging 7½, and the Gulf Stream seems to be with us. Water temperature 76°.

At night a very trying motion, with the ship most uncomfortable.

Spoken by a B.O.A.C. airliner this afternoon, flying high towards New York. Dipped to him in salute.

Radiogram from London seeking to arrange a rendezvous with newspapermen off Bermuda, which we are already well past, and from one of the reception committees in Plymouth, asking to be told the precise hour of our arrival off Provincetown. No sailor and no sailing ship can be sufficiently in the Divine confidence to make such predictions! We shall be there when we arrive, and to "predict" anything is to mislead. No answer. (As for that, we simply haven't, and don't want, the electric capacity to use our radio much. It was intended for emergencies.)

FRIDAY, JUNE 7   *Noon: 35.50N. 69.44W.*
               Run: 149 miles

After the most rolling, jumping, utterly unrhythmic pitching and jerking and altogether motion-filled night—the worst even of this voyage—there is less wind in the morning, and we give her back all sail. The Gulf Stream sea throwing itself about in a spiteful and turbulent manner as if bored and fretful with the heat and the humidity, and the endlessness of its Europe-warming mission. The ship logging about six knots, the work proceeding.

About 9 A.M. a Royal Naval single-engined aircraft, identified by S/Lieut. Winslow as a "Night Raider" from the *Ark Royal*, flies round and stays with us some time. Sure enough, the *Ark Royal* herself shows up about an hour later, looking (to us) better in the distance than close to, accompanied by two very dashing Daring class vessels which the aforesaid S/Lieut. identifies as the *Diamond* and *Duchess*. These close us, coming very close, the *Diamond* leading, with a signal of greetings, and the ratings shouting across chitchat to our mariners. The *Ark Royal* flies off two extremely noisy helicopters, and passes close along our weather side, giving me an anxious moment. She towers above us and passes like the walls of Ancient Rome, and her decks are crowded with ratings who run about the flight deck to get a better view. Our S/Lieut., changed into naval uniform above the waist, is recognized by some of his squadron mates who are in the *Ark Royal*; and the *Ark*, with destroyers, makes a circle round us, while we dip to them and they reply. It is good to see them: they looked well, particularly the shapely hulled destroyers at speed around us. They tear off at length towards the western horizon, the spray and spume flying over the destroyers' bridges.

Afterwards, a typical Gulf Stream day—changeable, humid, trying, with the sea very lumpy and some of the people seasick who have not been so for six weeks and thought they were long over it.

I asked the *Ark Royal* for a position check, which he kindly gave us. Never having relied on our cross-staff and traverse board, our second mate's position is the same within a mile or two.

We are told by South Chatham Radio that an airship will visit us tomorrow, and the wireless operator has managed to repair our radio telephone, which is to be regretted. Somebody in Brooklyn, staging something, wants to know what film star the crew would most like to meet? Answer: none, which disposes of that matter.

SATURDAY, JUNE 8   *Noon: 37.05N. 69.45W.*
Run: 76 miles

Begins lumpy, confused, hazy, humid, after a wild middle watch with the wind jumping to northwest, then north-northwest and north, and the two tops'ls lowered in their gear but not furled. Some of the squalls were hard. The ship heading off east-northeast somewhere, on the port tack, which course is useless for progress: the wind drops and she bounces, jumping in the irksome and ill-tempered sea, with about as much for'ard way as a seesaw. At 7A.M. wear ship to the westwards, with the watch, keeping the ship under the courses. It is better to head west across the Gulf Stream, with the set on the ship's lee bow, than to sail to the northeast getting nowhere. Set the tops'ls again, the wind settling in the east and the glass (which has been low these past several days) at last rising. She comes up to the nor'rard well on the new tack, the wind going to east-northeast.

But early afternoon the wind freshens, in strong squalls. At 3 P.M., in a fresh squall, take in the fore and main tops'ls again and unbend and stow away the lateen bonnet, which was too much for her. The sea rising with the wind, and the ship jumping. Sea still rises, and wind (sea 76° F. with a great deal of Gulf weed about): rain squalls come, blinding, and stay. Post lookouts, start the foghorn. Take in the lateen, leaving the ship under the bonetless courses and the spritsail. What next may I do if the wind increases? Lie a'hull, as the old ships did? With bare poles and the helm down, hove-to virtually under the windage of the big aftercastle? It would be interesting to try that in a gale, just once, to see if it works.

The gale comes and I do try it, and it does work. In the last of the sullen, oddly colored daylight, squalls to gale strength, with a high beam sea and the ship laboring heavily, call out all hands. Port watch clew up sprits'l and have a lot of trouble, the bowsprit waving like a fishing rod with the thrashing of the sail. Adrian Small, Joe Lacey, Beric Watson, and Andy Lindsay take their lives in their hands out there.

The trouble is that unsupported bowsprit. The only way to give the stick adequate support would be to carry a heavy stay from it in to the cutwater, but to do that would mean that no sail could be set there at all. Therefore it must take its chance, and I remember that, after all, a good many thousand vessels must have found themselves in the same state down the centuries, and lived through many a gale of wind. Our spritsail is a big sail and the yard which carried it is big, too. There are only two buntlines on the thing, to smother the canvas a bit as it is bunted up to the yard, and the yard, the sail, and the whole of the bowsprit work and jump most alarmingly. It looks a pretty dangerous place to go, struggling almost uphill up the steep steeve of the waving bowsprit to fight a way on to the rolling, pitching, gyrating yard, with all the sea boiling furiously with anger under the bows, almost like a personal anger, as if it were eager to get at the lads working so close to it there and was flinging itself about in angry frustration until it did get them. The mate had life jackets on the boys, in case the bowsprit went and they all fetched up in the sea. What could I do for them then? What use are life jackets? The ship would run over them, with her bluff bows, and keelhaul them without the small advantage of a line to pull the bodies back inboard, and they would rise again far back in the long boiling wake, perhaps a cable astern or more—if they rose again at all. How could I get them back then?

Hurriedly I considered the problem. One must be prepared. The best thing I could do would be to fling out an inflatable life raft, (always ready), getting all way off the ship at once, and hope to pick them up again in the night or in the first light of the morning. It is dark when they finish. I am mighty thankful, and relieved, to see them come in again, wet through, smiling, and delighted with their work and the exultation of a difficult job well and quickly done.

The other two watches haul up the mains'l, then all hands to the fores'l. No sail gives the slightest trouble, except the sprits'l. This Elizabethan gear is good and does its work well. The canvas in, the helm lashed down, a little heavy oil going out very slowly to wind'ard, lifelines rigged, she lies splendidly in the sea, though at times she is still excessively lively. Even Felix the kitten cannot find a place to sleep. She is dry and safe, and we have 200 miles of sea room. The north-setting Gulf Stream should offset the lee drift, for the Stream's direction should be on our lee bow, holding us up.

All hands delighted with the way she lay to. It was quiet and peaceful in the great cabin.

"I never felt so safe in a ship in a gale of wind before," said the mate.

I had hoped to lie a'hull only an hour or so, but at midnight I am still hove-to and it is blowing furiously, with heavier rain squalls than ever.

The crew were splendid, as always. Everyone seemed really to enjoy the hard work of fighting the wet canvas on the reeling yards, with the sea jumping wildly.

SUNDAY, JUNE 9 *Noon: 38.26N. 70.05W.*

Run: 83 miles (130 to landfall)

Get under way again shortly after daylight, the wind still hard east-northeast, after lying a'hull and in perfect safety through the night. At 0500 set fores'l, at 0700 the mains'l, at 1100 the spritsail, having first rove a spilling line round that recalcitrant sail to tame it a little next time we have to take it in. Set the lateen at the same time, having previously tried the fores'l with the lateen, which was good balance, but the setting of the mains'l appeared to upset this. By early afternoon, both tops'ls on her again, and she logs about five knots. The observations, made in bright clear sunshine with a fresh east wind, show that the Gulf Stream current just about offset the ship's drift while hove to, and she was set about fifteen miles to the north as well. Which is very good.

At noon we have 130 miles to go to the Nantucket lightship and hope to see her some time tomorrow, but we are a little west of the landfall now and must rely on the Gulf Stream to put that to rights, for the wind will not permit us.

At 10 A.M. the usual Sunday prayers, and thanked the mariners for their good work yesterday.

Drying out the effects of yesterday's and the night's bit of a storm, for the cabins and everything became extremely wet. I lost stuff through leakage both from driven rain and sea which had managed to survive the rest of the voyage, and the cabin which the second and third mates share was awash (though it ought not to have been, for no weight of sea came aboard—almost no sea at all.)

Mate preparing anchor and cables. We have never anchored this ship, so great was the haste to get away. We had buoys in Brixham, Dartmouth, and Plymouth. The historically correct anchors are very heavy, and the windlass cumbersome.

An astonishing school of well-organized porpoises came near

the ship once, apparently engaged in a fish roundup. They formed a circle and many jumped high out of the sea, perhaps driving in stragglers among their prey fish. And there were more Mother Carey's chickens hovering about the ship than I have ever seen before in one place together—a hundred or so, all fluttering about and patting the water with their tiny feet. They rarely seem to land on the sea at all, strange little birds.

Going along well in the evening, but the wind is east-northeast and we cannot make the course directly towards the Nantucket lightship, nor do we know what the Gulf Stream is doing with us. We are still in the stream water, for the temperatures tell us that: but which way is it setting us?

The fine new tanker *Border Sentinel* comes out of her way to salute us.

MONDAY, JUNE 10   *Noon: 40.05N. 70.50W.*
Run: 106 miles

Fifty-one days out, and a disappointing day again. We are able to sail on our course only for a few hours in the morning but when we hope to see the Nantucket lightship, we see only some swordfishermen out of New Bedford. These close us, with five men strung on their masts looking for fish. One tells us that we are still sixty-five miles from the Nantucket lightship. Sixty-five miles! And mostly to the west'ard, with a northeast wind! There is no coming in today, then.

It falls calm and we loll about: a fog bank disperses before reaching us, which is something to be grateful for: aircraft fly about and one drops parcels which prove to contain canned beer and sundry messages. Later another drops something in the water just ahead but we miss that and, remembering the beer (which we did not particularly want), did not bother much. But that aircraft—a twin-engined private machine—came back again and again with someone waving quite a lot, but always up-sun and unrecognizable. Joe Meany thought it was his mother. Finally this aircraft went off towards New England.

Try to keep those interested ashore (who appear to be legion) informed of our lack of progress. Had we not been set to the west in that gale, we would have made our landfall, as hoped, quite well this morning—which is a little disappointing.

Spoken by a New Bedford dragger which passes across a sack of the most remarkable and enormous crayfish, much appreciated. In the evening a small power launch speaks the ship, with a couple of newspapermen aboard who want to talk to Joe Meany. They don't get much out of him.

A beautiful clear moonlit night, but not much progress. The ship slips along at perhaps a couple of knots, heading towards the Nantucket lightship, with a very quiet south wind.

And so ends.

TUESDAY, JUNE 11   *Noon: Off the Nantucket Lightship*
                    Run: 70 miles

Begins with the great liner *Queen Elizabeth* coming with the dawn from one direction and the U.S. Coast Guard training bark *Eagle* under full sail from the other. The roar of the giant Cunarder's welcoming siren must have astonished her passengers at five in the morning, and the sound of our cheering crew must have surprised them too, if they could hear it. The *Eagle* sailed very closely on our quarter, and I talked to Captain Karl Zittei, getting a bearing and distance on the Nantucket lightship. The *Eagle* looked splendid and it was grand to see her.

Soon afterwards the sky is filled with U.S. Navy blimps, jet aircraft in formation, great Super-Constellations singly and in pairs, and all kinds of aircraft until the air so full of noise that orders could not be heard aboard. Just at noon, rounded the

Nantucket light vessel at last and hauled up for Cape Cod, going well on the port tack with a southwest breeze. All afternoon the welcome and the good progress continue. Two U.S.C.G. cutters escort us, shipping and aircraft salute us; the sun shines and the sea flattens; in the evening under a full moon the ship, as if proud of herself and showing off, races on towards Cape Cod. And everyone, in a way, is sorry, because the sailors know that this may well be her last night as a real, living ship, a proper sailing ship in full commission with a good crew: she will arrive to become a wooden static thing, unmanned except by warders and girls in Pilgrim costume showing tourists round, and it will soon become incredible that she ever sailed.

The mate's fifty-eighth birthday: the watches sang him greetings at midnight, to his surprised delight. Singing for the mate! I never heard the like. But these cheerful fellows sing before breakfast. They are a grand crew.

WEDNESDAY, JUNE 12

Sailing with a freshening west-southwest wind and averaging 7.7 knots all night, in flat water, the U.S.C.G. tug *Yankton* accompanying.

At 0600 abeam Cape Cod, and the passage done.

CHAPTER

16

TUMULTUOUS WELCOME

I WAS offered, and accepted, a tow from abeam of Cape Cod lighthouse into the sheltered harbor of Provincetown, for the wind was ahead and the weather boisterous. For the crew's part, we all hated the idea of having to accept a tow when within sight of our destination, but the ship might have beat about there for days and the various reception committees were becoming impatient. For this we could not blame them. They had been waiting some time, the grandstands had been ready at Plymouth for weeks, and it would be maddening to keep the ship beating outside their port almost in their sight. For all practical purposes, the westwards passage was completed with landfall, anyway. We had then been directed to enter the ship at Provincetown, for the place had been especially opened in that capacity in the new *Mayflower's* honor, and the idea was that we would continue thence to Plymouth after the minimum delay. It was just across Cape Cod Bay.

The actual elapsed time from off Plymouth, Devon, to abeam of the Nantucket lightship was fifty-one days, and the navigational records showed that the ship had made 5,420 miles. This was not at all bad going. We might well have been fifty-one days, or sixty-one, on the northern passage, and no one could say that any time was really lost by sailing the southern way. It could, more likely, have been gained. Strangely enough, the average rate of advance over each twenty-four hours worked out at practically the same rate which most modern large sailing ships managed, right to the end of the sailing era. The *Mayflower's* daily average was 106 miles, the same as the ship *Joseph Conrad's* on a passage from Tahiti towards New York in 1936, and the *Joseph Conrad* was built in 1882. Most of the big grain ships averaged about that speed under sail, too, over their round-the-world voyagings. It is odd to reflect that, for all the Christmas-card appearance of the 1620 ship (to say nothing of the pessimism of so many of her critics) she did as well as latter-day vessels, although some of them were capable of bursts of twice her speed. Perhaps we were lucky, though we had certainly not gained much from the indifferent trade winds.

I do not think the explanation is luck at all. It is far more probable that we had underrated the Elizabethans. This new *Mayflower* had shown herself to be essentially a handy little bark, despite the odd leads of much of her rigging and the too shallow mast-doublings, and so forth. She sailed well for her size, and she handled well. It could be, too, that I may have underrated the capacity of her apparently slender spars to stay with her. They had survived the Gulf Stream storm all right, without a trace of damage. They had indeed survived the whole voyage (except for that one broken fore-topsail yard) without any adverse effect at all. I had nursed them a bit, but I remembered old sailors, when first I went to sea, speaking of their preference for wooden ships of what they called the real days of sailing ships, with wooden spars and hempen rigging. Such ships, they used to say, came to life in the sea in a way that no iron wire-rigged sailing ship ever did or could, with the rigidity of her hull of iron and her masts of steel, and as much of her rigging as possible of the same materials. I don't know. Brought up in the iron and steel ships, I trusted them, and I liked the feeling of constancy and strength against the sea that their strong hulls and stout rigging gave. The only wooden sailer I had ever been in before was the schooner *Hawk*, and she was a little witch. It was the gyrations of the *Mayflower's* sticks which bothered me, and her stiffness, of course, had made this problem worse by imposing such a violent motion on her.

Well, there she was at any rate, all in one piece and looking splendid, and my reflections on her behavior and how much better a few things might have been, were cut short by her arrival at a special buoy in Provincetown harbor. As soon as she was secured a horde of officials came aboard, most of whom had come down especially from Boston or across from Plymouth to clear her in—a formality of importance to all ships arriving from foreign. Our welcome was terrific, colossal, magnificent! Ever since speaking the beautiful *Queen Elizabeth* off the Nantucket lightship ours had been almost a triumphal progress. Little fishermen and great liners, oil tankers, tramps, ships, vessels and craft of all sorts, air-borne and sea-borne, came out of their way to exchange salutations, dipping their ensigns and blowing on their sirens if they were ships, flying past us at the dip if they were big aircraft, whizzing about to what seemed the peril of whoever might have been aboard them if they were small. Soon the photographers came by airship and four-engined transport aircraft, and the air was full of the sound of powerful engines. As we approached Provincetown the sea was filled with yachts and fishermen who shouted their greetings in Portuguese as often as in American. Though the gale-warning flags were flying, all manner of small craft came out—not only small, for among them was the Norwegian full-rigged ship *Christian Radich,* which came storming by, a cloud of lovely wind-filled canvas listing her lovely hull.

In Provincetown itself it took an hour or more to secure to the buoy, so many craft were milling there in welcome, and at last the Coast Guard had to bring a fleet of fast and powerful launches to clear a way for us. The medical officer who came aboard to clear the ship began his duties by giving us a stirring speech of welcome which he delivered right there on the quarter-deck, while the customs and the immigration men all waited, listening, with another large launch full of elderly gentlemen in Pilgrim costume come to offer more speeches and to stage some reenactment of the signing of the *Mayflower* compact aboard.

Soon, when the medical director was done, the quarter-deck, the little poop, and the whole main deck became a milling crowd of welcoming officials and committee members from Provincetown's Mayflower II Reception Committee, while a much larger launch full of pressmen and women circled the scene, being kept off by the Coast Guard until the formalities were completed. *Mayflower* or no *Mayflower*, this was a foreign ship arriving at an American port, and the formalities must be complied with. In truth, the ship might have been carrying a cargo of hashish and manned by a crew of Communist agents, and she would have been cheerfully accepted by the officials just then. They danced about, peering here and peeking there, like schoolboys to whom a great story of history had suddenly, somehow, come to life, and it thrilled them to the bone. Many had their cameras with them, and they made pictures everywhere while carrying out their duties. The ship was entered in record time and with delightful simplicity and cooperation, which I could not help wishing might be applied in other ports all round the world.

The genuine pleasure of these good New Englanders and their very real and tremendous delight in seeing the little ship come in, were rather moving to us, just in from sea. Of course, struck by the ship's extraordinary smallness, they imagined the voyage to have been one of great hardship and risk, neither of which it had been at all, and when I had a moment, I reminded the crew that they must not permit themselves to be swept off their feet by all this (and the lovely girls waving to them from all manner of craft, on all sides), for in truth the welcome was for the symbol, not us. We had served the symbol and the service was our true reward. For a moment, I feared that the spontaneous and tumultuous enthusiasm all round us might go even to the heads of my good crew, for the test of character was considerable and was to go on for some time.

I really need not have worried. They were all right then, too, as they had been all right at sea. Their mail was aboard, by the sack, and telegraph boys were bringing telegrams and cables by the carton. I had not even time to glance at them. When I had, I saw that many were from exalted persons, including Presidents and Prime Ministers, which surprised me. There was a welcome arranged at Plymouth which would last ten days, a very nice man from Chicago who was president of the Society of Mayflower Descendants was telling me, while a Western Union boy shoved another hundred or so telegrams in my hands, and the kindly Mayor of Provincetown outlined his arrangements. For the first time, I could see how those 105 Pilgrim passengers had fitted in the vessel, for we had a hundred or so humans crowded on the quarter-deck alone, and more jumping over the bulwarks in the waist, despite the guard which the efficient Coast Guard had put there.

It was all most sincere and wonderful. It was moving and it was unique. But we had not come in from sea in fifty-odd days by getting a sufficiency of sleep, and the last nights towards landfall are rough in any vessel. When was I going to get some rest, or even some time to read through all those telegrams? They were not for me: they were the ship's. But I would have to answer them. In the meantime, another official was already giving a warm and heartfelt speech preparatory to presenting the ship with a citation, a septuagenarian dressed as a Pilgrim Father was leading the signing of the Mayflower Compact (I suppose) on the Elizabethan binnacle, a Senator from Washington was pressing an invitation to the ship to open the St. Lawrence Seaway, and another man was demanding that I go forthwith to New York (in a chartered aircraft which he had somewhere nearby) to appear that evening as his "mystery guest" in some television program which he declared was of the utmost importance. I would not, for many reasons, the least of which was that I expected to be on the way towards Plymouth before nightfall.

There was some slight hiatus about the press, which was unfortunate. The fact of the matter all along had been that it was Plimoth Plantation, in Plymouth, Massachusetts, which was going to receive the ship and to look after her, in perpetuity. To do this properly, a considerable sum had to be raised, and the Plantation organizers had undertaken an expensive campaign. To help with this, it was considered to be essential that the news stories of the *Mayflower's* arrival should emanate first from Plymouth and not from Provincetown, for obvious reasons. The little ship meant national headlines, and the dateline from Provincetown would bring no publicity to Plimoth Plantation. (She got the national headlines all right. One great Boston daily splashed its front page next morning with the simple statement SHE'S HERE!, in black letters two and a half inches high, assuming that automatically every citizen would know what "she" was meant.)

But, whatever the well-meaning dignitaries of Plimoth Plantation might wish, there was the ship right there in Provincetown under the noses of several hundred pressmen and presswomen, many of them with nationally known names. They had already been waiting for some days, they knew that *Life* magazine would be on the newsstands that very day with an exclusive account of the voyage written by a correspondent who had been aboard and was, indeed, still there, and their editors were insistent and forceful in their demands for news.

So the laudable purpose of Plimoth Plantation came to nought, and the pressmen came aboard, a few of them—very few—glowering about an "iron curtain" round the ship and wanting to know who was selling the story? No one was doing that. Bereft of first blood on the real news of the voyage, such as it was, many of them made a bee-line for Joe Meany, the American boy who had been built up as the only American aboard (there were in fact five, including the *Life* representatives), and based their stories on him. They were all most friendly to the ship and her enterprise, despite their chagrin over the news "beat," and the press coverage next morning was such as never had been accorded a Red Ensign ship before in all history. The freshly arrived *Mayflower* appealed to the American nation as a good-will gesture and as adventure too, and there was no doubt of that.

And then we sailed across Cape Cod Bay to the glorious welcome at Plymouth. If the welcome at Provincetown was wonderful, that at Plymouth was indescribable. None of us had seen so great or voluminous a crowd of vessels—some full of enormous TV cameras, some full of pressmen, but mostly full just with industrious and extremely happy members of the general public, who shouted their congratulations and their delight that at last the promised replica of their wonderful *Mayflower* had safely arrived and was sailing into their port. With Pilot Kendall Holmes' advice, I took a tow along the narrow and rather tortuous channel that leads to the special buoy off the Pilgrims' landing place, which had been dredged out for the ship. The little tow-

boat was so excited that he forgot we had a spritsail-yard
(for which he was hardly to be blamed) and the top of his
mast became mixed up with our anachronistic headgear in
a horrible fashion. Even assailed in this manner, the headgear all stood, and the towboat came out of the encounter
worse than we did. The towboat extricated herself and we
came along in, slowly securing to the buoy almost within
a biscuit's throw of the canopied Plymouth Rock. A shallop of the same period as our ship, especially planned and
built and now manned by mariners in the same Elizabethan
dress as our crew, took our lines and helped us to secure,
and the populace roared its delight.

Then came the landing. It was a hot and dusty day but
the crowds were enormous, and they stayed like that for the
following ten days, during which my wife and I had pre-
cious little time to sleep or eat. The Vice President came
from Washington, a tribe of Red Indians came from Oklahoma (and gave us certificates declaring us to be chiefs of
their tribe), everybody came, notably school children by
the score of thousand. There were parades, receptions, din-
ners, lunches, engagements of all sorts. The mail was impossible, though we had some welcome help and I had a
rule that I must answer at least twelve of the most important letters before breakfast. What use were twelve
when a fresh hundred came? The result was that I got no
breakfast, for then the telephone would start to ring and
it never stopped. There were television programs, radio
programs, sports fixtures, visits to ceremonies and functions
at Boston and all sorts of places, with never a quiet moment. Plymouth staged Indians' Day, New England Day,
Scouts' Day, Unloading Day (to receive the treasure chests

out of the hold), and a joint religious festival of thanksgiving on the first Sunday. There were functions all day and a pageant half the night, and it was all sincere and wonderful.

It was also extremely tiring, for the crew never did get the chance to catch up on sea-lost sleep. My valiant wife (who flew over from Oxford) and I had a dreadful taste of what it must be like really to be persons thought of importance in this publicity-crazed world, and how essential it is, for very sanity, that such persons be surrounded by at least some protection. We had no protection and we had no staff. We were however surrounded by a host of splendid friends, and that was much more important. Everyone was our friend, and that was delightful. We could accept the wild rush.

Plymouth was not ready with a permanent berth for the ship, for the simple reason that Plimoth Plantation's fundraising campaign was just getting into its stride (their need was a million dollars), and Plymouth itself can be an unsafe harbor for ships. It was therefore considered necessary to go elsewhere, if only briefly, and the ship was invited by Mayor Robert Wagner of New York to be an attraction at New York's Summer Festival. I was unaware that the city had a summer festival, always having avoided the place in the hot season and regarding Manhattan more or less as a business center, and little else. I was quite wrong, for New York is a great tourist attraction, one of the sights not only of America but of the modern world, and over a million Americans alone visit each summer in appreciation of that fact. Therefore it was a good place for America to see the new *Mayflower,* and she was towed through the Cape Cod Canal and down Long Island Sound, stopping at Newport, Rhode Island (more functions), and the King's Point Merchant Marine Academy overnight. Many of my sailors had left by then, perforce to get on with their share of the world's work, and some King's Point cadets were helping aboard.

In New York there was the traditional harbor welcome, on July 1, and the ship suffered the indignity of being taken aback in the confused draft caused by a hovering helicopter, which took station off her quarter and stayed there too long. Sailing ships can make effective use only of one wind at a time, and two were too many. It was an awkward moment while we struggled to get control of the ship again, for the wind was strong and the channel crowded with tugs and sightseeing vessels and craft of all descriptions. The aerial display, the fire-fighting craft, and hooting ferries made so much cheerful bedlam that it was extremely difficult to make an order heard aboard. However, we did get control back again, somewhere off the Statue of Liberty, and tremendously enjoyed the whole experience.

Almost as soon as we had landed there was a ticker-tape parade up Broadway, with the remaining crew members marching on foot, dressed in their Elizabethan clothes and Scotty Anderson Bell carrying Felix the cat, who thought so little of the proceedings that he had to be restrained or he would have deserted ship forthwith (Felix found a good home with Joe Meany at Waltham, Massachusetts, where he proceeded in due course to found a new line of feline *Mayflower* descendants.) My wife and I shared the luxury of an ultra-large car with Admiral Gordon McLintock of the King's Point Academy and Jim O'Brien, the city's official greeter, both of whom were old friends of mine. At the City

Hall, after appropriate speeches, the Mayor gave all hands citations from himself to commemorate the voyage, and somebody mentioned that it was about time the *Mayflower* came to Manhattan, for Captain Jones' original charter had been to take her there. Instead, he had double-crossed the Pilgrims and gone to New England.

Be that as it may, there was no doubt about the warmth and sincerity of New York's welcome. The ship was berthed at a convenient pier belonging to the Hudson River Day Line, in midtown Manhattan, hard by the Cunard piers where all the great liners berth from Europe. There she stayed through the summer months, and was thronged with visitors from every state in the Union, even a few from Virginia. The British crew left, excepting a handful of professional sailors who cared for her rigging through the hot months, and the intention was that the ship should go from New York to Plymouth to be handed over permanently there to Plimoth Plantation, on Thanksgiving Day, free of debts, to be their pride and joy for ever.

Handed over she was, according to promise, though not free of debt and not then to stay in Plymouth, for she had to go on tour. The Stars and Stripes flew from the peak, looking oddly different to us who had become accustomed to the Red Ensign there. The tangled skein of her finances was far from unraveled. She would have to go to Miami and other places on a money-raising cruise—perhaps to the Great Lakes. The public trust never had been formed, and I had seen no published accounts of the London enterprise. Some facts seemed to be sufficiently obvious. The ship had cost considerably more than the London promoters had for-seen, and the foregoing of revenues from further exhibition of the vessel at great British ports was a serious loss to them.

Had she been allowed to say in Britain another twelve-month, she certainly would have cleared all her costs. There were many of us, on both sides of the Atlantic, who regretted very much that this had not been done. A vast amount of work went into straightening things out, and there was some criticism. However, it is to be remembered that, but for Mr. Charlton and his supporters, there would still be some oak trees growing at beauty spots in Devon, but there would be no *Mayflower II.* Considering some aspects of the matter and the trouble they were put to, some people might prefer the oaks, but after all, the promoters did what they set out to do. Whatever may be said, they are not the first to fail to raise the full sum required for their enterprise.

This was the over-all view taken by Plimoth Plantation. I quote from the Annual Report to members issued by the Plantation for the year 1957:

Mayflower II was turned over to Plimoth Plantation in Plymouth, Mass., at Thanksgiving, by Project Mayflower, London, the builders of the ship. . . . The ceremony was televised on Dave Garroway's program. It was a brilliant, cold, sparkling day. The ship, moored in an almost flat calm near the Rock, was a beautiful sight in the early morning sunlight.

Although *Mayflower II* was supposed to be turned over to Plimoth Plantation free and clear, Project Mayflower found itself unable to carry out the commitment. The principal reasons were that:

1. The vessel cost almost twice the amount originally esti-

mated, so that the fund-raising schedule adopted at the beginning proved nowhere near adequate. Actually Project Mayflower raised about the sum initially budgeted.

2. Construction was not finished until just before the scheduled sailing date so that plans to raise further monies through exhibits of the ship in English ports had to be cancelled.

However, debts or not, Plimoth Plantation is now the proud possessor of a beautiful ship, built to our own specifications from designs of our own naval architect, William A. Baker. It could not possibly be replaced for less than $300,000.

There it is—historical accuracy to the last. After all, the first Pilgrim Fathers were in debt to their promoters in London for many years, after the arrival of the ship in America—though perhaps in a different way. Their *Mayflower* was a valiant little bark which delivered them safely, and the debts were no fault of hers. We of the crew could all reflect that our new *Mayflower* had also shown herself a valiant bark. We had delivered her in good faith, by God's grace, and the crew owed no one anything. We had done our best, and the ship we sailed was welcomed and accepted in good faith, and spendidly.

This is what mattered, and the symbol of the ship will abide.

CHAPTER

17

A SHIP TO SAIL?

WHATEVER else she might have been, for me the *Mayflower* was a ship to sail, and interesting, but I hoped that no one would regard her voyage as my swan song. Yet where was there another ship to sail, an ocean-going square-rigged ship, large or small, to keep the ancient skill of such sea-faring alive? It was odd, indeed, that at fifty-five years of age I should be among the last exponents of it, at the end of so long and illustrious a line. Perhaps it was time for it to die.

Perhaps, indeed. The terrible loss of the German four-masted bark *Pamir* was no help. Like most seamen who knew anything about the vessel, I heard the news that the *Pamir* was in distress in the North Atlantic, in September 1957, with incredulous amazement. I knew the ship well. When Captain de Cloux and I bought the "P" liner *Parma* in Hamburg in 1930, the *Pamir* was also for sale and was offered to us. We considered for a while which ship we might take, and turned down the *Pamir* on the grounds only of her excessive strength. She was so strong and well built a ship, even for the Cape Horn nitrate trade, that there were 200 tons more steel in her than she required to carry full class, by any rules. This meant that, so heavy and strong was she, that she could carry 200 tons less freight than she should have done. The *Parma*, by comparison (perhaps because she was a Scots-built ship) carried some 500 tons more than her dimensions indicated, but there was nothing weak about her. The late Captain Erikson bought the *Pamir* soon after we concluded our deal for the *Parma*, and he had no complaints about her. She was a good sailing and a powerful ship, designed and built to take hurricanes in her stride (as she must, if she were to be of any use in the Laeisz nitrate trade with its westwards rounding of the Horn on every voyage).

Now here was my BBC radio speaking of the ship being on her beam ends and in dire distress. Even if she were on her beam ends, I considered that she ought to come up again, and that without much serious damage. The *Parma* had done it and so had the *Herzogin Cecilie,* to my personal knowledge. So had many other big square-riggers. But the *Pamir* was doomed. She did not right herself. She took in water and down she went. At first it seemed that all hands had gone with her (which if she had to go, surprised no seaman: for how could a crew or anyone survive a hurricane without their ship, or inflatable life rafts of the latest description?) but—and this was another astonishing feature—there *were* survivors. A handful of boys was picked up from broken lifeboats, after an exhaustive search lasting many days.

Further news indicated that the vessel had been loaded with loose barley from Buenos Aires towards Hamburg, and this loose grain had been stowed also in her deep tanks. (We never touched loose grain and we had no deep tank. Our grain cargoes were invariably in sacks.) A few tiers of sacks had been put above the loose grain with the idea of keeping the whole cargo steady as it settled down during the ship's long voyage. No officer survived, and it was therefore difficult to understand just what sail the ship had been carrying—it seemed, from the survivors' reports, to be a lot—or why the master had not been able to avoid the center of the hurricane. He was dead, poor man, and could give no answers.

In due course there was an exhaustive, and fearless, inquiry into the causes of the loss of the *Pamir,* and the court was outspoken in its findings. Four principal causes of the disaster were enumerated as follows:

1. The sails were not properly handled.

2. The cargo of loose grain was not stowed properly, and shifted.

3. The ballast tanks were filled with grain instead of water, thus upsetting the ship's stability.

4. The ship was not properly battened down, so that when she heeled water broke in through the superstructure.

In its report, the court further said that the master's lack of acquaintance with the *Pamir's* special characteristics, and the inexperience of the first officer, may have con-

34. First fresh meal for fifty days!

35. The *Pamir* on her last voyage, spoken by the *Christian Radich*.

36. Mr. Prölss has come up with a splendid idea for a new kind of sailing-ship.

tributed to the tragedy. The *Pamir* had twelve sails set
when she was struck by the storm. The wind in the decisive
hours had not reached extreme force, but because of the
way the sails were set and the inadequacy of the ballast,
the *Pamir* took a severe list. The loose grain then slid to
one side and the ship took in water through her superstructure, which was awash. In these conditions the ship
would have capsized, even in a less severe storm. The court
also found that as a sailing ship the *Pamir* was inadequately
manned, commenting that a crowd of willing beginners was
no substitute for an adequate and fully trained crew.

The court recommended that sailing ships should only
be entrusted to captains who had had long experience as
watchkeeping officers in sail. All officers should have had
basic sailing-ship training. The master was a substitute, in
place of the regular captain who had been left behind in
Hamburg on sick leave, and the acting master, who was
sixty-two, had not been in that kind of sailing ship for many
years.

The court's findings, in a way, were more staggering even
than the vessel's loss, and they were not acceptable in their
entirety to the ship's management committee. Certain obvious facts stood out. If a big steel bark like that could be
lost in a storm (of undoubted severity but even so a storm,
which she should have survived) or because it was no longer
possible to provide such ships with the all-important officers
and nucleus of skilled crew without which they cannot, or
ought not, go to sea, then the outlook for big sailing ships
is bleak indeed. The German court had taken that view. If
the port of Hamburg, one of the last strongholds of deep-
sea sail, was compelled at last to accept the fact that the

tradition was broken or in immediate and final danger of that fate, what hope had an individual in Britain to do anything about the restoration of a square-rigged ship, or the retention of unwanted sailing skills? The Germans had lost three sailing school ships in twenty years, with about 200 boys and seamen. Except for the two Soviet Russian four-masters which as far as I know carry no cargoes, anyway, the *Pamir* and the *Passat* were the last big working square-rigged windjammers anywhere. At the time of writing, the *Passat* is laid up in Germany and her future is uncertain, but the consensus on the Hamburg waterfront is that she will not sail again.

When we bought the *Parma,* the other members of the group were Finns, and we all knew what we were doing and how to do it. It is too late to find any syndicate such as that now. Our venture was in the early 1930's when there was still a live deepwater sailing tradition in Finland, when many countries still insisted that merchant-service officers should be trained in sail and so provided a reservoir of eager cadets, and when there were still experienced Cape Horn shipmasters by the score, less than fifty years old— perhaps, even then, by one score. The *Parma* cost us something like £3,000. Crew costs and so forth came to about £100 a week. The *Passat* has had something like £100,000 spent on her *twice,* since the end of the war. For any private individual or group of individuals to stand that sort of finance under today's taxation, with no hope of making ends meet, is impossible.

I was aboard the *Passat* in the Hamburg docks in October, 1958, with my good sailing-ship friends Captain Herman Piening (who used to command the *Padua* and is now

marine superintendent for the house of Laeisz) and Captain
Dominik, to have a look at her. Captain Helmut Grubbe
was in command, with a good maintenance crew aboard.
Captain Grubbe is an enthusiast, and the *Passat's* condition
was splendid. I would say she was good for another thirty
years, and it is to be hoped that some way may be found
for her to continue as a training-ship, if not in Germany
then perhaps elsewhere, though her German owners would
be most reluctant to part with her. It seems a sad, almost an
underhanded, blow of fate which took the *Pamir* from them
so tragically, when they were doing a magnificent best to
keep up a great tradition and a source of national seafaring
strength.

Nor is this idea dead in Germany, by any means, for also
in the Hamburg docks at the time of my visit was a new
square-rigger, the bark *Gorch Foch,* launched recently at
the yard of Blohm and Voss, to restore sail-training in the
German Navy. The *Gorch Foch* is a sister-ship, more or less,
of the U. S. Coast Guard's auxiliary training bark *Eagle,* and
the decision to build her was made after the loss of the
Pamir. The *Gorch Foch* will carry no cargoes and will not
have to try to compete upon the seven seas as the *Pamir* and
the *Passat* had to do. It was, in a sense, the cargo-carrying
that killed the *Pamir.* She was an excellent sailing school-
ship and, without the need to try to earn freights on a com-
petitive market, both she and the *Passat* would have done
very well. But to sail without freights is expensive, and
these are large ships without a naval vote to support them.

As for other big ships, besides the two Russians (which
are used exclusively as school ships, I understand) there is
the worn-out hulk of the four-masted bark *Omega* lying at

Callao, or was until fairly recently, and there are the permanently laid-up four-masters *Viking* at Gothenburg, and *Pommern* at Mariehamn. And that is all. None of these, except the Russians, goes to sea. None is likely to, and there is certainly nothing that I can do about it. The day of the engineless big square-rigger is over.

Well, a small ship would do. According to the news that comes to me, some of the square-rigged sailing school ships may not sail for much longer, either. It was reported that the *Danmark* is to be laid up, in Denmark, and in future boys may be trained aboard her without going to sea. The little ship *Georg Stage* finds it more and more difficult to recruit the necessary number of petty officers, without whom she cannot function. These are recruited from likely lads who themselves began in the little ship, but with wages and conditions so good at sea these days and (until very recently, at any rate) work so plentiful, youth is reluctant to accept the harsher and less materially rewarding life of the school ship. The Norwegian ships *Sörlandet, Statsraad Lehmkuhl,* and *Christian Radich,* though still sailing, find it difficult to recruit both officers and petty officers, for it is a long time now since big sailing ships were scrapped in Norway—well over thirty years. I was aboard the *Christian Radich* at Madeira in the early part of 1957, when she was under charter for Louis de Rochemont's Cinemiracle *Windjammer,* a film in a new and compelling medium which really does bring reality to the screen and has served sailing ships magnificently. Some lack of leadership aboard was sadly evident. If a school ship cannot be run properly, it is better not to run her at all.

As for other sailing ships fit for ocean-going, they are few and far between. There are the Portuguese Grand Bankers, which form a splendid fleet doing a great job of work, and there is a fleet of Spanish motor schooners, two- and three-masters, operating in the corner of the Mediterranean between Alicante and Marseilles. Such ships may still be built in the Balearic Islands, but today they are motor schooners well on the way to becoming motor ships, as the tendency always is once "auxiliary" power is accepted. The schooners out of Newfoundland have long been nothing but motor ships with the traditional schooner hull, carrying a little steadying sail. One would search the whole South Seas without finding a schooner better than the passenger-carrying ex-yacht *Te Vega*, which for all practical purposes is a luxury dude transport.

The *Te Vega*, a really lovely auxiliary schooner, cruises between Fiji, Tonga, the Cook Islands, Bora Bora, Raiatea, and Tahiti, more or less on regular schedule. This must be delightful and I wish I could join her, but it is scarcely sailing as I know it. The copra ketches, the recruiting schooners (if permitted to go to sea at all), the district officers' vessels are all powered, and so are all most other vessels, except the odd yacht, that wander about the beautiful South Seas. Some of these may come to bad ends, like the mysterious *Joyita*, but they would never again be taken for sailing ships. Many of the native craft have been driven out of business, except for fishing, by the spread of the big launch and small motor ship. To find a last representative of the seagoing crab-claw-sailed double canoe now, one would have to go to the Reef Islands, east of the Solomons and, as far as I know, there is only one such ship still sailing there.

There is one bright spot in all this world-wide picture, and that a brilliant one. This is the prodigious increase almost everywhere in the active pursuit of the sport of yachting. Not a stretch of water anywhere in the United Kingdom, be it sizable lake, disused old barge canal, or minute reservoir, but carries its quota of sailing yachts and enthusiasts to sail them. No vagary of the English weather can keep them ashore. Men, women, and children by the thousand find their sport and their recreation in sailing today, who never sailed before. Once considered to be a rich man's province, now yachting is for everyone. The statistics are astonishing. The Royal Yachting Association had some 370 affiliated clubs in Britain in 1947. Ten years later, the number had grown to 909, all active, and this number is steadily increasing. From 336 individual members in 1947, ten years later there were 5,177. The greatest increase is in the class of small dinghies and the like. One such class, the Cadet, was designed ten years ago and now has over 2500 boats in the United Kingdom alone.

This I like to see, for dinghy sailors are active sailors who would never mess about in their small, exposed, and uncomfortable craft if they did not feel the real thrill of sailing. Many such small vessels are built by the owners themselves. Other classes have doubled their numbers, already substantial, within the past five years. So it goes on, until it is calculated that one person in every 100 in Great Britain spends at least some leisure messing about in some kind of sailing craft, boat, or vessel. In Britain, some of this is explained usually by the fact that no one in those islands can live more than 100 miles from the sea, but this is not the whole explanation if, indeed, it is any part of it. The same phenomenon is to be observed in the United States of America, and throughout most of Europe, where the sea is quite often almost inaccessible.

All of this is highly encouraging. So are the well-organized and well-sailed ocean races, which sometimes attract the best part of a hundred entries—the races to Bermuda, to Honolulu, round the Fastnet Rock, to Tasmania from Sydney, to Heligoland, and so forth. The business of ocean racing under sail, once considered solely the domain of the glorious clippers, may now be almost for every man. I learn that a race across the North Atlantic is being organized for singlehanded craft, to set out from Cowes in the Isle of Wight towards City Island, New York, on the third Saturday of July 1960. There will be no rules of measurement and no handicaps. The few rules simply specify that any sort of vessel may enter provided that she has a crew of one man or woman only, amateur or professional, that during the race she "must be propelled only by the wind and/or the manpower of the crew," and that all entered craft must qualify by first sailing, singlehanded, the tough course from Cowes nonstop to Bantry in southwest Ireland and back again. Further particulars are to be had from an American gentleman residing in Peru and, I understand, already there are many entries.

This race is not intended as a stunt. It is a serious and logical development, aimed at the further improvement of boats and gear. I must add that though I wish it well, a transatlantic racing singlehander is one form of ship that I have no desire to sail. Not only is such racing a feat of endurance of heroic proportions which I fear now are beyond me, but the excessive, endless, and hopeless motion would make me violently seasick. While men and women can be found who are willing to accept this sort of thing, there is no fear of the loss of the art and science of sailing. Far from it!

But this is all fore-and-aft searfaring—gaff-and-boom, staysail, or jib-headed stuff. I may be biased, but I think there is also a place for square-rig—square-rig for ocean work, square-rig for training—and that is dying while we stand on the sidelines and watch. I am glad to notice that, as the ships in being disappear from the seas, at least there is a growing collection of real ships "preserved," here and there about the world, for posterity, if interested. Indeed there is a group of them from which the student will be able to learn much of maritime history, ranging from the replica of the *Santa Maria* at Barcelona through the *Mayflower II* at Plymouth, the *Constitution* at Boston Navy Yard and the *Victory* at Portsmouth, the clipper *Cutty Sark* at Greenwich near London, the full-rigged ship *Balclutha* (saved by the San Francisco Maritime Museum in that beautiful Californian bay), and the ship *af Chapman* at Stockholm to the four-masters *Viking* and *Pommern*. This is all magnificent though, like the *Mayflower*, perhaps at times more costly than the promoters dreamed. It can be an expensive business, preserving old ships.

I would like to see the *Hans Egede* rigged again, preferably as a small and handy bark, or one of those Sicilian brigantines, which were converted into frigates for the film based on the life of John Paul Jones, kept when the filming was ended. She should continue then at sea as a joint Anglo-American venture for the training of boys, and the further retention of time-honored deepwater square-rigged sailing skills. When such a ship was worn out, I would prefer to see her replaced, rather than preserved.

It would be an expensive matter to convert one of the film ships for training purposes to today's rigid standards. Good ships as the *Serapis* and *Bon Homme Richard* were for their purpose, they are old, and American shipping regulations are severe as to the seaworthiness, life-saving apparatus, and so forth for vessels carrying youth to sea— necessarily so, but also, one fears, rather hopelessly. The beautiful little stays'l tops'l schooner *Yankee,* for example, which the well-known Captain Irving Johnson, U.S.N.R., sailed successfully round the world with crews of boys several voyages, was put out of business in 1958 by sudden insistence on the full observation of a horde of regulations— all very sound, no doubt, but in their cumulative effect, ruinous. The *Yankee* had shown her seaworthiness, one would have thought, and was doing a good job. She was a former German pilot schooner from the tough old North Sea. Irving Johnson, than whom no world-wandering sailing man could have a better reputation, had spent considerable sums on keeping her in the best of order, just for the purpose of youth-training under sail. He had been able to keep her going because she was accepted for registry as a private yacht, and the youth aboard were paying guests (no one could finance such voyages as a philanthropy). But a new ruling declared that she must comply with the prohibitory regulations of a commercial vessel, and the change of status would so increase her costs, both for further conversion and manning, that she could not operate under the American flag at all. I don't know, but I would have thought that here was a sailing venture which, provided it continued in good hands, could have been fostered rather than hindered.

One aspect of the new *Mayflower* voyage which all the sailing-ship men aboard regretted was that the good little ship was asked only to sail once. Her "voyage" was no voyage at all, in the time-honored sense, but a one-way delivery passage which being made left us again with no ship at all. But I will weep no tears over that. Engine-less square-rigged ships now belong on greeting cards, and I accept that, if I must. But it would surely be foolish to throw away all that has been learned about the ocean winds and their use to seafaring man. What about modernizing deepsea sailing? How about applying something that has been learned from aerodynamics, with airfoil sails of modern materials, simplified and modernized gear to control the sails, new alloys for masts and yards to save weight and improve performance? Would it not be possible to design a great and truly modern sailing vessel which could harness the ocean winds better than that has ever been done before, and transport heavy cargoes more cheaply than mechanical vessels can? I thought so, indeed. Square-rig development had stopped with the five-masted full-rigged ship *Preussen*, just when it was really getting somewhere.

Then I heard of Mr. Prölss. Indeed, Mr. Prölss came to see me. I had not before ever heard of Mr. Prölss, who was neither sailor nor shipowner, but he had a folio of drawings, graphs, and data with him for a six-masted full-rigged ship of truly modern design, which could carry 13,000 tons of cargo and sail twenty-five knots. Here was the answer! Wilhelm Prölss of Hamburg is no sentimental sailor, languishing for sight of some glorious but has-been sailing-ship. He

is an engineer, a scientist, a painstaking truth-seeker in quest
of facts, and he had produced a wholly modern concept of
the wind-driven ship at sea—a big steel carrier of good and
graceful lines, bowsprit-less and tripod-masted, the "masts"
set on turntables controlled by push button and designed
to stay upright despite the vessel's heel, the spars of alloy
carrying sails of perfect airfoil designed to accept the force
of the wind at all times in the manner that would do most
good, and yet all controllable from the deck at the touch of
a lever. Here were no external running gear to shout for
costly upkeep and disturb fast cargo-handling, no maze of
supporting stays and shrouds and all those things, to impede
the angle of attack of the sails—no braces, for the whole
mast turned keeping the leading edges of all the sails and
the sails themselves set perfectly for all winds: no halyards
or downhauls, for the yards kept their hoisted positions:
no profusion of gear upon the sails, for they brailed in snug
and safely to the center, requiring no perilous labor aloft to
stow them and get gaskets round.

Here was an eye-opener! This quiet scientist from Germany was *thorough* all the way through. His folio did not
contain just an airy idea. He had made models, conducted
tests, worked endlessly with graph and slide rule both to
evolve his design and compute and test its expected performance. His figures and his computations had been
checked by some of the best mathematical brains in West
Germany and faulted nowhere. Among those able to con-
ceive just what scientist Prölss had done there was, indeed,
a little quiet enthusiasm.

I joined that small band forthwith. I am for Mr. Prölss
and his modernized six-masted full-rigged ship, push but-

ton job as she may be and no glamorous beauty for a Christmas card. He has worked out her power, her capacities and her speed painstakingly. With the daily weather maps from the German Hydrographic Office there in Hamburg and his graphs of her performance, Mr. Prölss is plotting his big ship steadily on passages between Hamburg and Hampton Roads. She made Hampton Roads only twenty-five days out from Hamburg a month ago, carrying 13,000 tons with ten less crew than a comparable modern motor-ship now must carry, at a freight a dollar and a half a ton less than the minimum such a motor ship could accept with hope of paying. All this, of course, in theory only—but theory painstakingly evolved, worked out with the utmost thoroughness, and faulted by no expert who has studied the data.

I believe whole-heartedly in the sailing school-ship. But, for practical purposes, I am prepared to concentrate on helping Mr. Prölss. There may be the answer. With his ideas, the wind-driven ship may still be in business.

TECHNICAL APPENDIX

TECHNICAL APPENDIX

THERE are excellent books which throw light on the rigging and other technicalities of ships such as the bark, or barque, *Mayflower*, of 1620. Notably there is Dr. R. C. Anderson's classic *Seventeenth-Century Rigging*, recently reprinted in London by Messrs. Percival Marshall, and Mr. William A. Baker's new book about his work and its results. I shall therefore confine myself to some remarks on the sailing and handling of such ships, as we found it. First I must say that we did not find out all there was to be learned on the subject, by any means. There was too much hurry about the passage. There were no sailing trials. Apart from a few hours in New York harbor, the ship sailed only in one trim. At no time could I have the ship and just bash about, beating in a hard wind, trying the old-fashioned idea of giving the sails great pregnant bellies the better to hold the wind, lying "a'try" with the lee clew of the mains'l used as a lateen. I had a passage to make and I had to get on with it, to the exclusion of all else. The promoters had no interest in the sailing qualities of that or any other vessel, except as they affected the *Mayflower's* probable date of arrival, and she was set an impossible schedule. However, we did learn something.

The *Mayflower* we sailed was in essence a small bark, sailing just like any other bark—a vessel with square sails on fore and main masts, and any sort of fore-and-after sail or sails on the mizzen, is a bark—and better than many. Any sailing ship sails because her canvas balances and can be made to give her ade-

295

quate forward way, and to maneuver her. Speaking very broadly, she has sails aft which tend to hold her up to the wind, sails right forward which tend to blow her off the wind, and the principal driving sails in between. The two sets of balancing sails, forward and aft, also add to the forward motion as well as being the principal maneuvering sails. If you require to bring the ship up to the wind, you can flatten in the aftermost sail and let the forward sail (in our case, the spritsail) shake, if you wish. Then she will come up very well. If you want to fall off—"pay" off, sailors say—then you can let the mizzen sheet fly, or take that sail off the ship altogether, and the spritsail will blow her head off the wind. You then trim the main yards and those sails will also help.

The square sails, as in square-riggers right down the centuries, were trimmed by means of ropes called braces attached to the ends of the yards to which the sails were bent (secured). These sails were set by means of ropes at their lower corners, called tacks and sheets, and hauled up, clewed up, bunted up—unset, in a manner of speaking—by means of other ropes which passed across the front of them, were then secured to the bottoms of the sails, and could be hauled upon from the deck. The topsail yards were hoisted by means of hall-yards—haul-yards, a self-explanatory term like all sea terms, if one goes back to origins: these haul-yards have become halyards—and the main and fore yards, for all practical purposes, were fixtures aloft. They spread their sails and stayed where they were. In the *Mayflower's* case, they could be lowered fairly simply, and were fitted with a sort of primitive but effective halyards called "jeers" for this purpose. These jeers were rove through the sheaves in the tops of big balks of timber set upright in the hull and protruding three feet or so above the main deck. These timbers were called knights, possibly because they were powerful and had to be relied upon to do important work.

We made little use of the jeers, preferring to do all the work aloft on the yards there, as we were accustomed to this method. To achieve this, footropes—stout hempen cordage stretched along below the yards at a convenient height for sailors to balance on and do their work—were rigged on all the yards. I understand from Sir Alan Moore (who knows his subject) that possibly even as late as 1620 there were no footropes aloft at all, at any rate not permanently. The big sails could be handled by lowering their yards, I suppose, and the tops'ls were deep but narrow, and they could be handled by a few boys working one astraddle on each yardarm (where they would have the lifts to cling to, if necessary) and the others pulling the bunt of the canvas into the commodious round tops, where there was plenty of room to make a well-stowed bundle of it and lash it properly. We worked the tops'ls aloft, too. Boys could do that work very well because the topsails were just what their name implies—*top* sails, not principal sails at all. The principal sails were the courses. The topsails came off the ship first in any increase of wind, and for all practical purposes the ship handled—in this sense—like a schooner. The foresail was considerably smaller than the mainsail and could therefore be held much longer, and the main without its bonnet was not an outsize sail. It is possible that, historically, our unbonneted mainsail may have been a trifle large.

There never was any trouble with any of these sails or their gear, and they all set and did their work splendidly. Elizabethan seamen had a curious idea that all square sails pulled harder if they were not set too taut. Indeed, to our way of thinking, they did not set their sails properly at all, nor cut them well either. They liked them baggy because they then held more wind, and the fact that they made less effective use of it did not occur to anyone, apparently, for several centuries. Even braced sharp up, on a wind, they still set the sails as flowing big bags, keeping the luffs—the weather leaches, the leading edges—taut by means of awkward bowlines led clumsily to somewhere forward where a stress could be put on them, either to the mast next ahead or, if there was no mast, to a stay. As the stays were all made of rope, and the entire fabric of the rigging was rope-supported, this business of using ropes to put stress on more rope led to an absence of rigidity unknown in later days. It also caused an almost constant requirement to set the rigging up, to tauten it again.

Nonetheless, it worked, and it may even have been better in one sense, as the old sailor in the *Rothesay Bay* had pointed out to me in 1919. Wooden-hulled and rope-rigged sailing ships were alive. They *lived* in the sea, and lived in the wind too, in a way we never knew in modern steel vessels. Our *Mayflower* sails were well cut for the simple reason that a good sailmaker like Harold Bridge of Brixham, working with good Scots materials, was incapable of turning out a badly cut sail, and we found the bowlines superfluous. Neither did I try to get a belly on the sails except sometimes on the tops'ls in a squall, but my purpose then was not to increase the pressure on them (and so the ship's speed, according to the Elizabethan notion) but to *decrease* it temporarily, while the squall passed. This worked. The Elizabethan notion must have been wrong.

As for the spritsail, this was so good a maneuvering sail that I could well understand how it had persisted down the centuries, even after the use of jibs, set on stays from the foremast to the bowsprit and jib boom, had long been general. Jibs were all very well, but a square-rigger man looked on his square canvas as his real sails. The spritsail was square, and the pressure it could exert, and so the swinging power it imparted in ship-handling, were immediately apparent. Our spritsail threw the ship's head off the wind far more effectively than a bowsprit full of fore-and-aft headsails could do, when we required it. You could see it at its work and the ship responding, and there was no doubt about it.

The same thing applied to the lateen, to bring her up to the wind. It was a good, long sail with a long effective leading edge and (without its bonnet) a small aspect ratio—just the thing for its job. The long lateen yard was in effect the leading edge of the sail, like a tall mast in a Bermuda-rigged yacht. Because of the standing rigging on the mizzen, under which the lateen yard, of necessity, had to be tucked, it was impossible to swing the mizzen before the wind as the Arabs (and of course the Maldivians, the Indians, and every other sailor using the same rig) could do with their great lateens. This made the mizzen a useful balancing sail and of driving value with winds from the quarter to a couple of points forward of the beam, but no use before the wind. Naturally, the lateen yard was always on the lee side of the mast. There never was any trouble to get it there, though we always brailed the sail in before shifting the yard. A cumbersome but effective type of topping lift, called simply the mizzen lift, which was led to the main topmast-head with its operating tackle led back to the mizzen rigging, topped the lateen to the vertical and simplified the business of swinging the yard round the back of the mast. You let go the two tackles on the foot of the yard which kept it trimmed when the sail was set, and simply manhandled the yard, slung at its point of balance and kept vertical by the lift, round the back of the mast, regardless of the standing rigging. You could do it just as well with the sail set, though the canvas would then thrash about and make the job more awkward. We were against avoidable awkwardnesses in all jobs.

The spritsail was harder to trim and to handle, but on a wind the sail set quite well even though the tack—the weather clew—was in the empty air, and could be bowsed down to no place. The sail set with two sheets, one on either side, led well back along the ship's sides and, as long as the weather clew was well out to windward (which was contrived as in any other square sail, by trimming the yard, by means of the braces, more towards the fore-and-aft line), the sail stood well and did its work. Because of the bowsprit's entire lack of standing rigging, it was also possible to improve its set by canting the spritsail yard, even to the vertical, and then setting the spritsail as a sort of quadrilateral jib. We tried this and it worked quite well. The multiplicity of the spritsail gear made this always a rather difficult sail to trim but, once trimmed, it stayed set very well and worked splendidly. To secure the spritsail, we clewed and bunted it up to the yard like any other square sail, and worked at the canvas on the hoisted-out yard, from footropes. It could also be run in to the beak. Here again, the multiplicity of the necessary gear, and its unavoidably awkward leads, made this a difficult business, especially on a black night, and that was why we rarely tried to handle the sail in that manner. I suppose that was the real reason why the spritsail finally went out of fashion, leaving the ship's headsails to the staysail and jibs, but I can remember seeing big square-rigged ships which still spread something of a spritsail yard, well into the twentieth century, though one of its principal uses (if not its only use) then was to spread the guys which helped to support the long jib boom.

With the spritsail, the lateen mizzen, and the good positioning of the masts carrying the real driving sails, our *Mayflower* both tacked and wore very well, swinging either across the wind or round before it very fast, with little loss of way. Although such a chunky little ship and—to our eyes—so disproportionately high aft, there was nothing wrong with her maneuvering ability. She handled as well as the sweet old iron bark *James Craig* ex-*Clan MacLeod*, which was the best handling square-rigger I had been in. She went to windward well, in a good sailing breeze, and she could be made to lie up six points. Because of the cordage rigging, which however well set up always slacked a bit to lee-ward, especially on a wind, the yards could be braced more sharply—near the fore-and-aft—than in a modern ship. There were simple lines and tackles called catharpins with which you could gather the lee rigging in, and brace up even sharper, if you didn't mind the increase of chafe of yard against shroud. Both the mainstay and the fore-stay, although cut from the best of Gourock's heavy hempen rope, bellied out with the lift of the courses behind them, and I never saw that this did the ship any harm. There was a great deal more chafe than in a vessel with a more modern rig, of course, but this could be much relieved (though never prevented) by the liberal use of chafing gear— baggywrinkle, leather, ropeyarn mats, and so forth.

The height of the hull kept the main deck well above the water. She shipped no heavy seas, not even in the chops of the Channel nor in that Gulf Stream gale. On a wind, she would steer herself. Running, she was no more difficult to steer than any other square-rigger, except perhaps when the wind took her on either side of the tall aftercastle. Then she would swing. The fact that the mainsail was so much larger than the foresail was inclined to make her a little hard-mouthed, at times.

She was all in all a good little sailing ship, able, smart, and weatherly. Elizabethan seamen knew the business of ocean sail-ing, and they were tolerable navigators too. As for the period instruments we had, the traverse board was a simple and ex-cellent means of recording the day's work (which we also did in the log, of course) and the dry-card compasses were reliable. But the accurate use of the cross-staff rather defeated us. It was altogether too approximate, and the best latitude we ever got from it was ten miles out. Perhaps, having the modern instru-ments at our disposal, we did not take sufficient pains to become properly accustomed to its use. It was an uncomfortable instru-ment, not easy to use, and hard on the eyes.

INDEX